# BEING A BOY AGAIN

# BEING A BOY AGAIN

Autobiography and the American Boy Book

## MARCIA JACOBSON

THE UNIVERSITY OF ALABAMA PRESS

Tuscaloosa and London

Copyright © 1994
The University of Alabama Press
Tuscaloosa, Alabama 35487-0380
All rights reserved
Manufactured in the United States of America

∞

The paper on which this book is printed meets the minimum requirements of
American National Standard for Information Science-Permanence of Paper for
Printed Library Materials, ANSI Z39.48-1984.

The illustration used as a frontispiece is "Wating for a Bite," by Winslow Homer,
published in *Harper's Weekly*, 22 August 1874.

**Library of Congress Cataloging-in-Publication Data**

Jacobson, Marcia Ann.
  Being a boy again : autobiography and the American boy book /
Marcia Johnson.
    p.    cm.
  Includes bibliographical references (p.   ) and index.
  ISBN 0-8173-0764-8 (alk. paper)
    1. Autobiographical fiction, American—Men authors—History and
criticism.   2. American prose literature—Men authors—History and
criticism.   3. Boys—United States—Biography—History and
criticism.   4. Boys in literature.   5. Autobiography.   I. Title.
PS374.A88J33   1994
813'.409352054—dc20                                    94-14510

British Library Cataloguing-in-Publication Data available

*To Steve and Nate*

One of the best things in the world to be is a boy; it requires no experience, though it needs some practice to be a good one. The disadvantage of the position is that it does not last long enough; it is soon over; just as you get used to being a boy, you have to be something else, with a good deal more work to do and not half so much fun. And yet every boy is anxious to be a man.

—Charles Dudley Warner,
*Being a Boy*


A man, if he is any good, never gets over being a boy.

—Sherwood Anderson,
*Tar: A Midwest Childhood*

# CONTENTS

# ACKNOWLEDGMENTS

I am grateful to the journals that gave my work a hearing when I was still formulating my ideas. Half of Chapter 4 and the whole of Chapter 5 first appeared in *American Literary Realism* and *Western American Literature;* they appear here in revised form.

Two National Endowment for the Humanities Summer Seminars were particularly helpful to me. John Demos's "Theory and Practice in Psychohistory" directed my attention to the meaning of the boy books I was concerned with in the adult lives of their authors; James Olney's "The Forms of Autobiography" broadened my understanding of autobiography as a genre and gave me tools with which to examine the boy books. And Summer Support from NEH gave me additional time to work on this study.

My friends—Jim Cox, Fred Crews, John Crowley, and Bill Veeder—were, as they have been many times, provocative and helpful critics. It is a pleasure to record my thanks here.

It is a pleasure, too, to acknowledge the professional staff at the University of Alabama Press for their help with my manuscript, their responsiveness to my concerns, and their enthusiasm for my boy book.

# BEING A BOY AGAIN

# THE BOY BOOK

## The Historical Context

In January of 1870 a delighted William Dean Howells reviewed Thomas Bailey Aldrich's *The Story of a Bad Boy* for the *Atlantic.* "Mr. Aldrich has done a new thing in . . . American Literature," Howells began enthusiastically and continued:

> No one else seems to have thought of telling the story of a boy's life, with so great desire to show what a boy's life is, and so little purpose of teaching what it should be; certainly no one else has thought of doing this for the life of an American boy. The conception of such a performance is altogether his in this case . . . and it is one that will at last give us, we believe, the work which has so long hovered in the mental atmosphere a pathetic ante-natal phantom, pleading to be born into the world,—the American novel, namely.
>
> Autobiography has a charm which passes that of all other kinds of reading; it has almost the relish of the gossip we talk about our friends; and whoever chooses its form for his inventions is sure to prepossess us; and if then he can give his incidents and characters the simple order and air of actual occurrences and people . . . his success is assured. We think this is the open secret of the pleasure which "The Story of a Bad Boy" has afforded to boys themselves, and to every man that happens to have been a boy. (124)

As Howells undoubtedly knew, some of our humorists— George Washington Harris, Johnson Jones Hooper, Benjamin P. Shillaber—had already given us boys whose mischievous and even destructive behavior made them anything but models to be emulated. But he was correct in noting that Aldrich's work was the first sustained presentation of such a boy. With his usual prescience, Howells also recognized that "the story of a boy's life" was a subject that would be provocative for American writers and would inspire at its best that fixation of the late nineteenth century, "the American novel": *Adventures of Huckleberry Finn* was only fifteen years away.

Shortly after the turn of the century, Frank Norris looked back at what had followed in the wake of Aldrich's work:

> The ten year old—who always went in swimmin' and lost his tow—appeared in the magazines. There is no sentiment about him. Never a tear need be shed over the vicarious atonements of Pinky Trevethan or Skinny McCleave.
>
> It is part of the game to pretend that the Pinkys and Skinnys and Peelys and Mickeys are different individuals. Error. They are merely names of the boy that perennially and persistently remains the same. Do you know who he is? He is the average American business man before he grew up. That accounts for his popularity. The average business man had clean forgotten all about all those early phases of primitive growth, and it amuses him immensely to find out that the scribe has been making a study of him and bringing to light the forgotten things that are so tremendously familiar when presented to the consideration. It is not fiction nor yet literature in the straightest sense of the word, this rehabilitation of Skinny McCleave. It has a value vaguely scientific, the same value that a specimen, a fossil insect, has when brought to the attention of the savant. It is the study of an extinct species, a report upon the American boy of thirty years ago. (86–87)

As Norris's generalizations, his mocking tone, and made-up names suggest, the genre became commonplace, conventional enough to be imitated easily. And so it continued until approximately the beginning of World War I when, like so much else from the nineteenth century, it no longer spoke to the needs of Americans. What Norris does not note is that along the way to this end, the genre also fulfilled Howells's expectations for it. Mark Twain's *Tom Sawyer* and *Huck Finn,* Hamlin Garland's *Boy Life on the Prairie,* Howells's own *A Boy's Town* and *The Flight of Pony Baker,* Stephen Crane's *Whilomville Stories,* and Booth Tarkington's Penrod books

were all part of a literary landscape that included the Pinkys and
Skinnys.

Taken together, Howells's and Norris's remarks nearly span the
history of the genre and outline its development from something
personal and innovative to something thoroughly conventional.
In addition, they define the genre. The boy book, to use the
modern term,[1] is, as both writers make clear, a book for adults,
although children can read it. Its special appeal lies in its autobiographical aspect. Howells uses the term "autobiography" with
a degree of looseness that is particularly appropriate. When he
speaks of autobiography providing almost "the relish of . . . gossip," he directs us to think of the book in question in terms of its
relation to the author's life: like gossip, such a book will provide
us with the real "lowdown" about another human being. When
he goes on to speak of the author's choosing the autobiographical
form for his invention, he asks us to think of autobiography as a
fictional genre[2]: the protagonist's story will be presented in such
a way as to engage our emotions and imaginations and so speak a
deeper truth than a mere transcription of fact. And when he
observes that the boy book appeals to "every man that happens to
have been a boy," he points to a level of generalization that will
permit all (male) readers to feel an identification with the protagonist and his experiences. The boy book, as Howells defines it,
is a multidimensional autobiography. Norris, too, notes that the
boy book "is not fiction" and goes on to make the middle-class
origin and appeal of the genre explicit by explaining that the boy
book is every man's autobiography, for its protagonist is "the
average American business man before he grew up." It offers
pleasure specifically because it uncovers what was thought to be
lost: "the average business man had clean forgotten all about
those early phases of primitive growth." Norris's observation becomes an extended metaphor: this early period is fossil-like; it
belongs to an "extinct species." The evolutionary terms were
common to late nineteenth-century discussions of child development. Here, in the context of Norris's remarks, they alert us to
something poignant in the genre: in describing the past, the boy
book evokes a condition of being that is truly vanished forever.
The boy book also evokes a vanished social condition, for it is, as

Norris says, "a report upon the American boy of thirty years ago"—that is, a boy who was almost invariably a small-town or farm boy.

When we think of some of the other literary fashions of the second half of the nineteenth century and the early twentieth century—the religious crisis novel or the new woman novel, for example—we realize that the boy book is an anomaly in a period that embraced one new genre after another and elevated each to best-selling heights. The boy book was not so obviously topical as those forms that became best-sellers. Nor, with its life span of about fifty years, was it as short-lived.[3] A few works attained the widespread popularity of the best sellers: Twain's, Peck's *(Peck's Bad Boy)*, Tarkington's. But for the most part, the boy book occupied lesser heights, its longevity testifying to the fact that it spoke to persistent and apparently insoluble needs on the part of Americans. What those needs were and how the boy book addressed them is the secondary subject of this book. The autobiographical element which Howells and Norris point to I take as the central clue to the meaning of these books and therefore as my primary subject. In doing this, I respond to the still unanswered invitation Edwin H. Cady issued in *The Road to Realism,* his 1956 study of Howells, in which he defined the boy book:

> The American boy-story, which has never been properly studied as a literary phenomenon, was more or less founded by Thomas Bailey Aldrich and consolidated by Mark Twain, with Howells to help him clarify what he was doing. It is distinct from the "story for boys," though ordinarily sold to editors and librarians as such, in that it contains a depth level at which an imaginative exploration of the nature and predicament of the man-child is carried out. The importance to American literature and to American cultural self-awareness of the body of writing in this genre has never been fully realized. (12)[4]

The years spanned by the boy book encompassed enormous economic and social changes. These changes and the problems they created for American men in particular make up one context for the boy book. America moved from a state of relative isolation in 1869, the year in which *The Story of a Bad Boy* was published, to that of a world power in the years after 1914, the period in which the Penrod books were published. In the course of those same years, the American West was explored and settled, and the frontier—both a literal and symbolic promise of "new life and freedom"[5]—was officially closed. America went from being a nation of small businessmen and, primarily, farmers, to one that was increasingly urbanized. Advances in technology meant that farm work required fewer people and that farmers could move beyond subsistence farming to specialization in one product. The result was that increasing numbers of Americans migrated to the cities—joining an ever-growing number of foreign immigrants—seeking jobs in factories and in the skilled professions that support an industrialized nation. A laissez-faire notion of government, deeply rooted in American culture, encouraged the growth of corporations that controlled all phases of manufacturing and distribution of goods. The small businessman and the small farmer were frequent casualties of such growth. The inevitable result was that the gulf between rich and poor grew wider than it ever had or has been in American life.[6]

A man, eager to succeed in the marketplace, to fulfill the role his patriarchal culture told him was his, had a more difficult time than ever (Dubbert 81–84, Filene 69–80, Hantover 287–93). Howells, contrasting America in the early nineties with his country forty years earlier, thought in terms of opportunities lost, of possibilities foreclosed, and of masculinity threatened:

> If a man got out of work, he turned his hand to something else; if a man failed in business, he started in again from some other direction; as a last resort, in both cases, he went west, preëmpted a quarter section of public land, and grew up with the country. Now, the country is grown up; the public land is gone; business is full on all sides, and the hand that turned itself to something else has lost its cunning. The struggle for life has changed from a free fight to an encounter of disciplined forces, and the free fighters that are left get ground to pieces between organized labor and organized capital. (*Altruria* 121)

Henry Adams, always more self-dramatizing and pessimistic than Howells, saw the change in terms of the dehumanization of life and personal disempowerment: "My country in 1900 is something totally different from my own country in 1860. I am wholly a stranger in it. Neither I, nor anyone else, understands it. The turning of a nebula into a star may somewhat resemble the change. All I can see is that it is one of compression, concentration, and consequent development of terrific energy, represented not by souls, but by coal and iron and steam."[7]

As these quotations remind us, individual lives also encompassed many changes. Nearly all of the boy book authors experienced some of the changes that transformed America, and nearly all found that experience painful. This is most dramatically so in the cases of Twain and Howells, whom we might think of as the first generation of boy book writers. Their life stories read like American fairy tales. Starting out as poor, semi-educated boys in small midwestern towns, both went East to distinguish themselves as writers as well as businessmen and self-publicists and so to enjoy a degree of wealth, popularity, and intellectual prestige that they could not possibly have anticipated in their wildest youthful fantasies. Yet neither found the pressures of such an adulthood entirely congenial, and both were haunted by a sense of not having lived up to the best that was in them. Aldrich and Charles Dudley Warner (author of *Being a Boy*), writers of the same generation, who spent most of their lives in the Northeast and who were more conservative in political and social matters than Twain and Howells, did not feel that they had straight-jacketed themselves to enter the Eastern literary establishment, but they did know the pain of finding the once-respected role of genteel writer increasingly marginal in relation to public affairs.[8] The writers from the next generation, Garland, Crane, and Tarkington, rejoiced in escaping their stifling childhoods. For Garland adulthood brought release from the drudgery of midwestern farm life, for Crane a break with the propriety expected of the son of a small-town minister, and for Tarkington triumph over his passive, bookish childhood. But the ferocity with which these writers threw themselves into contemporary urban and political life and the insistence with which Garland and Crane, particularly, championed realistic literature suggest a profound discontent with late nineteenth-century America and a need to prove themselves more than mere writers. To cite this handful of writers is not to exclude the numerous others who wrote boy books; it is rather to suggest how widespread and difficult was the encounter with massive, disruptive social change. It is also, significantly, to remind us that the encounter was primarily a man's experience, since, with fewer chances to move and with few careers available, only a small number of women experienced such profoundly life-altering experiences as the writers I cite here.

It is not surprising that the boy book is a nostalgic look at the past—though often the nostalgia is a bit rueful, since that simple and secure past somehow did produce the troublesome present. In emphasizing the nostalgic element in these books, we recognize that they are one of the many forms of escapism and implicit social criticism spawned by the late nineteenth century. Contemporary historians see in such disparate phenomena as the mythologizing of the past in regional literature, the cult of the strenuous life, the new interest in nature, the arts and crafts movement, and the passions for things medieval or Oriental a desire to infuse vitality or spirituality into a culture that was mind-numbing and sense-dulling in its monotony and complexity (Higham 25–48; Lears; Martin, *Harvests* 81–88; Tomsich 27–50). Less discussed, but of equal import, is the adult interest in books about children (Jacobson, *James* 104–09). This interest became a fad in the nineties as American adults devoured the work of Rudyard Kipling, Robert Louis Stevenson, James Barrie, and Kenneth Grahame. In this environment, the boy book flourished and, meeting with success in the marketplace, inevitably inspired the cliché-ridden products that Norris complained of.

A column in *Scribner's* in January 1898 made the particular appeal of books about children clear. The author began by reflecting that Grahame's book, *The Golden Age,* is based on his memory of childhood, and then went on to more grandiose thoughts:

> perhaps the *Recollection of Childhood* is the real golden age, the age at which men most nearly approach the pure gold of indestructible joy. I call it second childhood, this season of life when the spirit of youth lives in men, kept alive by the glorified memories of childhood days and the yearning to "be a boy again." . . . Not until he has known what sin is and what is shame do the other days take hold on a man's remembrance, and bring back the spirit of eternal boyhood by which man must enter the Kingdom. . . . Little by little this widespread awakening of intelligent interest in childhood is finding expression in literature. In the wastes of tawdry "real-

ism," iconoclasm, cynicism, and shamelessness, men have lifted
up voices of regret for the epic age, and cried aloud for the times
when life was simpler. (123–24)

Recollection of childhood is posited here as a source of revital-
ization, very nearly of salvation, akin to the immersion in
medievalism that brought Henry Adams an appreciation of Ca-
tholicism and emotional renewal. The passage hints at more. It
speaks from a pre-Freudian world that pictured childhood as a
time in which one is free from a burdensome sexuality, a judgment implied in the notion that knowledge of "sin" and "shame"
is what separates one from childhood and thereby provokes a
longing for a return to that innocent time. The masculine terms
in which the passage as a whole is couched suggest that immersion in childhood memories—a vicarious return to a presexual
time—might be of particular relevance to a man whose culture
values assertive masculinity as the outward expression of male
sexuality and yet at the same time is so competitive as to frequently deny a man validation through his work. The boy book,
by virtue of its subject, escaped some of the maudlin excesses a
redemptive view of childhood could lead to. At the same time,
again by virtue of its subject, it could speak to the need for escape
and renewal as well as trace the roots of male discomfort with the
present.

The economic changes of the last half of the nineteenth century
brought changes to the American family that altered the meaning
of childhood and so created another, quite different, context for
the boy book. Demographers and family historians note that as
the century progressed, family size declined among the urban
middle class, the births of children were spread over fewer years,
and children remained at home, dependent on parents, for a
longer period (Wells 85–94). Although such factors as a gradual
enlargement of woman's traditional sphere and improved medical
care—which meant a decrease in child mortality—contributed to
the decrease in family size, the change was primarily a response to
the growing number of skilled jobs that support an industrialized
nation: the technical, clerical, and managerial jobs that require
special training. Then, as now, such jobs were more desirable

than factory jobs. A family, therefore, could do most for its children if it could forego the economic contribution working children might make and send those children to school instead. This was normally possible only if family size was limited (Handlins 161–62, Kett 232–34).

Paradoxically, the family that adjusted itself for the future benefit of its children lost some of its integrity as the children necessarily turned to schools and social groups to teach them the skills they would need to secure desirable employment and to fill their time as they awaited their delayed entry into the job market (Lasch, *Haven* 12–21). Faced with a wholly new economic situation, parents could not guide their children—a situation that was particularly hard on boys, whose adult lives would differ more from those of their fathers than girls' lives would from those of their mothers. The result of such parental failure was what Philip Slater calls "a child-centered society and a democratic family system"—that is, one in which "the child emerges as the receptacle for future hopes and hence bears a higher status than her elders, whose authority is weakened by its doubtful relevance to this future" (61). (I appreciate Slater's egalitarianism, but as I have noted, the child in question in the second half of the nineteenth century was most often male.) The result of such a situation, Slater continues, is that social change is further accelerated as the child comes to the fore in economic and social life and that the same situation obtains in the next generation. A pattern established after the Civil War thus continues on to the present.[9]

Henry Adams is our great spokesman on the subject of pain suffered by the "miseducated." But the subject was discussed in less intellectualized terms as well. Randolph S. Bourne, writing in the *Atlantic* in May 1911, answered a February piece by Cornelia A. P. Comer, "A Letter to the Rising Generation," in which Comer criticized Bourne's generation for its lack of purpose and its failure to respect tradition. Bourne, who identified himself with the younger generation (he was born in 1886), noted that its character had been shaped by the failures of its parents:

> The rising generation has practically brought itself up. School discipline, since the abolition of corporal punishment, has become almost nominal; church discipline practically nil; and even home

discipline, although retaining the forms, is but an empty shell. The modern child from the age of ten is almost his own "boss." The helplessness of the modern parent face to face with these conditions is amusing. What generation but the one to which our critic belongs could have conceived of "mothers' clubs" conducted by the public schools, in order to teach mothers how to bring up children! . . .

I do not use this assertion as a text for an indictment of the preceding generation; I am concerned, like our critic, only with results. These are a peculiarly headstrong and individualistic character among young people, and a complete bewilderment on the part of the parents. (592)

Bourne's use of the words "headstrong" and "individualistic" and his characterization of the parental generation as helpless and bewildered give substance to Slater's assertion that the failure of parents was empowering for the younger generation.

At the same time, as Bourne's example of "'mothers' clubs' conducted by the public schools" indicates, adults—primarily mothers, but fathers as well—were not readily willing to give up the opportunity to influence the lives of the next generation. If they could not train their children in practical skills, they could try to influence their moral and psychological development. The last decades of the nineteenth century consequently saw a new emphasis on the responsibilities of motherhood and a quickening of interest in the development and welfare of the child and adolescent. The number of books on child rearing increased dramatically (Wishy 105–07, 197–99). The child became an object of scientific study, primarily under the auspices of G. Stanley Hall, who launched the Child Study Movement in the 1880s and formulated our modern concept of adolescence in the 1890s (Ross 279–340). New social activities developed to augment the work of the schools by providing a masculine influence to balance the influence of female teachers and mothers and to fill up the leisure time of unemployed young people, especially young men. These included organized sports, church-related programs that reached out to embrace the adolescent, clubs that promoted wilderness activities, paramilitary clubs, and—the most successful organizations of all—the YMCA and the Boy Scouts, which were followed in due time by their sister organizations (Dubbert

147–53, Kett 173–211, Macleod). As even this bare listing makes clear, these activities for young people were based on the same activities that appealed to adults as escapist and regenerative. When adapted to young people, however, the point was not to relieve them of the stress created by their environment—sheltered, still-dependent middle-class youths had barely entered the environment adults complained of—but to nurture in them qualities that adults saw jeopardized in themselves. Scouting, for example, could teach the urban boy nature lore and crafts and could instill in him a manly as well as a moral approach to life.

Because the pastimes of rural and small-town boys figured so centrally in the boy book, the boy book itself became a part of this context. In his account of the boys' activities that developed at the end of the century, David I. Macleod notes that "by the 1890's adults were complacently embracing an artificial cult of the 'bad boy'" (54)—a cult fed by the boy books. These books, Macleod argues, set up a model of boyhood that was immensely attractive to parents and teachers. It was steeped in nostalgia, it idealized the past, but it also presented a view of boyhood that could be used by the present. The small-town values, the active outdoor life, and the harmless "gang" that educated and supported its members were all things that could be incorporated into such activities as Scouting (53). That the boy book typically dealt with younger boys than organized boys' activities addressed themselves to was not a problem because the end of childhood was becoming increasingly blurred. The boy book usually ended when its protagonist reached the age of twelve or fourteen. Often its author had gone to work at that age; equally often, the author of a book of this nostalgic genre was disinclined to recall a time when adult feelings and responsibilities were beginning to impinge on his life. Although the adolescent who was courted by the Scouts or a similar group was rapidly leaving childhood behind, he was not an adult because he was not employed. Structured activities with their emphasis on outdoor activity and individual achievement could offer an adolescent boy "a simulacrum of manliness" (55) and perhaps distract him from his developing sexuality at the same time. In short, application of the boy book values could keep the adolescent a boy until he was ready to enter the job market.

This second context greatly increased and complicated the adult audience for the boy book. The audience included not only the reader responsive to the author's autobiographically based account of himself, such as the troubled businessman seeking escape from the present and a profounder self-knowledge, but also the reader—the teacher or parent of either sex—who saw the boy book as a blueprint by which to juvenilize a growing boy rather than as an implicit critique of the present. If the troubled businessman most nearly apprehended the original spirit in which the boy book was written, its authors and publishers as good businessmen were not averse to courting those readers who read through the lens of their own need to assert social control as well.

How successful they were is evidenced by how comfortably the boy book took its place in the juvenile book market. Some writers found outlets in the influential children's magazines of the period. Howells, who presumably would have had relatively easy access to adult magazines, published *A Boy's Town* in *Harper's Young People* (8 April to 26 August 1890) and parts of *The Flight of Pony Baker* in *Youth's Companion* (1 December 1898, 16 November 1899, 10 May 1900; one chapter was published in *Harper's Weekly*, 5 July 1902). Publishers were able to enlarge the juvenile market further. In addition to regular reprintings, some of the boy books were reissued as school texts. Aldrich's *Story of a Bad Boy* was reissued this way in 1887; Edward Eggleston's *The Hoosier School-Boy* was first published in 1883 and reissued as a text in 1890; Garland's *Boy Life on the Prairie* was first published in 1899 and reissued in 1926; and Warner's *Being a Boy* was first published in 1877 and reissued in 1896. Boy books with the apparatus of schoolbooks—notes, a special introduction, study questions— joined with the how-to pages of children's magazines and such books as D. C. Beard's *The American Boy's Handy Book* (1882) and Ernest Thompson Seton's Boy Scout Handbook (*Boy Scouts of America: A Handbook of Woodcraft, Scouting and Life Craft*, 1910)[10] to become guides to boyish activities that flourished spontaneously in a previous age and could be revived in this. Awareness of the prescriptive use to which the boy book was being put also influenced the writing of later authors who worked in the genre. Crane's *Whilomville Stories* (1900) and Tarkington's *Penrod* (1914), to take the best examples, successfully capitalized on the market for boy books even as the genre was becoming increasingly threadbare.

That the boy book could simultaneously be accepted as offering a vicarious escape from and implicit critique of the culture that produced it and as an instrument for furthering the ends of that culture can be explained in large part by the developmental notion of childhood that informed such books. Contemporary psychology held that the developing individual recapitulates the course of development taken by the entire species—a notion summarized in the still-familiar phrase, ontogeny recapitulates phylogeny. Childhood of the individual reenacts childhood of the race; maturity brings the individual into congruence with that acme of civilization, late nineteenth-century Western man. Such pseudoscience drew on Romantic metaphor, evolutionary thought, and Christian meliorism. This recapitulation theory was popularized most strenuously in the United States by G. Stanley Hall, whose goal as a psychologist and educator was to describe each stage that the growing individual passes through and to prescribe the sort of education appropriate to each stage. Hall concentrated most of his energy on adolescence—a reflection of his own troubled youth (Ross 338–39)—but in the process described the "juvenile," the boy between about eight and twelve. This boy is a savage. He is inclined to outdoor activities such as hunting, fishing, and loafing and is not yet capable of developing such higher qualities as creativity, spirituality, and altruism. A proper education would stress rote learning and drill in fundamentals—there is no point in reasoning with a "savage"—and, ideally, would be conducted in the country, in circumstances recalling Hall's own rural upbringing in the 1840s and 1850s (Gould 135–43; Hall ix–xiii; Ross 147–48, 289, 307, 314–15). Once this period was passed, an educator could go on to encourage the development of higher instincts, but he could be assured of success only if the savagery had been fully indulged so that it would not seek expression at a later period (Gould 142, Hall xi, Ross 372).

These notions struck an immediately responsive chord. They seemed to account for the wildness of boy behavior in a time when boys were not yet part of the male world of work but were no longer a part of the family world of home (Rotundo 32–34). They appear in the child nurture material of the period as well as in popular writing. They are explicitly cited in nearly all of the boy books and are the literal subject of two of them: Charles Eastman's *Indian Boyhood* (1902) and Seton's *Two Little Savages* (1903). John T. Trowbridge, managing editor of *Our Young Folks* (1870–1873) and author of several books for boys, though not boy books as I am using the term, conveys the emotional appeal of these views in an essay on the American boy in the *North American Review* of February 1889. He begins by defining the boy in contrast to the man he will become:

> Whether man has emerged from monkeydom, may be a question. But that civilization has been evolved from savagery, there can be little doubt. And as the race has risen from ruder conditions, so the epitome, the individual, begins with the native wildness of the stock, and develops later whatever sweetness of humanity he may be capable of. The man is an enlightened being, the boy is a barbarian. He inherits not only the mild parental possibilities, but also the cat-like or tigerish traits which enabled his progenitors, in the dim past, to make the struggle for existence. Sometimes it seems as if his humanity were as thin as his jacket, and fitted him as loosely. The wild animal is underneath; strip him and you find the stripes. (218)

The last three sentences, with their repetitive stress on the animal in the boy, reveal an author titillated by the escape from civilization that the boy represents. Not surprisingly, this description is followed by a list of representative and implicitly condoned forms of boyish naughtiness—in the course of which Trowbridge observes that "the boy is nearer barbarism than the girl, for the reason that the fight for existence has fallen chiefly upon the male of the race, and that kindliness is earlier developed in the sex that keeps the home" (220)[11] and so helps us to understand why girl books, with their emphasis on growing up and becoming little women, do not parallel boy books in purpose or content.[12] The notion of boyhood savagery celebrated here is what makes contemplation of boyhood—as in the boy book—a revitalizing escape from the present.

At the same time, since the savagery is only a temporary condition, an adult can rejoice in knowing that it must give way to something better. The second half of Trowbridge's essay examines ways in which the boy can be guided toward the future. Sensitive parents and teachers who respect the child's natural inclinations help, as does vocational or practical education. Trowbridge observes, "The effect upon a boy, especially if he has been what we call a 'bad boy,' of turning his energies in the right channel, can be likened only to the supposed miraculous conversion of sinners." He then asks rhetorically, "Is not every reckless young spendthrift of golden days capable of such a conversion?" (222). Change for the better is inherent in the recapitulation theory; boyish savagery is earnest of responsible adulthood. The recapitulation theory provides for the salvation of the adult—recall the *Scribner's* article I quoted earlier—as well as of the child.[13] That the carnage of the Civil War and the wholesale slaughter of the American Indian did not challenge widespread acceptance of the recapitulation theory reminds us how adept Americans are at denying unpleasant truths about themselves. But the strenuous maintenance of the recapitulation theory spoke to more than a refusal to accept responsibility for the past. In so neatly compartmentalizing boyhood, the recapitulation theory also comfortably obscured the central fact of everyday adult male life in the period: that it was ferociously competitive— "free fighters . . . get ground to pieces between organized labor and organized capital," as Howells put it—that it was in fact boyhood savagery writ large.

After examining the antimodernist gestures of the end of the nineteenth century, T. J. Jackson Lears discerns a common pattern:

> Though none imagined the alternatives as starkly as Dostoevsky, nearly all antimodernists sensed (however dimly or fleetingly) that they somehow had to choose between a life of authentic experience and the false comforts of modernity, between Christ and the Grand Inquisitor. But ironically the pursuit of authentic experience in a secular age often became circular and self-referential. In the West, particularly the United States, intensity of feeling— physical, emotional, even spiritual—became a product to be consumed like any other. Recoiling from the vision of the Grand Inquisitor, antimodern dissenters furthered its fulfillment. (300)

Restating this thesis even more starkly, Lears observes that anti-modernism "promoted accommodation of new modes of cultural hegemony while it preserved an eloquent edge of protest" (301). The examples are many. The arts and crafts movement and the cult of the strenuous life became recreational outlets for businessmen. The passion for things medieval disintegrated into the empty symbols of clubs and schools. The interest in exotic cultures created new forms of consumerism as the well-to-do became collectors. The desire for a heightened inner life led to increased self-absorption on the part of intellectuals, with a consequent devaluation of political participation and an inevitable moral vacuum in which professional and managerial elites flourished (Lears 301–02, Trachtenberg 30–52). The boy book, as I understand it, is a variation on this theme. In offering a vicarious escape from the present, the boy book was an expression of the culture's longing for the vitality and authenticity that contemporary life excluded. In presenting an entertaining and sometimes sentimentalized picture of a bygone age, the boy book distracted from the difficulties of the present and paradoxically allowed for unreflecting accommodation to it.[14] And in presenting a text that could be used as a blueprint for educators, the boy book explicitly served the needs of a developing capitalistic society. It was thus doubly a product of the age that created it. Looking backward, it was a part of a progression onward.

## Fiction and Autobiography

In the pages that follow, I will look at the ways in which the impulse to write autobiography first helped to define the boy book and then, as the genre became increasingly conventional, found ways to express itself within conventional lines. In the course of doing this, I will trace the history of the boy book from Aldrich's "new thing in . . . American Literature" and Warner's equally new venture to Crane's and Tarkington's self-conscious reworkings of the genre, which highlight the growing bankruptcy of its conventions and portend its death. Although I will glance at a number of the ephemeral boy books of the period, my focus will be on the work of canonical writers who defined the

genre, inspired others, and wrought a series of memorable inno-
vations within their self-imposed limitations. My study is more
or less a chronological account, which is to say it is somewhat
distorted, since the life of the genre is only approximately described by chronology. The constant reprinting of particularly
successful books, like Aldrich's and Twain's, makes the marketplace look different at any given time than mere chronology
would suggest. Additionally, the work of the early humorists
gained new life from the sustained examinations of boyhood that
constitute my subject. This work, in turn, very likely fed interest
in the boy book, further complicating the history of the genre.[15]
Moreover, the fact that the boy book was a product of its varied
authors' personal histories within an encompassing cultural situation is cause for some caution in generalizing about the development of the genre as a whole.

If we must be cautious literary historians, we can be more
confident in turning to the boy books themselves. I have referred
to these books simply as fictionalized autobiographies, but a
more precise definition is possible. I have quoted Cady's observation that the boy book is "distinct from the 'story for boys,'
though ordinarily sold to editors and librarians as such" and cited
Norris's observation that despite the high degree of conven-
tionality the boy book assumed, it was nevertheless felt to be
autobiographical. If both Cady and Norris are correct, the boy
book is a literary form that we read with mixed generic expectations. We expect a degree of imaginative license appropriate to
fiction; we also expect the boy book to honor what Philippe
Lejeune has called "the autobiographical pact"—the promise that
what we will be reading is an account of the life of the author, a
promise we apprehend, ideally, without recourse to the world
outside the printed text ("Autobiographical Pact" 14). To some
extent, of course, all fiction is autobiographical, and all autobiography is fictional. A novelist draws on material that he knows
and that speaks, in some way, to his personal condition; an autobiographer necessarily selects and rearranges what he remembers
(or thinks he remembers) and wishes to communicate to us. But
we can better understand what the boy book is if we look to both
sides of it—first to the fictional "story for boys" and then to the
autobiographical account of childhood.

The category "story for boys" had a more restricted meaning in the nineteenth century than it would today. We think of books like *Treasure Island* (1883) and *Kim* (1901) as coming under this rubric (or in a more egalitarian age, as coming under the rubric stories for children), but we know from book reviews and memoirs of nineteenth-century readers that these books appealed to adults as well as children. To look at some examples that are unambiguously stories for boys and are superficially close to the boy book, we might consider Trowbridge's Jack Hazard stories and Eggleston's *The Hoosier School-Boy*. Trowbridge acknowledged that "very faithful descriptions of the farm life and scenes in which I was brought up" were contained in some of his Jack Hazard stories, but he also insisted "you will not find much of me personally in those stories" (Rideing 29). Eggleston offered a similar disclaimer: he acknowledged that he had "drawn my native village" in *The Hoosier School-Boy* and observed, "my stories are full of the reflections of my childhood," but added "of undiluted autobiography there is little" (Rideing 73). What distinguishes *Jack Hazard and His Fortunes* (1871; the first of the series) and *The Hoosier School-Boy* from the boy books are their clear didactic aims, which limit their appeal to a juvenile audience and require the author to treat childhood recollections as mere background to his moralistic concerns. It is fair to say that these authors take advantage of the credulity of their young readers. The realistic settings command assent, but the gullible reader finds himself in a world inhabited by familiar character types and governed by the most improbable plot coincidences, which in turn make possible sentimental scenes and moralistic observations. The reader of *Tom Sawyer* who recalls Huck and Tom fortuitously discovering the existence of the evil half-breed Injun Joe's treasure will realize that the boundaries between the story for boys and the boy book are not impassable. Nevertheless, it would be impossible for this same reader to confuse *Tom Sawyer* and a Jack Hazard book: even the titles, *The Adventures of Tom Sawyer* and *Jack Hazard and His Fortunes* point to a telling difference in focus.

If the boy book is not a story for boys, it is not an autobiography of childhood either. Such an autobiography differs significantly from the life story of an adult, and the difference is not simply one of scope. Roy Pascal distinguishes helpfully between accounts of childhood contained within longer autobiographies and accounts limited to childhood alone:

> When the childhood is merely the preface to the account of the mature man, experiences tend to be singled out that fore-shadow the later development. There is then a double selective principle, on the one hand what is remembered, on the other, what is considered of relevance to the later achievement. One can admit that the latter principle is never utterly absent, but in autobiographies that are limited to childhood, it is much less imperious. Such autobiographies show the formation of a temperament, not a public or even a private character. (85)

Whereas Pascal acknowledges that "relevance to the later achievement" cannot be "utterly absent," Richard N. Coe, with an apparently more modest definition of "later achievement," argues that consciousness of this relevance is what gives the work its distinctive character. To him, the childhood autobiography is

> *an extended piece of writing . . . in which the most substantial portion of the material is directly autobiographical, and whose structure reflects step by step the development of the writer's self; beginning often, but not invariably, with the first light of consciousness and concluding, quite specifically, with the attainment of a precise degree of maturity. . . .* The formal literary structure is complete at exactly the point at which the immature self of childhood is conscious of its transformation into the mature self of the adult who is the narrator of the earlier experience. (8–9)

Both critics recognize that the informing point of view of the childhood autobiography, like that of all autobiographies, is necessarily that of the remembering and recording adult. Yet expression of the unmediated responses of the child (so far as it is possible for the adult to recapture these) is a central part of the childhood autobiography. Both critics find room for these responses but see them finally contained within the overriding story of growth, whether it be the "formation of a temperament," "the attainment . . . of maturity," or, if we prefer the language of the period of the boy books, the development of character. The structure that will follow from such an end is necessarily chronological. As Pascal notes, "The common structure of accounts of childhood is given by its common theme—growing up" (84). Garland's *A Son of the Middle Border* (1917) and Sherwood Anderson's *Tar* (1926) are examples of such autobiographies.

The boy book is sometimes organized to present a series of adventures or experiences over time, but it does not concern itself with the development of the boy into the man who narrates the story. The subtitles of many of the books point to the specific focus on boyhood and boyish adventures: Rossiter Johnson's *Phaeton Rogers* (1881) is subtitled *A Novel of Boy Life;* Joel Chandler Harris's *On the Plantation* (1892), *A Story of a Georgia Boy's Adventures During the War;* and Ellis Parker Butler's *Swatty* (1915), *A Story of Real Boys.* At the same time, these books and the canonical works I listed earlier differ from the story for boys because, despite their sometimes heavy admixture of fiction, they are essentially autobiographical. Instead of detailing the process by which the boy becomes the man who writes the book, they use the return to boyhood as a way of confronting those issues from the past that remain alive in the present—what Cady called the "predicament of the man-child." In so confronting the past, and interpreting and inevitably recasting it in light of present needs, a work—necessarily a fiction to some extent—emerges that is an autobiography, not of childhood, but of the adult engaged with his childhood. The engagement with the past takes a different form than it does in the autobiography of childhood. In the passage above, Coe speaks of the autobiography of childhood culminating in the convergence of two viewpoints—that of the developing child and that of the narrating adult. Because the boy book is the work of an author who perceives his childhood as profoundly distinct from his adulthood, the two viewpoints do not converge. Instead, we have a genre in which the narrator and the younger self, the boy protagonist, occupy separate realms.

Because the boy book struck so responsive a chord with the public, the genre appealed not only to writers seeking to explore autobiographical issues, but also to writers eager to profit from the market these books created. I have already spoken of the willingness of authors and publishers to reprint boy books as schoolbooks and of the new life the boy book gave the work of literary humorists. Another aspect of the widespread desire to profit from interest in the boy books is the proliferation of books similar to the autobiographical boy book in appearance but lacking the personal urgency that informed the genre as it originally developed. Many authors of successful boy books wrote sequels that carried them increasingly away from the autobiographical impulses that had first informed their work and into a simple series of adventures. [16] Many now-forgotten or seldom-read male authors also contributed to the rising swell; even some female authors wrote books that were contenders in the same market. Many of these works were frankly imitative of the autobiographical boy book, but without the author's personal motive were little more than a series of boyish escapades. Others seem to have a different agenda: the books by women, in general, seem to be offered as correctives to accepted male behavior. [17] Still others, such as those of Johnson and Butler mentioned above, refer occasionally to a younger "I" and so alert us to the author's personal involvement in his story, but that story is not presented self-consciously or skillfully enough for us to disentangle it from the more or less conventional boy adventures that occupy the bulk of the books. In short, the boy books that stand out for us because of their investigation of autobiographical issues became, as time went on, increasingly embedded in a welter of what Norris, making no subtle distinctions, called "Pinkys and Skinnys."

My central concern, as I have indicated, is with the boy book as it first appeared, an autobiographical form essentially defined by a separation of narrator and protagonist. Contemporary theoretical work on autobiography alerts us to the formal consequences of such a separation in autobiography and enhances our understanding of what that distance means. Reflecting on the fact that there is always a distance between the narrating "I" of an autobiography and the self of whom he speaks, Lejeune observes that the distance "may become excessively wide in a narrative or in autobiography which rests on an articulation and a perpetual interchange between discourse and history." Because of the experiential differences between man and boy, an autobiography of childhood and a boy book, of course, are superlative examples of such works. Lejeune sees the distance between narrator and protagonist as providing creative opportunities for the writer as he seeks to recapture or, more accurately, reinvent, his past self: "The inherent duality of the narrative voice corresponds to gaps in perspective between the narrator and the hero. These discrepancies of information and appreciation facilitate the games of focalization and voice typical of this kind of narrative (for example, limitation of one's field of vision to that of the character, use of the narrator's intrusions, presentation of lyric or ironic passages, etc.)" ("Third Person" 31). The boy book authors try all of these "games" and add some others as well. We will see examples of liberties taken with the placement of biographical facts to allow the narrator to emphasize important events, of narrative frames to distance and comment on the story, of protagonists split into two characters to afford the narrator two responses to his younger self, and of poems—literally lyric passages—inserted in the text to mark the presence of a voice removed from the story.

Even where the narrator and protagonist are not characterized as distinct individuals, as will be the case in some of the boy books I examine, the presence of the narrator as someone apart from his protagonist is felt through his use of a style and tone that is sometimes faithful to a boyish perspective, but is equally often inappropriate, or, more accurately, ironically appropriate, and therefore appropriate to the adult. Lejeune is helpful in describing what is happening in such a text. After looking at the accounts of childhood by Jules Vallès, which he finds anomalous in French literature for their blurring of the distinction between narrator and protagonist, Lejeune speaks of the mixed texture of the narrative. Again he emphasizes game playing on the part of the author: "The blends of voices between the narrator and the hero appear less like the articulation of two chronologically different cases, than like the result of a work within a voice that mimes, reverses its mimes, jeers, plays naive, a *made-up* voice that no longer makes any 'natural' (that is to say, believable) sound but that perhaps invents a new form of the natural" ("Ironic Narrative" 69). Unlike the unity achieved at the end of the autobiography of childhood described by Pascal and Coe, the unity of past and present achieved by a text constructed like Vallès's—and some of the boy books—is apparent rather than real.

Recognition of the autobiographer's dual perspective and the devices through which he expresses his two points of view thus provides us with a powerful interpretive key to autobiographies in general and to the childhood autobiography and the boy book in particular. But making use of this key is not a simple matter of discerning how the narrator feels about the past as opposed to how the protagonist feels about the same events. As Lejeune notes, there is a "perpetual interchange between discourse and history"—a constant shifting of attitudes as the narrator relives his past in recalling it and brings his present condition to bear on it in interpreting it. A reader must take into account the varied texture of the books and recognize that they are as much—or more—about the present as they are about the past.

Jean Starobinski, in his discussion of the most famous of all childhood autobiographies, Rousseau's *Confessions,* provides an example of such a flexible reading and an explanation of the shifting moods he finds. He discerns in the *Confessions* a mixture of elegiac and picaresque episodes, the equivalent of the "lyric or ironic" passages to which Lejeune refers. He understands this mixture, as Lejeune would, as an expression of the dual perspective of the narrator, that is, as the response of the narrator who identifies himself with his child subject, but who also recognizes his distance from that earlier self. Starobinski then goes a step further, relating the two voices to Rousseau's "system"—a "system" that clearly underlies the nineteenth-century boy books as well: "According to that philosophy, man originally possessed happiness and joy: in comparison with that first felicity, the present time is a time of degradation and corruption. But man was originally a brute deprived of 'light,' his reason still asleep; compared to that initial obscurity, the present is a time of lucid reflection and enlarged consciousness" (83). Childhood, when seen from the remembered perspective of youth, is consequently presented in a lyrical or elegiac mode, a perspective that implicitly casts an ironic light on the present; when seen from the unillusioned perspective of adulthood, it can only be treated in a picturesque or ironic mode. Starobinski's explanation has the virtue not only of explaining the fluctuating moods of the childhood autobiography and the boy book, but also of suggesting why the inclusion of fictional material in these autobiographical genres does not compromise their standing as autobiography. The book he describes may well not be faithful to the facts of the past yet may be faithful to the present condition of the writer as he recalls his past and so honor the autobiographical pact.

With this in mind, we can return to the world that gave rise to the boy book and to the particular authors I will examine. The nostalgia for a world lost to the Civil War or to the imperatives of nineteenth-century industrialism accounts in good part for the elegiac strain we find in all the boy books. And the recognition that if the past was paradise lost, the present is a fallen world in which the race is to the swift accounts for the ironic strain with which boy books writers view their own past innocence. Within this context, the writers I will examine confront their particular problems. As I will argue, a particular crisis of male adulthood is the motive and the shaping force behind each of the boy books. My authors look to their roles as fathers or would-be fathers, as husbands, as breadwinners, and find themselves wanting. The mixture of attitudes that the boy book comfortably encompasses makes the retreat to boyhood a retreat from and a critique of present difficulties and—though this seems to be realized on an intuitive rather than a conscious level—an opportunity to confront the sources of the difficulty. Inevitably, as we will learn, this means a confrontation with the author's father, the person who should have taught him how to be a man, who should not have bequeathed him so ill-fitting a world. Inevitably, given the discontent that informs these books, that father will be found wanting.

To think of the boy book in the terms I suggest here is to understand better why Howells found *The Story of a Bad Boy,* and by implication the other boy books, appealing to "every man that happens to have been a boy" and why Norris saw in the highly conventional Pinkys and Skinnys the life of "the average American business man before he grew up." The boy book not only portrayed widely shared boyhood experiences and so allowed each male reader to flesh out the page before him with his own memories, but also spoke to the particular difficulties of being a man in late nineteenth- and early twentieth-century America.

2

# THOMAS BAILEY ALDRICH AND
## —— CHARLES DUDLEY WARNER

In turning to the particular boy books that constitute the substance of this study, my approach will be to look first at the situation of the author at the point at which he recalls his past and writes his book. Doing so should make it possible to identify the concerns of the adult that most likely prompted his reengagement with his childhood and that, in turn, shaped the book he wrote. In the case of my first two examples, Aldrich and Warner, we must work without detailed biographical studies.[1] Nevertheless, we can make reasonable guesses as to each writer's motivation.

Aldrich was thirty-two and close to the beginning of his career when he wrote *The Story of a Bad Boy*. An expectant first-time father, he spent the summer of 1868 in Portsmouth, New Hampshire, his own boyhood home after his father's death, working on his book. He returned to Boston in the fall, put the finishing touches on the book, and, in a happy juxtaposition of events, became the father of twin boys the day after completing his manuscript (Greenslet 89). The prospect of fatherhood, along with a summer spent in a much-loved boyhood home, would be powerful incentives for any man to recall his past. For Aldrich recollection was undoubtedly complicated because that happy boyhood home was his in consequence of his father's death. He now faced fatherhood without a father on which to model himself and with memories of a boyhood that was happy enough to suggest that perhaps a father was not so very necessary.

For Warner the immediate motive is less clear. He was older than Aldrich—forty-eight—and well established, ensconced in the comfortable society of Nook Farm in Hartford, Connecticut, and known as Mark Twain's one-time coauthor and as an editor and essayist in his own right. With memories of his own childhood rather than children of his own to inspire him, he put together *Being a Boy* (Fields 13–14, Lounsbury iii–iv). What specific crisis triggered those memories, however, is lost to us. Kenneth R. Andrews, the historian of Nook Farm, has noted that nostalgia for the past was a central motif in the best books of that literary community (206); we might assume therefore that reminiscences played a significant part in the conversations of so many like-minded friends. A reference to *Being a Boy* as "My Only Boy" suggests that disappointment in not having children of his own was an important incentive to Warner to create a literary child.[2] If he needed further encouragement, the successes of Aldrich's book and of Twain's *Tom Sawyer* would have provided it.[3]

These different circumstances and motives led to different kinds of books. Between them, Aldrich's and Warner's works define the two general categories to which boy books belong, a fact that makes them, in addition to their early dates of publication, proper introductions to this study. Aldrich's reinvolvement in Portsmouth life evoked specific, detailed memories. The result was a book that, as we have seen, Howells praised for its realistic treatment of a particular boy's life: "No one else seems to have thought of telling the story of a boy's life, with so great desire to show what a boy's life is, and so little purpose of teaching what it should be." It was "a new thing in . . . American Literature." Warner's *Being a Boy,* the product of more distant reminiscence— its author being separated from his subject by more time and space than was Aldrich—also earned Howells's praise in his review in the December 1877 *Atlantic* as something "new in kind" (764). Its distinction was that it was a generic account of a boy's life: "What is expressed is the essence of a country boy's life in a New England hill town thirty or forty years ago. In the process, many facts must be stated, but they are those which characterize the average boy John rather than any particular boy John" (763).

These two approaches—the particular and the generic—carry with them a variety of consequences in terms of form and content. The particular story tends to be linear in form, each chapter presenting an event unique to the individual boy. This structure is common to the majority of boy books, for it is probably the easiest of all literary forms to follow, it can be readily serialized, and it is particularly accessible to a young reader. The main difficulty it presents for an author who is not concerned with tracing his boy protagonist's progress to adulthood is how to conclude his book. The generic story, in contrast, tends to be cyclical in form because it focuses on the typical and therefore recurrent patterns in a boy's life. It is easier for an author to conclude such a book, but harder for him to find ways to incorporate his unique story. Both forms proved provocative and fruitful for the autobiographically minded boy book author.

*The Story of a Bad Boy* was first published in *Our Young Folks* in twelve serial installments, from January to December 1869. It appeared in book form the next year. Although Aldrich was to assert in his 1894 Preface to the book that "a generous destiny provided him with ample material for his autobiography, and he invented next to nothing" (iv), his book is not an autobiography of childhood; it is written with only perfunctory reference to the author's adult life. It is also less faithful to biographical fact than Aldrich's remarks suggest. He included an apparently fictional account of a reunion between a maid and her long-lost sailor husband to provide some comic relief after a tragic episode and to help move the book toward closure. He also shifted the central fact of his life in Portsmouth, the life recounted in *Story of a Bad Boy,* from the time preceding his years in Portsmouth to the conclusion of those years. As Aldrich's biographer tells us, Aldrich spent three years, from age eleven to fourteen, in Portsmouth after the death of his father, living with his mother and maternal grandfather and attending school in preparation for a college education that was finally deemed beyond the financial reach of his family (Greenslet 11–16). In the book, Tom Bailey—the name Aldrich went by, but also one that distances the boy protagonist from the adult narrator and thereby opens the way for a dual perspective on events—spends several years in Rivermouth (the name is another distancing gesture), living with his grandfather and attending school. His parents remain in New Orleans, and at the end of the book, his father dies offstage. The rearrangement makes the happy years in Portsmouth seem all the more idyllic because they are not purchased with the father's death. It also serves the formal end of providing Aldrich with a logical stopping point for his story. Most important, it allows Aldrich to explore his feelings about losing a father and, by implication, about becoming a father.

Tom Bailey's story begins with Tom in New Orleans anticipating his journey north. We travel to Rivermouth with him and are introduced, as he is, to the town, Grandfather Nutter's household, a new school, and new friends. It is a congenial environment for Tom, and he flourishes, which is to say, he learns how to be a boy without his father present—a reflection of Aldrich's own experience that, as an anxious father-to-be, he must have found both comforting and disheartening. Tom's grandfather, "who knew what a boy loved, if ever a grandfather did" (41), encouraged the boy's mildly aggressive nature by decorating his room with an old shotgun and by supporting his fighting with the school bully. The companionship of his friends, who formed a gang for the sole purpose of creating mischief, provided an influence under which Tom "became more manly and self-reliant" (59).[4] With these friends he engages in a series of activities ranging from a play put on in the barn to a Fourth of July prank to a marathon snow fight—typical boy adventures particularized by Tom and his friends and by the Rivermouth setting of the book.

The events do not work toward any particular end. Aldrich follows Tom through a year in Rivermouth—we are frequently made aware of the particular season or holiday at hand—and then vaguely notes the passage of another year and more. These years bring additional adventures, including a grand prank played on the townspeople and a crush on an older girl. For the most part, each event is a discrete adventure having no necessary connection with any other. Tom consequently does not appear to age at all. The position of the boyish romance near the end of the book suggests adolescence, but Aldrich is not interested in this sort of maturity in *Story of a Bad Boy* and does not explore it. Like all boy books, this one minimizes the passage of time.

The linear structure of the story is particularly congenial to the dual perspective inherent in all autobiography, since each event is independent of what precedes or follows it, and the narrator's shifting attitudes need not be harmonized. Aldrich begins his book by calling our attention to its dual perspective as he both allies himself with and distances himself from his younger self in a passage that anticipates both Lejeune's and Starobinski's remarks about the shifting nature of the narrator's involvement with his protagonist: "This is the Story of a Bad Boy. Well, not such a very bad, but a pretty bad boy; and I ought to know, for *I am, or rather I was,* that boy myself" (3; my emphasis). Most often Aldrich, as I will refer to the barely characterized narrating persona, simply recounts an event with good-natured gusto, evoking the delight he took in the affair as a boy yet remembering too that his book will be sold as a story for boys and so moralizing ever so slightly for their edification. Aldrich's moralizing never becomes the overriding concern it is for Trowbridge or Eggleston; it is rather a minor part of the older and wiser narrator's character. In that self-conscious role of adult looking back, he also reflects on his childish limitations. We become most aware of his adult presence through his occasional direct interventions in his story. More often we feel the adult presence through his gentle, forgiving irony as he recalls such things as his uncritical admiration of the garish wallpaper in his grandfather's house, the innocence that allowed him to be very nearly gulled into treating all of his friends to ice cream on the Fourth of July, or the mixture of fear and eagerness with which he approached his initiation into the gang, the Rivermouth Centipedes.

Even the episode that occasions the most extensive ironic treatment of his younger self is a cause for compassion. When an older cousin, a young woman of nineteen, comes to stay with Grandfather Nutter for a short time, Tom falls hopelessly in love with her. Though he must have been about thirteen at the time, and though in the previous chapter he has scared the entire town out of its wits by setting off a dozen of the old cannons that the city had abandoned along one of the wharves, Tom suddenly becomes "a small boy" (229) observing a beautiful lady. He suffers genuine torment: "How I despised little boys! How I hated one particular little boy—too little to be loved!" (232). Foreshadowing Tom Sawyer, he becomes a "Blighted Being" (238)—a role he has learned from the fiction he has read and one that suits his present mood though, as the adult narrator clearly realizes and perhaps the child lover too, it was not congenial to his basic temperament:

"A translation of The Sorrows of Young Werther fell into my hands at this period, and if I could have committed suicide without killing myself, I should certainly have done so" (242). Lest we miss the tenderness that accompanies the mockery of the younger self, Aldrich also intervenes to remark: "I smile over this very grimly even now. My sorrow was genuine and bitter. . . . The burdens of childhood are as hard to bear as the crosses that weigh us down later in life, while the happinesses of childhood are tame compared with those of our maturer years" (232).

Occasionally, Aldrich's irony is directed at the adults who governed his young life. His great aunt, Miss Abigail, who recommends hot drops as a cure for every ailment (as Aunt Polly will later prescribe a spoonful of Pain-Killer) and who faints at the sight of Grandfather Nutter "smoking" an empty pipe in spite of her prohibition against smoking indoors, comes in for some good natured ribbing. Kindly Grandfather Nutter is handled more gently and less directly, as is evident in Aldrich's account of a typical Sunday. He begins by commenting, "Sunday was *not* a cheerful day at the Nutter House. You shall judge for yourself" (66). Then he goes on to judge for us. Throughout his account we hear his adult voice, distant from the child who suffered the soul-stifling boredom of the life-denying Sabbath, witty now at the expense of those who inflicted such torture on him. The shift to the present tense marks this episode as one of those "games of focalization" that Lejeune mentions in which the adult narrator adopts the child's perspective, but the extensive hyperbole reminds us of the adult narrator's freedom to pass judgments that the child could not, and by extension, of the distance between the protagonist and the narrator:

> At seven o'clock my grandfather comes smilelessly down-stairs. He is dressed in black, and looks as if he had lost all his friends during the night. Miss Abigail, also in black, looks as if she were prepared to bury them, and not indisposed to enjoy the ceremony. Even Kitty Collins [the maid] has caught the contagious gloom, as I perceive when she brings in the coffee-urn—a solemn and sculpturesque urn at any time, but monumental now—and sets it down in front of Miss Abigail. Miss Abigail gazes at the urn as if it held the ashes of her ancestors, instead of a generous quantity of fine old Java coffee. The meal progresses in silence. (67)

After Sunday school and two church services, Tom and his grandfather go for a walk: "We visit, appropriately enough, a neighbor-
ing graveyard. I am by this time in a condition of mind to become
a willing inmate of the place" (69). The wit is sharper here than
elsewhere in the book because it is informed by a memory of
recurrent childhood discomfort, but Aldrich's stance is one of
good-humored understanding and forgiveness. He concludes his
chapter by shifting back into the past tense and into his more
neutral narrative voice: "This is the way Sunday was observed in
the Nutter House, and pretty generally throughout the town,
twenty years ago. Persons who were prosperous and natural and
happy on Saturday became the most rueful of human beings in
the brief space of twelve hours. I do not think there was any
hypocrisy in this. It was merely the old Puritan austerity cropping
out once a week" (69).

In contrast to the lively adventures and the ironic backward
glances is the death of one of Tom's playmates, Binny Wallace. The
death of a childhood playmate is a commonplace of nineteenth-
century children's fiction, but in this case, the death was a real-life
event (Greenslet 12), and Howells recognized its authenticity. He
praised the chapter recounting the death as "the best in the book,"
"the simplest and directest piece of narration . . . singularly
touching" (Review of *Story* 125). The account is colored by Aldrich's knowledge of its tragic ending, but that does not prevent
his real reinvestment in the experience, which Howells acknowledged in his praise and which we feel in the disappearance of the
distancing ironic voice. Aldrich begins with a comment that
alerts us to the coming change in his narrative stance: "My
thoughts revert to this particular spring more frequently than to
any other period of my boyhood, for it was marked by an event
that left an indelible impression on my memory. As I pen these
pages, I feel that I am writing of something which happened
yesterday, so vividly it all comes back to me" (152).

He recalls an outing he took with three friends. The boys took
proper precautions: they rowed instead of sailing to avoid the
danger of sudden squalls, and they took a fifth oar. Aldrich comments, "The scent of the new clover comes back to me now, as I
recall that delicious morning when we floated away in a fairy boat
down a river like a dream!" (159). They found an island, pitched a

tent using all five oars, fished and made chowder, and settled down to a delectable feast to be eaten from clam-shell saucers. "How happy we were, we four, sitting cross-legged in the crisp salt grass, with the invigorating sea-breeze blowing gratefully through our hair! What a joyous thing was life, and how far off seemed death—death, that lurks in all pleasant places, and was so near!" (160). After the chowder Binny returns to the boat to get some lemons for lemonade—but a storm comes up and the boat breaks adrift carrying Binny to his death without an oar to save himself.

Aldrich ends the chapter, which has been narrated with an impressive directness and economy, with some degree of sentimentality and triteness as he tries to interpret its meaning for his adult self: "Poor little Binny Wallace! Always the same to me. The rest of us have grown up into hard, worldly men, fighting the fight of life; but you are forever young, and gentle, and pure; a part of my own childhood that time cannot wither; always a little boy, always poor little Binny Wallace!" (171–72). It is hard for a twentieth-century reader not to fault Aldrich for the sentimentality of his observation that death "lurks in all pleasant places" and his contrasting "pure" boyhood with "hard" manhood. But in context this sentimentality is offset by the simplicity with which the whole episode has been narrated, giving substance to Aldrich's comment that he feels as if he is writing about what happened yesterday. It is also offset by the paradox that Binny's death has preserved not only Binny's youth as we might expect, but also a part of Aldrich's own childhood. The entire episode is a reengagement with the original experience that stands in marked contrast to the ironic distancing from childhood experience we see elsewhere in the book.

Within a page of the opening of the chapter following Binny's death (we are now about two-thirds of the way through *Story of a Bad Boy*), we hear news of Tom's father for the first time since the beginning of the book: the New Orleans banking house with which he is connected is in financial trouble through the default of a major customer. Within a short time, the weakened bank itself will fail, and Tom's father will be detained in New Orleans to settle his affairs. Unable to flee a cholera epidemic, he will die without ever seeing his son again. This catastrophe is delayed until the end of the book by the comic reunion of Kitty Collins and her sailor husband and by Tom's crush on his older cousin.

The question must arise, why did Aldrich introduce his father's business problems so close to Binny's death? There seems to be some associative connection between that death, which keeps part of Tom's childhood alive into his adulthood, and the death of Tom's father, which follows directly from his business problems. Aldrich is not explicit on this matter, but near the end of the book, he describes Tom's reaction to his father's death. Like the account of Binny's death, the passage is in sharp contrast to Aldrich's earlier accounts of Tom, in particular to the ironic accounts of Tom mourning in the guise of Blighted Being. There is no narrational distance from the subject now as Tom Bailey's grief becomes Thomas Aldrich's: "As the days went by my first grief subsided, and in its place grew up a want which I have experienced at every step in life from boyhood to manhood. Often, even now, after all these years, when I see a lad of twelve or fourteen walking by his father's side, and glancing merrily up at his face, I turn and look after them, and am conscious that I have missed companionship most sweet and sacred" (268). The death of the father is in effect an unhealed wound; because of it, a part of Tom's childhood cannot be completed as it should have been. Significantly, the adult Aldrich, the father-to-be, identifies with the young boy and not his father "even now, after all these years." We understand at this point that Binny's death does more than introduce Tom to death; in its effect, it is the prototype of the loss he suffers when his father dies. Aldrich's rearrangement of events for his book, an act of fictionalizing of far more significance than the Kitty Collins plot, allows him to acknowledge through his protagonist not only that he has missed having his father, but also that the loss left him childlike, which is to say, vulnerable. For all the remembered pleasures of boyhood in this book, for all its good-natured irony, the central story it has to tell is one of pain and insecurity.

Yet Aldrich's genial temperament forbids his dwelling on this matter. To do so would be to insist that a father matters more than the general tenor of this book has suggested, and to so insist would feed the anxieties of the first-time father. So Aldrich retreats. The offstage death spares him, as well as the reader, what his childhood did not: direct confrontation with the horrors of death from cholera.

The death of Tom's father also provides Aldrich an opportunity to express his anger at his altered prospects, but true to his temperament, he does so in a rather repressed form. With a seeming lack of bitterness, Tom accepts the change in family plans occasioned by his father's death: he gives up his cherished dream of being a Harvard man and prepares to leave Rivermouth to go into his uncle's countinghouse. The uncle is eager to enlist Tom's services: he is afraid delay will encourage the boy to embark on a literary career. But Aldrich, recalling his similarly delayed career as a man of letters, exacts a small bit of revenge on business life. He literally has the last laugh. Shifting into a distancing irony again and mocking Tom's uncle as he enters into his point of view, he notes that the uncle's fears were based on his having seen some of the boy's poetry: "Now, the idea of a boy, with his living to get, placing himself in communication with the Moon, struck the mercantile mind as monstrous. It was not only a bad investment, it was lunacy" (271). We have already seen Tom's father fail in business and have no reason to feel particular confidence in the mercantile mind. In fact, we see immediately how limited that mind is, for it misjudges Tom. We know he will continue as a man of letters—even the child reader knows this, for he has Aldrich's book in hand—and we applaud when Tom wryly comments, "We adopted Uncle Snow's view *so far* as to accede to his proposition forthwith" (271; my emphasis).

The book ends as it began. The first chapter opened with an adult Tom introducing himself as one who was once "a real human boy . . . no more like the impossible boy in a story-book than a sound orange is like one that has been sucked dry" (4) and reminiscing about the past, telling us what has become of each of his boy friends whom we will come to know. The last chapter also reaches beyond Tom's Rivermouth years to tell us how other characters in the story have fared and concludes, "So ends the Story of a Bad Boy—but not such a very bad boy, as I told you to begin with" (278).

Although *Story of a Bad Boy* has received little modern critical attention, it is worth noting that Aldrich's differing attitudes toward his past have allowed for widely varying responses to the book. Albert E. Stone, reviewing the treatment of childhood in literature that preceded Mark Twain's work, observes that nostalgia for his boyhood past distinguishes Aldrich's treatment of childhood from that of Jacob Abbott (author of the Rollo books) and Nathaniel Hawthorne: "With Aldrich, boyhood for the first time is a past, not a present, condition of life to be celebrated" (27–28). He also notes the shifts in point of view in the work from that of "experiencing boy" to "remembering adult" (29) and concludes: "This shifting back and forth between boyish character and adult author becomes actually the underlying theme of the novel" (28). Stone is surely correct in linking Aldrich's nostalgia to his reengagement with his younger self— no such feeling emerges, for example, from *An Old Town by the Sea* (1893), Aldrich's account of his beloved Portsmouth. But by ignoring the irony that so often characterizes the adult voice in *Story of a Bad Boy,* Stone suggests a more somber and more sentimental book than we actually have. Ann Beattie errs in the opposite direction. She observes, "The general mood of the novel—and of its main character—ranges from cheerful to ebullient. In part, this may be explained in terms of perspective: Tom Bailey writes the book as an adult, and adults, in America, learn to overlook the bad (how else can we forge new frontiers?) just as little boys learn not to cry" (vi). As I have argued, *Story of a Bad Boy* encompasses several attitudes toward the past, for the "remembering adult" is not constant in his relation to his past self.

Of course, we must accept Aldrich's claim that he was presenting "a real human boy" with caution: Tom lacks complexity, and his mischievous behavior will soon be as conventional in nineteenth-century literature as that of the angelic child Aldrich was implicitly criticizing. Yet because Aldrich was dealing with autobiographical issues in creating Tom and telling his story, he brought his past and present to the character. When he looked back at Tom Bailey, he saw himself, and made his claim to realism in good faith. In his identification with Tom and his gentle irony, he reveals a generally comfortable maturity from which he can acknowledge past pleasure and accept past limitation. At the same time, his positioning of Tom's father's death and his identification with Tom's grief signals a troubling vulnerability that seems to have assumed new life as he approached fatherhood.

Next to *The Story of a Bad Boy*, Warner's *Being a Boy* seems flaccid. Not surprisingly, it has merited only the most perfunctory critical discussion. The book seems to have been put together casually and carelessly. Thomas R. Lounsbury, editor of the *Complete Writings of Charles Dudley Warner*, tells us that "*Being a Boy* was published at the end of November, 1877. Portions of it had probably appeared previously in various periodicals, and possibly most of it; but with the exception of one chapter, which came out in the 'St. Nicholas' for January, 1874, none of them have been traced" (Note [i]). Such an origin suggests that Warner did not think in terms of a book at first. His remark on the "waywardness" of his collection of essays on boyhood (viii) in the Preface written twenty years later certainly lends retrospective support to the notion that the idea of a book was something of an afterthought. Given the fact that we cannot locate the first appearance of the various essays, we have no way of knowing how much, if any, revising and rearranging he did when he collected them. Judging from the end result, he did very little: *Being a Boy* is a more rambling book than Aldrich's, and its protagonist is handled inconsistently. Nevertheless, like Aldrich's book, Warner's has something to tell us about its author as he recalls, admittedly indirectly, a parentless childhood and a childless adulthood.

The biographical facts that inform Warner's book are surprisingly similar to those that shaped *Story of a Bad Boy*. Like Aldrich, Warner lost his father when he was young and spent several important boyhood years—in Warner's case, from his eighth to twelfth year—in the care of a relative. Unlike Aldrich, however, Warner was taken to live on a farm in western Massachusetts and was separated from his mother (Fields 11–13). When Aldrich wrote about his boyhood, he fictionalized slightly. Warner, whose boyhood experience must have been more painful because of what amounted to the loss of both parents at once, chose instead to depersonalize his experience, even going so far as to refrain from characterizing the people with whom his boy lives. "The rural life described is that of New England between 1830 and 1850, in a period of darkness before the use of lucifer matches," he wrote in the 1897 Preface to the book; "There was no attempt at the biography of any particular boy; the experiences given were common to the boyhood of the time and place. While the book therefore, was not consciously biographical, it was of necessity written out of a personal knowledge" (viii–ix). The claim that he is not writing autobiography is insistent enough— Warner states twice that he is telling a generic story and then apologizes for having to add any personal element—for us to suspect that Warner is trying to protect himself. While he rightly recognized that he had not written a childhood autobiography, he knew that his book did deal with autobiographical issues.

The book itself suggests that it took Warner a while to figure out how to present the generic story he set his sights on, for we see him groping for both a suitable structure and a proper pro- tagonist. *Being a Boy* begins with several loosely related essays or chapters on the pleasures of rural boyhood. Eventually, however, the book settles into an account—with some interruptions—of a year in a farm boy's life. Warner describes such typical events as a Thanksgiving feast, a lonely winter evening, a maple sugar camp in the spring, and a revival that comes in the summer. Events are included, not because they are particular to an individual life, but because they are recurring and representative. As is appropriate to such a structure, Warner takes care not to specify his boy's age, merely suggesting at one point that ten is ideal for a farm boy and at another that what he recounts is applicable to a boy between eight and fourteen. Warner's emphasis on the recurrent has the further effect of freeing boyhood from the constraints of time. Even though he locates his story in a particular time and place, the events, and by implication the boyish experiences, he dis- cusses are as enduring as the passage of the seasons.

While Aldrich's linear structure readily accommodates bio- graphical particulars, Warner's cyclical structure is more resistant. At first glance it looks as if Warner has found a way around this difficulty. Like Aldrich's work, his book is narrated by an older man looking back, another slightly characterized persona who frequently reminds us of his presence by such remarks as "as I remember" (152) or "a generation ago" (199), as well as by his occasional moralizing. He narrates events in the lives of both a distinctive younger self, "I," and a representative boy, "the boy" or John. "I" gives the cows he herds the names of Roman numerals, tries to convince himself that his pet fox is above stealing chickens, and fantasizes about laborsaving devices that will enable him to stay in bed on winter mornings. John does routine farm chores, longs to go fishing, and attends school. But the distinction breaks down rapidly: "I" too does some chores and dreams of fishing, while John has what surely must have been an experience particular to Warner: when the revival comes to town, John, alone of his friends and family, fails to find a conviction of sin. Like Tom Bailey, he is simply a good bad boy—"you could n't find a much better wicked boy than John" (182), Warner tells us— basically decent, if impatient with his chores and a bit hot-tempered. It seems as if "I" and John are not really two distinct characters at all but an inconsistency left over from the original publication of the essays that were collected for the book. In allowing that inconsistency to remain, however, Warner points to the possibility of treating the protagonist of a generic boy's story as two people who together represent the author's historical and personal interests. Both Howells and Garland would exploit this procedure to very provocative ends.

If Warner could not turn his protagonist to real advantage, he could indulge the dual perspective of the autobiographer, distancing himself from his protagonist at times, identifying closely with him at others. Warner sometimes views his younger self with irony—especially in his timid relationships with girls. More often Warner stands at an even further remove from his story than does Aldrich at his most ironic. Warner's desire to write an impersonal account of boy life probably explains some of this distancing, but an inability or disinclination to get too close to himself must also be at work. His device is the aside, a form of reflection that is certainly detrimental to his work, because it takes us away from the protagonist's life. But Warner's asides are of interest to us as students of the boy book, because Warner touches on so many things other writers were to pick up. He muses on the pleasures of boyhood: "One of the best things in the world to be is a boy; it requires no experience, though it needs some practice to be a good one. The disadvantage of the position is that it does not last long enough; it is soon over" (1). He observes that a boy is a "natural savage" (198): "He has the primal, vigorous instincts and impulses of the African savage, without any of the vices inherited from a civilization long ago decayed or developed in an unrestrained barbaric society" (198–99; we might note in passing the Romantic view of savagery expressed here). And he is drawn to warlike sports and games, "not alone from his love of fighting," but "from his fondness for display" (199). Perhaps with a nod to Mark Twain, Warner includes an anecdote about a good boy who comes to a bad end, reflecting that "John was a very different boy from Solomon [the good boy], not half so good, nor half so dead" (99), and another about a bad boy who comes to a good end (169–70).

Although he holds back in these many instances, Warner does occasionally reinvest himself in the past. This is particularly true in passages describing the appeal of outdoor life. In one typical instance, he begins, "John, it is true, did not care much for anything that did not appeal to his taste and smell and delight in brilliant color; and he trod down the exquisite ferns and the wonderful mosses without compunction" (175–76). Then the judging voice of the adult narrator recedes as Warner continues: "But he gathered from the crevices of the rocks the columbine and the eglantine and the blue harebell; he picked the high-flavored alpine strawberry, the blueberry, the boxberry, wild currants and gooseberries and fox-grapes; . . . he dug the roots of the fragrant sassafras and of the sweet-flag; he ate the tender leaves of the wintergreen and its red berries" (176). He goes on and on, giving us more than a page of sensual delights in one long, incantationlike sentence that suggests a memory fully invested in the particulars of that time and place. In this passage Warner also indirectly addresses his condition as a parentless child: New England herself literally becomes the nurturing parent, providing what is otherwise missing from Warner's young life.

Despite such moments of indulgence, Warner makes clear that successful maturity is validated finally by one's leaving New England, as he did when he became an educated and well-traveled adult. Even New England herself, that nurturing parent, who now in Warner's characterization shades into a frustrating lover, recognizes that this is the desired end:

There is everything in the heart of the New England hills to feed the imagination of the boy, and excite his longing for strange countries. I scarcely know what the subtle influence is that forms him and attracts him in the most fascinating and aromatic of all lands, and yet urges him away from all the sweet delights of his home to become a roamer in literature and in the world,—a poet and a wanderer. There is something in the soil and the pure air, I suspect, that promises more romance than is forthcoming, that excites the imagination without satisfying it, and begets the desire of adventure. (163–64)

Why it is necessary for Warner to insist on the importance of leaving New England is evident despite his lyrical accounts of New England life. Although he says early in the book, "There are so many bright spots in the life of a farm-boy, that I sometimes think I should like to live the life over again" (21), we must understand that this is an infrequent sentimental moment, and even then, one compromised by the word "sometimes." When Howells reviewed *Being a Boy,* he observed, "The work John was set to do was what a less rigorous and more enlightened generation would think rather too much for a boy" (763). Although the book details John's schemes for making his chores less burdensome—including game playing and daydreaming—the drudgery prevails. Warner notes, "Say what you will about the general usefulness of boys, it is my impression that a farm without a boy would very soon come to grief. What the boy does is the life of the farm. He is the factotum, always in demand, always expected to do the thousand indispensable things that nobody else will do. . . . His work is like a woman's,—perpetual waiting on others" (31–32). John eventually escaped, though the means of escape is not alluded to in *Being a Boy.* Before Warner's father died, he insisted that Charles must go to college, and money was set aside from the sale of the family farm for the purpose (Fields 11).

What a life of "perpetual waiting on others" would have been like is hinted at in the story Warner tells of Cynthia Rudd, a beautiful, auburn-haired girl John admired. Although a little older than John, she did not reduce him to the comic Blighted Being Tom Bailey becomes under the influence of his cousin. Instead, she somehow enlarged his world. She figured for him as the embodiment of grace and goodness: her tact smoothed over awkwardnesses at his first boy-girl party; her singing in the church choir during the revival moved John to think, "There she is . . . singing away like an angel in heaven, and I am left out" (187). Years later, John, now the adult narrator, saw her again; she was the wife of a farmer, the mother of red-headed children, and "she looked tired and discouraged, as one who has carried into womanhood none of the romance of her youth" (220–21). Of course, a farm boy becomes a farmer, not a farmer's wife. But Warner was not really a farm boy; his being destined for college meant that he was treated as extra help, a "factotum," rather than an apprentice farmer. It probably also meant that the farm family entertained some suspicion of effeminacy on the part of the boy destined for college. It is no wonder that Warner equates his boyhood work with that of a woman and insists on the importance of escape from New England.

*Being a Boy* thus seems to refer obliquely to Warner's parentless state by positing New England as a fit parent; it also moves on to address, even more obliquely, the present childless condition of its writer by drawing attention to his successful manhood. Having made these points, it would seem that Warner's cyclical book could simply end with the completion of the one representative year or with an allusion to the recurring cycles that will follow. But Warner evidently wanted something more emphatic and, despite his commitment to telling a generic story of boyhood, needed something of more personal relevance. He reminds the reader at several points that he grew up to travel far beyond the narrow life of a farm boy: "Years after it happened to John to be at twilight at a railway-station on the edge of the Ravenna marshes" (190); "John was reminded of [a tree that grew from a surveyor's stake] years after when he sat under the shade of the decrepit lime-tree in Freiberg" (223–24). Then he expands an allusion to his adult condition into the essay that concludes the book. In this conclusion, entitled, "A Contrast to the New-England Boy" (234), he recounts seeing several groups of beautiful children— "like one of Correggio's pictures of children or angels" (237)—in a church in Genoa on All Souls' Day. His attention is caught by one boy in particular, a "ravishingly beautiful boy," "skylarking like an imp," "pouring out the most divine melody" (242)— much indulged by his comrades and the monk leading the choir:

"The jolly monk loved him best of all, and bore with his wildest pranks. . . . He knew his power, that boy; and he stepped forward to his stand when he pleased, certain that he would be forgiven as soon as he began to sing" (242–43). Warner is as much attracted by the boy as the monk and then is frightened by his own reaction. He recoils defensively, blaming the boy rather than himself: "Were he twice as lovely, I could never think of him as having either the simple manliness or the good fortune of the New England boy" (244). "Manliness" in this context carries the common nineteenth-century meanings of not childish and not feminine. New England boyhood in itself thus becomes a warranty against immaturity and effeminacy, and perhaps against homosexuality as well, though Warner seems unconscious of what his defensiveness is saying. New England boyhood finally is a promise of the successful male adulthood Warner would like to claim.

*The Story of a Bad Boy* and *Being a Boy* are superficially rather genial books. Although the loss of the father that underlies both seems singularly free of any dark consequences, the fact that each author felt the need to write about his childhood at some point in his adult life and thereby assure us of his successful maturity is suggestive of the magnitude of the loss. More certainly could have been revealed had either author the talent or the temperament to do so. Twain's and Howells's boyhood experiences as simple experiences do not seem to be significantly different from those of Aldrich or Warner, yet in the hands of those more complex and more gifted men they became the substance of much richer books. But Aldrich and Warner were doing something new. In his review of Warner's book, Howells focused on its virtues rather than its limitations. He characterized the book in terms that apply equally well to Aldrich's work: "The reminiscences are not sentimentalized, but they are touched with the greatest tenderness,—with the kind of compassion which one feels for one's own childhood, the sort of smiling regret one has for it. Something at once very delicate and very free is in the recognition of the narrowness of past joys and hardships; a humorous surprise that they should have ever sufficed to elate or depress, and a gentle wonder that one should have been the restricted being one remembers" (763). Howells's sympathetic identification with both the author's past suffering and present equanimity suggests how provocative this book was for him, just as it along with Aldrich's would be for others. Indeed, all future boy book writers owed a debt to Aldrich and Warner. Together they evolved a genre that allowed for a reevaluation of boyhood. In their contrasting forms and correspondingly differing presentations of the boy protagonist and in their different modes of intervention by the narrator, they provided models that would accommodate many individual needs and inspire new forms.

# 3

# MARK TWAIN

Aldrich's *Story of a Bad Boy* delighted Howells, but he had an even greater treat in store when he came to Twain's first boy book. After reading a late draft of *The Adventures of Tom Sawyer,* he wrote the author: "I finished reading Tom Sawyer a week ago, sitting up till one A.M., to get to the end, simply because it was impossible to leave off. It's altogether the best boy's story I ever read. It will be an immense success" (*Mark Twain-Howells Letters* 1: 110). In the review he wrote for the *Atlantic* (May 1876), he pointed to what seemed to him to be the distinguishing feature of Twain's work: "The story is a wonderful study of the boy-mind, which inhabits a world quite distinct from that in which he is bodily present with his elders, and in this lies its great charm and its universality, for boy-nature, however human-nature varies, is the same everywhere" (621). The particularity and peculiarity of the boys' world were notions Howells and, after him, Tarkington would exploit to great advantage in their boy books. These two writers were to focus on what they believed to be the innate savagery of boys, a quality that makes kinship with the adult world impossible. Twain's Tom Sawyer is never spoken of as a savage (although he does live in a superstition-filled world and plays at being an Indian); in fact, he shares many of his community's values (Fetterly 301–02, Robinson 22–27). The singularity of the boy mind that Twain was so able to grasp is that of an imperious imagination that redeems mundane life and in *Tom Sawyer* helps to set in motion the several plots that occupy the last two-thirds of the novel.

That so much of the novel is concerned with the working out of these plots—the murder in the graveyard and its consequences, the runaway boys and their funeral, the search for treasure, and the courtship of Becky Thatcher—reminds us that *Tom Sawyer* is not autobiographical in any traditional sense. Critical accounts of the composition of the book also make this clear (Gerber, Introduction 7–18; Hill). There are autobiographical motives and incidents aplenty, but there is also much fictionalizing and much that is indebted to other literary sources, including Aldrich's book (Gribben, "Boy-Book Elements" 152–59, 161–62; Stone 30–31, 62–63). It is with the autobiographical motives, however, that I begin, and my concern will be with the way in which they shape the fiction so that it in turn becomes a response to Twain's adult needs.

Tarkington, whose own boy books combined the factual and the fictional, offers us one way of understanding a heavily fictionalized book as autobiography. In his Introduction to *Huck Finn,* Tarkington justifies reading the boy protagonist of such a book as a projection of the adult author. Like Howells, Tarkington is taken by Twain's reinvestment in the boy mind:

> Mark Twain, writing *Tom Sawyer,* transposed himself backward through time into the boy he was in Hannibal, felt and knew again all that the boy had felt, said again what the boy had said, and then, with a masterly craft, evoked the portrait of that boy on paper. Moreover, this portrait is none the less true for the unreal background of plot against which it is seen, and I think the reason for this truthfulness is that the fantasia of romantic events seemed real to Mark Twain as he wrote, and that he had no doubt of its reality since it was built out of stuff fashioned in the mind of the boy. That is to say, although Mark Twain spoke of Tom Sawyer as a composite, the portrait is mainly of Mark Twain as a boy; it is essentially autobiographical, though by no means literally the record of Mark Twain's own youthful adventures and circumstances. (8)

In describing Twain's work this way, Tarkington makes the case for a book about childhood as autobiography if it is at some essential, but not necessarily literal, level a faithful re-creation of the author as child. Tarkington's observation is valuable as a corrective to the impulse to measure fiction against biography in appraising the value of such a book as autobiography. What Tarkington omits, however, and what I want to stress, is that the nature of the author's engagement with his past, as it is revealed in the book, is what makes the book an autobiography. Twain's work, like Aldrich's and Warner's, recaptures the past, but more important for my purposes, it also tells the story of an author responding to his past in terms of his present needs.

*Tom Sawyer* seems to have begun as a sketch, posthumously published under the title "Boy's Manuscript." It dates from 1868, when Twain was thirty-three and courting Olivia Langdon (*Unfinished Stories* 265–66). It is a first-person account of what eventually became Tom's courtship of Becky—in its heavy-handedness it is in Bernard DeVoto's words, "*Tom Sawyer* untouched by greatness" (7). It is also, as we know from Twain himself, a distant reflection of his own childhood romance (Wecter 181–83) and, we can guess, an oblique comment on the difficulties of his adult romance. But Twain's courtship prospered, and "Boy's Manuscript" was set aside. Then, a few days after the marriage itself, which committed him to domesticity and life in the East, Twain wrote a long letter in which he "rained reminiscences" on his childhood friend Will Bowen (*Letters to Will Bowen* 18). The constraints of adulthood evidently recalled memories of a freer time. But it was not until the winter of 1872–73, apparently stimulated by the death of his son, that Twain sought to turn his reminiscences into a book. In short, the ardent suitor whose perseverance had been rewarded, the transplanted Westerner whose move entailed some discomfort, and the loving father whose protectiveness was not enough to save his son all participate in the making of *Tom Sawyer*. The book is their autobiography; it addresses Twain's doubts about his success as a husband and father.

It is likely that the first eight chapters came easily, with Twain's drawing heavily on childhood memories and presenting his material in the anecdotal, linear form we saw in *Story of a Bad Boy*.[1] But when this period of inspiration was over, Twain put the book aside for approximately another year. Work on the sketches that made up "Old Times on the Mississippi" evidently stimulated Twain to return to his account of a Mississippi River boyhood;

work on *The Gilded Age* with his neighbor Charles Dudley Warner might have given him ideas about plotting. And perhaps the exchange was mutual, since Warner's own boy book was in the process of taking shape at the same time. Twain returned to the book in the spring and summer of 1874 and worked until inspiration flagged. He was now midway through the book, and he put it aside again. A year later he finished *Tom Sawyer*, writing the last half in a continuous effort. He debated a bit with Howells about whether he should take Tom into adulthood and whether his book was for boys or for adults—plausible concerns, because the book spoke to adult needs—but, in the end, he let the book stand pretty much as it was when he finished work on it in 1875.

Recapturing the past was never a simple matter for Twain. Years later Howells could recall him referring to his past as "so damned humiliating" (*Literary Friends,* "My Mark Twain" 274).[2] Twain's biographers and the autobiography he dictated in his old age offer an impressive account of childhood deprivation and suffering. Much of the difficulty might be attributed to his father, an emotionally remote man and a failure at each of the professions he tried. The often reiterated family myth of more comfortable days in the East, in the now irrecoverable past, could hardly have sweetened present poverty. And the bleakness of the present was confirmed by John Clemens's ultimate failure—his death when his son was only eleven. Jay Martin, speaking from the perspective of the psychoanalyst, concludes that "Twain's guilty feelings and troubled conscience were to a large extent the deformed products of his relation to his father; the accusations and rejection implied in his father's coldness toward him helped to create a conscience that in later life ever accused him of wrongdoing or inadequacy, even in times of success" ("Genie" 60). Yet, as Tony Tanner has observed, as Twain aged, he became obsessed with the past and recalled it in increasingly idealistic terms (143–49). We might attribute this obsession to Twain's mounting discontent with the pressures of late nineteenth-century American life along with, as Tanner hints, a pathological fear of old age. Whatever the reasons, the bases of this idealization are evident in the same material that exposes the limitations of the past (*Autobiography* 1–95, Paine 1–73, Wecter 1–119). If Sam Clemens's father failed him, his mother did not.[3] If the family lived in poverty, they lived in a small midwestern town where the extremes of wealth were not great anyway. If John Clemens's investment in Tennessee land realized as little for the family as all his other endeavors, young Sam still enjoyed the natural wealth provided by a Mississippi River town that boasted an island, a cave, and a steamboat landing, and by his uncle John Quarles's farm in nearby Florida, Missouri. To recall the past, for Twain, was necessarily to recall a time about which he felt profoundly ambivalent. The tricks of the autobiographer that Lejeune and Starobinski enumerate came to Twain's aid as he retold his boyhood through Tom Sawyer.

Like Aldrich, Twain announces his presence in his story at its onset, with the difference that Twain's narrating persona is more fully expressed as a personality. He is more aggressive and less genial than Aldrich, and his pseudonym is a promise to the reader that he will be entertaining. We meet him first in the Preface, where he authoritatively announces, "Most of the adventures recorded in this book really occurred." This, of course, is not true in any literal sense: at least half the book is pure fiction. And Twain must have known that his readers would not expect literal truth from a humorist. His next assertion is another "stretcher": "one or two were experiences of my own, the rest those of boys who were schoolmates of mine" (xvii). Critics—frequently citing Twain's autobiography itself—have shown how very many experiences Tom shares with his creator (Gerber, Explanatory Notes 469–99). It is evident that this is a narrator who wants to tell his boyhood story, but at the same time has reservations about fully implicating himself in it—a stance that distinguishes *Tom Sawyer* from Twain's account of his early years in his autobiography, where the confidence of the elderly public figure who has endured much enables him to exert considerable control over his presentation of his younger self. We see the ambivalence that characterizes *Tom Sawyer* again in the note on which Twain ends his Preface, where he promises his readers entertainment at the expense of the childhood he is to evoke: "Part of my plan has been to try to pleasantly remind adults of what they once were themselves, and of how they felt and thought and talked, and what *queer enterprises* they sometimes engaged in" (xvii; my emphasis). He warms eagerly to his subject and then condescendingly backs away from it. Although the Preface was undoubtedly added after the book was written, we hear the same condescension often enough as Twain intervenes in his story. We also hear a trace of it in the mock-archaic phrase that introduces the Conclusion to the novel: "So endeth this chronicle" (260). The context of this distancing formulation reminds us that this has not been a heroic epic after all, but merely the story of a boy's adventures.

Like Aldrich, Twain intrudes freely in his story, particularly in the first third of the book, which is the most dependent on factual autobiographical material. We can best understand his interventions by recalling Aldrich's ironic voice in his *Story of a Bad Boy*. Aldrich's is a forgiving voice. When he mocks his protagonist, it is for his ignorance, his gullibility, or his passivity—conditions that Aldrich recognizes as temporary afflictions of childhood even if the causes of real pain. Twain is a less forgiving narrator, and the range of subjects against which he directs his irony is much narrower. Tom Sawyer, unlike Tom Bailey, is never the butt of friends' jokes, and he is never subjected to unalterable parental decree. When Tom evokes Twain's irony, it is invariably because he is pretending to a state of emotional grandeur.

Our vocabulary for such behavior is informed by psychoanalysis: Tom is narcissistic, an exhibitionist, given to grandiose fantasies. In the simpler vocabulary of an earlier time, he was merely a willful child, showing off. Howells used such language in describing his friend in "My Mark Twain" (1910) when he spoke of Twain's lifelong boyishness: "He was a youth to the end of his days, the heart of a boy with the head of a sage; the heart of a good boy, or a bad boy, but always a wilful boy, and wilfulest to show himself out at every time for just the boy he was" (*Literary Friends* 257–58). Romantic veneration for children and Howells's fondness for his recently dead friend enter into this description. As our modern terminology indicates, we judge such eternal boyishness more harshly, and in this we are significantly one with Twain. Tom Bailey is not entirely free from self-dramatizing, but it is hardly the central motif of his life as it is for Tom Sawyer, and it is never the subject of such unflagging irony as it is in Twain's book.

Tom in love with Becky is paradigmatic. The role of Blighted Being is as diverting to Tom Sawyer as it was to Tom Bailey. But whereas Tom Bailey needed his admired older cousin to become engaged to a man her own age to set him off as a grief-stricken lover, Tom Sawyer's imagination of rejection is alone sufficient. Early in the novel, he slips easily from imagining Aunt Polly's grief at his death—his revenge for her failure to apologize for punishing him instead of Sid for breaking the sugar bowl—to imagining Becky Thatcher's grief. Becky has been modestly encouraging at this point—she threw Tom a flower before she went indoors—and there is no reason for Tom to cast himself in the role of unappreciated suitor. The fusion between Aunt Polly and Becky—between mother and lover—is, in fact, both strange and tantalizing. It has excited no comment because this is, after all, the story of a boy. But it is worth keeping in mind that it is also the story of a man near the beginning of his married life who expected his young wife to play a maternal role in her relationship to him: "But you will break up all my irregularities when we are married, and civilize me, and make of me a model husband and an ornament to society, won't you . . . ?" he had written, only half facetiously, to Livy during his engagement (quoted in Blair, *Mark Twain* 57).

As we might expect of a popular lecturer's surrogate younger self, Tom's fantasies typically tend to the theatrical. He imagines himself drowned and broods about Becky's response. Twain as narrator adopts the boy's perspective and makes a mockery of it by casting it in the inflated language of romantic fiction (plausibly known to Tom through pulpit oratory), notable for its tenuous relationship to reality: "He wondered if *she* would pity him if she knew? Would she cry, and wish that she had a right to put her arms around his neck and comfort him? Or would she turn coldly away like all the hollow world?" (24). Tom is so delighted with these melodramatic alternatives that he reworks the scene several times in his mind, relishing his imaginary power over Becky and his gratifying self-pity. He then makes his way to Becky's house, lies down under what he takes to be her window, and reworks his fantasy yet again: "Oh! would she drop one little tear upon his poor lifeless form, would she heave one little sigh to see a bright young life so rudely blighted, so untimely cut down?" (24–25). Instead of "one little tear," "a deluge of water drenched the prone martyr's remains!" (25) as a maid empties a slop bucket on the Blighted Being. Tom Bailey's suffering came to an end with the simple passage of time. The adult narrator's reflection that "in a quiet way I never enjoyed myself better in my life than when I was a Blighted Being" (245) turns being lovelorn into one of the many roles of boyhood and thereby grants Tom Bailey's suffering legitimacy. Tom Sawyer's experience, already mocked by the language in which it is cast, ends in further deflation stage-managed by the narrator. This is a pattern repeated again and again in *Tom Sawyer.*

We can observe this pattern of the self-glorifying imagination at work followed by rapid deflation in small episodes as well as large ones. In each instance Twain as narrator enters into Tom's inflated view of himself—a form of identification that amounts to a gentle mockery—and then steps back to disassociate himself more emphatically from Tom. When Tom and his friend Joe Harper take turns worrying a tick with a couple of pins as it crawls over Joe's slate in school, Tom decides that Joe is enjoying the tick too much of the time. He announces grandly, "'He's my tick and I'll do what I blame please with him, or die!'" Retribution follows: "A tremendous whack came down on Tom's shoulders" (58), as the schoolmaster punishes first Tom and then Joe. In a radically different but equally trivial incident of boy life—recounted in a much later chapter, but one that had its genesis in an earlier autobiographical letter (Hill 385)—Tom joins the Cadets of Temperance because he wants to wear the gaudy uniform of the order. He looks forward to the death of old Judge Frazer as an opportunity to do so: "Sometimes his hopes ran high—so high he would venture to get out his regalia and practice before the looking-glass" (161). But the Judge seems to be convalescing, and Tom resigns from the Cadets. Then the Judge dies, and once again Tom is deflated: "The funeral was a fine thing. The Cadets paraded in a style calculated to kill the late member with envy" (162).

More memorable, because of its larger scale, is Tom's presenting himself as claimant for a prize Bible in Sunday school. The Bibles were awarded for tickets, which were in turn awarded for verses of scripture learned, but Tom finds a more congenial method of getting what he wants. Rich with the profits gleaned from the previous day when he "sold" opportunities to whitewash his aunt's fence, Tom has the capital with which to amass enough tickets to qualify for a Bible. Amidst all the showing off that is going on to impress the visiting Judge Thatcher, Becky's father, Tom makes judicious trades and then steps forward to claim his prize: "It was the most stunning surprise of the decade; and so profound was the sensation that it lifted the new hero up to the judicial one's altitude, and the school had two marvels to gaze upon in place of one. The boys were all eaten up with envy" (34). But the rivalry with Becky's father is short-lived: Tom is tongue-tied in his presence, and we are reminded what a fraud he is (and what a fool the Judge is) by the Judge's praise of Tom and his confident assertion that "'knowledge is worth more than anything there is in the world. . . . you wouldn't take any money for those two thousand verses . . . no indeed you wouldn't.'" Mrs. Thatcher interrupts, asking the tongue-tied boy to name the first two disciples, and when Tom blurts out "'DAVID AND GOLIAH,'" the narrator intervenes: "Let us draw the curtain of charity over the rest of the scene" (36).

Tom's repeated humiliation is presented as comedy. The inflated language Twain uses to convey the boy's perspective and Twain's deflating intervention as either plot maker or commentator in his own voice provoke laughter and keep the reader at a distance from the boy's pain when humiliation comes. Twain's satire at the expense of Tom's community and Tom's characteristic buoyancy, which always makes him ready for the next adventure, further obscure the pain the boy suffers. Nevertheless, the frequency with which humiliation occurs in those parts of the book that are closest to Twain's real life experiences is striking. It seems as if Twain, writing out of the insecurities of his adult life, must blame the assertive and aspiring self that is embodied in Tom for its audacity—and at the same time must shield himself, through his comedy, from the suspicion that he is not worthy.

Although no one has commented on the pattern of assertion and humiliation in *Tom Sawyer,* a similar pattern has been discerned elsewhere in Twain's writing. In a suggestive article, Larzer Ziff discusses Twain's notion of experience. Using "Old Times on the Mississippi" as his text, Ziff suggests that for Twain becoming a pilot and thereby enjoying public acclaim and membership in a select fraternity paralleled the Presbyterian doctrine of salvation that Twain had grown up with. As a paradigm of human development this doctrine is precarious at best: "Growth was not continuous but pointed at an arrival. It was to be achieved through humiliation so that the second nature was proved, not simulated. Once the arrival was achieved further growth was secondary compared to the absolute distance between those who had arrived and those who were outside. And the fear always remained that the elite member had deluded himself and was a hypocrite whose new powers would be found wanting at a crucial moment and would lead to a catastrophic humiliation . . . thereby forcing him to prove himself anew" (252–53). The attainment of status repeatedly challenged by exposure to humiliation accurately describes Tom's case. Tom—and by extension Sam Clemens—is eternally vulnerable and therefore, in a very real sense, unable to grow. Ziff adds one other observation that is relevant to Tom. He relates Twain's view of experience not only to his Presbyterian background but also to his profound uneasiness with women: "His view of experience as something gained through and vulnerable to humiliation is very probably related on one level to a growth of which he never speaks in fiction or memoirs—sexual initiation and the dreaded laugh of the experienced woman at the incompetence of the adolescent" (251). *Tom Sawyer* is no exception to Twain's reticence on sexual matters, but once we are alerted to the link between humiliation and sexual timidity, it is no surprise to see that Tom is discomfited in his roles both as Becky's suitor and as her father's rival.

The places where Twain makes his protagonist a subject of humor or irony come mainly in the first third of the book. It appears that the self-doubt that went into the making of *Tom Sawyer* made Twain keenly aware of the humiliations of his childhood. But Twain also recalled his childhood fondly, and his sense of being straitjacketed by Eastern society must have intensified his memories of a less confined time and place so that writing out such memories became a source of emotional renewal. *Tom Sawyer,* like all boy books, includes a lyrical or elegiac strain. Hannibal has been renamed St. Petersburg, and Cardiff Hill on the edge of town "seem[s] a Delectable Land, dreamy, reposeful, and inviting" (10). It is spring and summer, and adventures crowd so thickly in on Tom and his friends that a rational calculation of the time scheme of the novel proves impossible (Byers, Peterson). In fact, no time scheme really fits the book: Tom is young enough to lose a front tooth and old enough to have a crush on a school-mate. He is any and all ages of boyhood. In later years, Twain would look back at the novel and claim that "*Tom Sawyer* is simply a hymn, put into prose form to give it a worldly air" (*Mark Twain's Letters* 2: 477 [1887]). His overstatement ignores the debunking to which Tom is subjected in the first part of the book and the real danger posed by Injun Joe in the second part, but it captures Twain's need to deny the humiliations of his childhood and to escape from the present.

Life in St. Petersburg receives its most lyrical expression when Tom and his friends run away to Jackson's Island. The freedom from such onerous restraints as school and parents and clothes and manners and the uninhibited play that follows is only a part of the island's charm. Even more significant in fixing this episode for us as an idyllic interlude is the presence of the narrator. His lengthy description of Tom's awakening at dawn calls attention to itself by its rather bookish beginning: "Gradually the cool dim gray of the morning whitened, and as gradually sounds multi-plied and life manifested itself. The marvel of Nature shaking off sleep and going to work unfolded itself to the musing boy." But as he proceeds, his language is less self-conscious, and he estab-lishes a delicate rapport between the boy and the natural world, entering into Tom's childish fantasies, gently mocking, yet at the same time justifying. As we read, we are constantly aware of the dual perspectives of child and adult, no longer at odds, but har-monized to create what Starobinski would call an elegiac episode:

> A little green worm came crawling over a dewy leaf, lifting two-thirds of his body into the air from time to time and "sniffing around," then proceeding again—for he was measuring, Tom said; and when the worm approached him, of its own accord, he sat as still as a stone, with his hopes rising and falling, by turns, as the creature still came toward him or seemed inclined to go elsewhere; and when at last it considered a painful moment with its curved body in the air and then came decisively down upon Tom's leg and began a journey over him, his whole heart was glad—for that meant that he was going to have a new suit of clothes—without the shadow of a doubt a gaudy piratical uniform. . . . A brown spotted lady-bug climbed the dizzy height of a grass-blade, and Tom bent down close to it and said, "Lady-bug, lady-bug, fly

away home, your house is on fire, your children's alone," and she took wing and went off to see about it—which did not surprise the boy, for he knew of old that this insect was credulous about conflagrations and he had practiced upon its simplicity more than once. . . . A cat-bird, the northern mocker, lit in a tree over Tom's head, and trilled out her imitations of her neighbors in a rapture of enjoyment; then a shrill jay swept down, a flash of blue flame, and stopped on a twig almost within the boy's reach, cocked his head to one side and eyed the strangers with a consuming curiosity; a gray squirrel and big fellow of the "fox" kind came skurrying along, sitting up at intervals to inspect and chatter at the boys, for the wild things had probably never seen a human being before and scarcely knew whether to be afraid or not. All Nature was wide awaken and stirring, now. (106–07)

If we laugh at Tom's notion that he will get a new suit—well, haven't we just seen the inchworm measuring? If we laugh at his belief that ladybugs are "credulous about conflagrations" (and Twain's language here does encourage us to laugh), haven't we just seen the ladybug fly away home? After taking these steps with Tom, it is an easy enough transition for the narrator, and for us along with him, to impute "consuming curiosity" to the blue jay and uncertain debate to the squirrels. So Twain makes us assent to Tom's imaginative perception of reality. It has become a critical commonplace to praise Huck Finn's description of dawn in his book, but our doing so should not obscure the celebration we see here.

The remaining two-thirds of *Tom Sawyer* move away from the mixture of defensive comedy and lyricism that mark the author's engagement in his story to more obvious fictionalizing and an emphasis on darker matters.[4] In what remains, the narrator's intervening presence is greatly diminished, though Twain cannot resist commenting critically on the genteel culture that produces maudlin schoolgirl essays (nor can he resist writing a parody of one himself on the stalactite that supplies Injun Joe with his last drops of water) and a committee of "sappy women" (241) who petition for Injun Joe's pardon. That Twain felt a need to go out of his way to mock these feminine aspects of his culture reminds us again of the uneasiness with women that we have already noted.

The plots that occupy the remainder of the book—the adventures of the runaway boys, the buried treasure story, and the childish romance—are all standard fare for children's books of the period. As developed in *Tom Sawyer*, however, these plots are shaped in accord with the central autobiographical issue of the first part of the book: Twain's suspicion that his achievement does not have a solid basis.

Twain provides Tom with opportunities for the public display and affirmation he has sought from the beginning of the novel. Tom returns from Jackson's Island twice, first to hear his aunt mourning for her "dead" nephew, then to hear the minister praising the "dead" boys, and he evokes the delight of the adult community and the envy of his friends when he is "resurrected" in church. He is once again "the pet of the old, the envy of the young" (173) when he testifies against Injun Joe in court, and he wins the admiration and envy of all yet another time when he finds the buried treasure. He makes his peace with Becky by taking her whipping for damaging the schoolmaster's anatomy book and is rewarded by her company at the picnic where he leads her astray in the cave, an episode that seems to replay the death-rebirth theme, but also hints symbolically at sexual initiation (Bridgman 220). He responds appropriately to her dependence on him by comforting her and leading her out of the cave, whereupon, his worth further confirmed by the treasure he has found, he wins her father's approval. When Becky tells Judge Thatcher that Tom lied to save her from exposure in school, "the Judge said with a fine outburst that it was a noble, a generous, a magnanimous lie—a lie that was worthy to hold up its head and march down through history breast to breast with George Washington's lauded Truth about the hatchet! Becky thought her father had never looked so tall and so superb as when he walked the floor and said that" (255). Judge Thatcher's language and posture acknowledge Tom as an appropriately aggressive rival for his daughter; the boy has become a man. It is wish fulfillment indeed.

But just as Twain persistently undercuts Tom's claims to grandeur in the first part of the novel, he does so here. Huck Finn emerges in the second part of the book to take over Twain's role as a critic of Tom. Twain could not have had such a role in mind for Huck when he first introduced him in Chapter 6 of *Tom*

*Sawyer,* since Twain himself did not know where his novel was going or how it was to get there. Yet Huck's entrance, dead cat in hand, his baggy, tattered clothes "in perennial bloom," is memorable. Twain tells us that "Huckleberry came and went, at his own free will. . . . he did not have to go to school or to church, or call any being his master or obey anybody . . . he never had to wash, nor put on clean clothes; he could swear wonderfully." We cherish the absolute freedom Huck represents, in part because "every harassed, hampered, respectable boy in St. Petersburg" (48) does so, and in part because we know what lies ahead for Huck in Twain's career. We can also respond to his introduction in the book because in his relationship with Tom—"Tom Sawyer's comrade," as his own book will identify him—he is our first memorable version of the boy pal; we will not meet another such pair until Tarkington's Penrod and Sam. Tom Bailey had a close friend in Pepper Whitcomb, but their relationship was not central to the story as is Huck's and Tom's.

The relationship, however, is not one of equals. Huck's manners and dress make him a corrective to the feminized domestic world in which Tom and his other friends live, but Twain embraces this prospect rather gingerly. Further, Huck's role is the secondary one typical of the boy pal. He is always a bit player in Tom's games, often a sounding board for Tom's ideas, and only occasionally a mentor to Tom—he knows some items of folk wisdom that Tom does not know (Tom, in turn, knows some that Huck does not), and he knows how to smoke. The patronizing diminutive, "Hucky," that appears frequently in the first part of the book puts him firmly in place. As a result of Huck's various disadvantages, his criticism of Tom is never as strong as Twain's in the first part of the book. We can also hypothesize that Twain, having moved farther away from the facts of his own childhood in later parts of the book, felt less need to judge his autobiographical protagonist so harshly.

If Huck's discordant voice never quite matches Twain's, Huck does acquire some force as the book progresses, growing in stature and occupying an increasingly larger role in Tom's story. He is eventually allotted a story of his own as he pursues Injun Joe and his companion to the Widow Douglas's house and enlists the Welshman and his sons to help her. At first Huck is only a silent critic. When the boys return from the island and announce their presence in church, "Aunt Polly, Mary and the Harpers threw themselves upon their restored ones, smothered them with kisses and poured out thanksgivings, while poor Huck stood abashed and uncomfortable, not knowing exactly what to do or where to hide from so many unwelcoming eyes. He wavered and started to slink away" (131). Huck, of course, does not have family to welcome him back from the dead, but his mute presence is not greeted with indifference or curiosity, but with "unwelcoming eyes." The community from which Tom seeks approbation is irremediably class-conscious; even in this wondrous moment in which they seem to have witnessed a literal resurrection, they cannot let down their guard. Later, when Tom anticipates getting rich by finding buried treasure, Huck is vocal and skeptical. He is willing to participate in the adventure of looking, but the money itself has no meaning to him. His Pap would lay claim to it, and as for Tom's notion that he could get married if he were wealthy, Huck's response is, "'Well that's the foolishest thing you could do, Tom. Look at pap and my mother. Fight? Why they used to fight all the time. I remember, mighty well.'" Tom insists his girl won't fight, and Huck, sounding jaded by experience he has not had, but that Twain certainly had had by the time he wrote the book, shifts the ground of his argument and observes, "'Tom, I reckon they're all alike. They'll all comb a body'" (179).

Finally, Huck rejects his new life with the Widow Douglas. After recounting Judge Thatcher's acceptance of Tom, Twain turns his attention to Huck: "Huck Finn's wealth and the fact that he was now under the widow Douglas's protection, introduced him into society—no, dragged him into it, hurled him into it— and his sufferings were almost more than he could bear" (255). He runs away after a few weeks, and Tom finds him. Huck regales him with a list of all the restraints the Widow has imposed on him—now he has the experience to back his claim that women "comb a body." And he unerringly points to the real source of his trouble: "'Tom, I wouldn't ever got into all this trouble if it hadn't a' ben for that money'" (258). The same money that brings Tom recognition and the promise of the girl he seeks brings Huck social acceptance, which he experiences as loss of freedom and a life dominated by a woman. His experience is Tom's transmogrified (recall the link I noted earlier between mother figure and lover); it is the dark side of successful male achievement—and perhaps an oblique reflection of Twain's own restiveness in marriage.

Had *Tom Sawyer* ended at this point, it would have ended with Tom's aspirations being once again undercut, now by Huck Finn's experience and voice instead of Twain's ironic voice. But Twain's comic mode prevails, and he allows Tom the final word. Tom persuades Huck to return to the Widow's, to lead a respectable life and thereby qualify for membership in Tom Sawyer's Gang of robbers. It is a more affirmative conclusion than the self-doubt that lies behind the book and that is expressed throughout it would seem to warrant. We might make sense of it as willed optimism in the face of self-doubt. A simpler explanation is that *Tom Sawyer* is, after all, an account of boy life that is aimed in good part at an audience of children. From this perspective, Twain's conclusion is perfectly appropriate, though it has the unfortunate effect of shifting our attention from the hitherto prominent theme of Tom's self-dramatizing to the theme of social conformity that always hovers in the background of the novel and tends to call into question the real value of Tom's achievement.

A psychologist looking back over Twain's account of Tom's history might conclude that Tom suffered from a weak ego that needed constant reassurance. He would see in Tom's narcissistic display a profound self-doubt masking itself in forever doomed, self-aggrandizing gestures.[5] He could look to Twain's later life and note Twain's self-conscious theatricality, his passions for financial speculation and lavish spending, his barely controlled rages, and his longing for and fear of death and see an unconscious anticipation of all this projected onto Tom. Perhaps, as Ziff suggests, Twain's insecurity was the legacy of Calvinism. More likely—as Jay Martin suggests and as my reading of *Huck Finn* will second—it was the one legacy Twain's failed father did leave his son, perhaps working hand in hand with his Presbyterian upbringing. By reading *Tom Sawyer* as an autobiography that moves into a fiction whose shape is determined by the autobiographical concerns the book begins with, we can refine the psychologist's insight. We can see that Twain himself, on an intuitive level, recognized the connection between his self-dramatizing and his vulnerability. But in this book, he was unable to plumb the sources of his two-sided character. What he could do was write a boy book in which the protagonist's life foreshadowed in its basic rhythm the pattern of its author's life—gaudy success undercut by humiliation, a much desired marriage undercut by the loss of a child.

*Huck Finn* followed readily—at least at first. It seems likely that Twain reworked material for the first chapter that had originally formed a discarded last chapter of *Tom Sawyer* (DeVoto 11, 46). Additional chapters followed in 1876, taking the story up to the point where the steamboat runs over Huck's and Jim's raft. After this, inspiration ran dry—which is to say, the pressures that produced the autobiography that shapes *Tom Sawyer* became less urgent. Twain worked on the book sporadically over the next seven years, completing it by working on it at various points between 1879 and 1883, with the chapters on the Sir Walter Scott episode written late in the process and worked into the first part of the book (Blair "When Was *Huckleberry Finn* Written?" Cummings 129–36). Partial serialization in the *Century Magazine* followed completion of the novel, underlining its linear and episodic structure.

In this prolonged gestation, the book became something more than a boy book. Although it began as a story of boyish pranks in the mood of *Tom Sawyer* and conducted under the aegis of Tom Sawyer himself, as Walter Blair has demonstrated in *Mark Twain & Huck Finn, Adventures of Huckleberry Finn* soon came to incorporate Twain's adult frustrations with his numerous social obligations and business dealings, his reflections on his widely varied reading and on contemporary politics, and his response to what he saw when he returned to the Mississippi River in 1882. We can think of *Huck Finn* as a form of autobiography in that it deals with the concerns of Sam Clemens's life, but much of it is not relevant to my concern with the boy book because it does not deal with autobiographical issues originating in childhood.

In one crucial respect, however, *Huck Finn* does deal with one of the same personal issues that *Tom Sawyer* does: beginning where that first book left off, it continues Twain's brooding on his suspicion of inadequacy. By the time he was at work on *Huck Finn,* Twain was an established and successful author, but one who was always regarded as something of an interloper among the New England literati whose preeminence in American culture had not quite reached an end. Twain's response was one of defiant resentment at being cast in such a role—a response that was memorably articulated in his satirical speech at the Whittier birthday dinner in 1877. But the ambivalent remorse that followed the speech and lingered for years suggests that Twain was not entirely confident about his own claims to authority (Howells, *Literary Friends* 295–97; Lynn, *Howells* 169–78; Smith, *Twain* 92–112). To the extent that *Huck Finn* continues Twain's examination of his ongoing self-doubt and links it with childhood material, it might properly be called a boy book in the autobiographical sense in which I have been using the term.

One might legitimately ask whether *Huck Finn* deals with Clemens's childhood at all. Certainly the first part of the book, with its St. Petersburg/Hannibal setting, the various descriptions of the river, Boggs's death, and the Phelps's plantation (John Quarles's farm moved to Arkansas), had its origin in Twain's childhood memories. But in his autobiography, Twain claimed that Huck was modeled on Tom Blankenship, son of one of the town drunkards, a boy who was "ignorant, unwashed, insufficiently fed; but he had as good a heart as ever any boy had. . . . He was the only really independent person—boy or man— in the community, and by consequence he was tranquilly and continuously happy" (73–74). This description more or less fits the Huck of *Tom Sawyer*. In his own book, Huck, checked by Tom Sawyer, by Widow Douglas, by Pap, and most of all by his own troubling conscience, is not a "really independent person" and, with his morbid thoughts, is not "continuously happy." He is, in short, a literary creation, only distantly inspired by Tom Blankenship. Given the differences in Huck's life and young Sam Clemens's life, critics have claimed him as an autobiographical surrogate only in a very general sense. My reading of his role in *Tom Sawyer* allows me to understand Huck's meaning to Twain more specifically as his adult self-doubt projected back onto his childhood.

Although we can grant that *Huck Finn* began as a boy book and incorporated boyhood memories at various points, the point at which it becomes something else is not readily definable. The opening chapters, which flowed so easily from *Tom Sawyer,* present Huck once again as Twain's self-admonishing side. In this role Huck again deflates Tom's pretensions, only now, because it is his book and his voice, Twain gives him all the energy and sharpness of the narrator at the beginning of *Tom Sawyer.* Tom's band of robbers is dismissed: "We played robbers now and then about a month, and then I resigned. All the boys did. We hadn't robbed nobody, we hadn't killed any people, but only just pretended. . . . I couldn't see no profit in it" (14). Tom's attack on "a whole parcel of Spanish merchants and rich A-rabs . . . with two hundred elephants, and six hundred camels, and over a thousand 'sumter' mules, all loaded down with di'monds" comes to a similar end: "It warn't anything but a Sunday-school picnic, and only a primer-class at that" (15). As for a lamp that will produce a genie when rubbed, Huck concludes that that too "was only just one of Tom Sawyer's lies" (17). But this role carries us only a short way into the book. In Chapter 5 Pap appears, and the book leaves the realm of childhood games and its correspondence with young Sam Clemens's life. We might consider the cruel Pap who victimizes Huck and the nurturing Jim who subsequently befriends him largely as fantasy characters, versions of the good and bad parents of fairy tales who embody the young protagonist's fears and wishes (Bettelheim 68). But Twain pours so much animosity into his portrayal of Pap and links him so convincingly to Huck's psychological makeup that I also read him as an exaggerated portrait of John Clemens. The concern with the past as it impinges on the present that characterizes the boy book is felt in this book after the story has left the immediate territory of the author's own boy life.

Whereas *Huck Finn* began as a continuation of *Tom Sawyer* and therefore as another boy book, it also offered an innovation in the genre: it was to be narrated by the boy protagonist himself. Twain conceived of such a narrative about the time he finished *Tom Sawyer.* In a letter to Howells he remarked, "By & by I shall take a boy of twelve & run him on through life (in the first person) but not Tom Sawyer—he would not be a good character for it" (*Mark Twain-Howells Letters* 1: 92). Presumably, Tom's egotism and imagination would color too vividly any story he might tell. Shortly after the publication of *Tom Sawyer,* Twain wrote to

Howells again, noting now that he was nearly half done with another "boys' book"; the title he mentioned—"Huck Finn's Autobiography" (*Mark Twain-Howells Letters* 1: 144)—implied the first-person narration he had adopted.

Appealing as the notion of having the boy protagonist tell his own story is, as compelling a way of rendering the boy mind as it seems, it was an innovation that was rarely picked up by other writers. Henry A. Shute's *The Real Diary of a Real Boy* (1902), Ellis Parker Butler's *Swatty: A Story of Real Boys* (1915), Grant Showerman's *A Country Chronicle* (1916) and *A Country Child* (1917), and Edgar Lee Masters's *Mitch Miller* (1920) constitute most of the slim shelf of such books.[6] Even though each of these writers shares Twain's perception that the boy's unschooled language and regional dialect are economical ways of evoking and elegizing the past, none of them handles boy language and perspective as brilliantly as Twain in *Huck Finn*. Henry James, in his Preface to the New York Edition of *What Maisie Knew,* his very different book about a child, recognized what the difficulty was: "Small children have many more perceptions than they have terms to translate them; their vision is at any moment much richer, their apprehension even constantly stronger, than their prompt, their at all producible vocabulary." James declined the challenge of restricting himself to "the terms as well as to the experience" (x) of the child, finding challenge enough in presenting the world his protagonist saw but did not fully comprehend in such a way that our understanding transcends hers.

Twain succeeded with a backwoods child narrator in large part because he created in Huck a character who was perfectly suited to his needs. Huck's dialect provided Twain with a stunning way of dealing with his professional insecurities, for it allowed him a direct challenge to the literary establishment that excluded him. Huck's speech allies him with such humorous predecessors as Sut Lovingood and Ike Partington, but these were marginal characters on the American literary scene and their creators acknowledged their marginality by allowing them to speak only within the space allowed by the genteel narrator who introduces them. Twain took the extraordinary step of writing an entire book narrated in dialect (Lynn, *Southwestern Humor* 61, 133–36; Smith, *Twain* 113). In doing so, in effect insisting that his language was as legitimate a literary language as standard English, he offered an affront to New England that outstripped the Whittier birthday dinner speech. Serialization in the *Century* and the popularity of *Huck Finn* must have made the situation all the sweeter for Twain.

The personality that made Huck a better narrator than Tom Sawyer was also suited to Twain's needs. Numerous critics have commented on Huck's passivity, his honesty, and his modesty— all of which enable him to present Mississippi River life with a kind of innocence that rejoices in its idyllic qualities (a fact that reminds us that this book, like other boy books, provided its author with a kind of psychic renewal) and, at the same time, records but sloughs off its appalling aspects. Consideration of Huck as narrator in turn opens up two other issues relevant to my concern with *Huck Finn* as a boy book. The first is related to a basic assumption of my critical approach: that the points at which the adult narrator in a boy book intervenes in the story are telling, for it is in this manner that he both empathizes with and judges his younger self. If the younger self is telling the story—that is, if the adult narrator hides behind the mask of the child narrator— we can appreciate the adult's dual perspective in those moments when we are made aware of the incompleteness of the child's perspective. This is of course what occurs in Huck's naively laudatory description of the Grangerford house. More to our purpose, it also occurs when we become aware of Mark Twain as the real storyteller. We are alerted to his presence the moment we open *Huck Finn*. His bust as the frontispiece of the first edition, his name on the title page, and his voice in the Notice and Explanatory remarks that precede the text all remind us that Huck Finn is his creation and not an equal as Huck pretends when he begins his story: "You don't know about me, without you have read a book by the name of 'The Adventures of Tom Sawyer,' but that ain't no matter. That book was made by Mr. Mark Twain" (1). Thus alerted, it is reasonable for us to ask where else Twain's presence is felt in Huck's narrative and what those instances mean. A second consideration has to do with the very nature of the protagonist. This is Huck's story; it is called *Adventures of Huckleberry Finn,* and Huck is necessarily on stage from the beginning to the end. But the role of protagonist is not compatible with Huck's humble character or with his meaning to Twain as a critic of flamboyant self-display. As my discussion will indicate, I think the issues of intervention by the adult narrator and the nature of the protagonist are related.

Twain proves himself remarkably consistent in maintaining Huck Finn's mask in the novel. Occasionally, readers point to Colonel Sherburn's denunciation of the would-be lynch mob as a place where the mask slips and we hear, not even Mark Twain, but Sam Clemens himself speaking (Smith, *Twain* 135–36). This identification is possible only if we go outside the book to Twain's other work; if we stay within the novel, Sherburn's speech can be read the way we read Pap's denunciation of the "govment" (33). We do not read this as a break in the narrative in which Poor White Trash voices its prejudices, but rather as an instance of that convention of all first-person narratives that allows the narrator exact recall of long passages of other people's speech. It is worth noting, however, that these two points in Huck's narrative stand out strikingly because anger is something denied to Huck's character. The usually deleted Raftsmen's Passage is another example of the same sort of narrative license, though I find it more troubling than either of these shorter interruptions because Huck is quiet for so long. Nevertheless, in its depiction of braggarts deflated and in its account of a man who kills his son, the episode has an obvious thematic relevance to the book as a whole.

I find only one genuine break in Huck's narrative, and that comes early in the book when Pap reappears in St. Petersburg.[7] A new judge, who does not know Pap, undertakes to reform him—much the way Clemens's own father tried to reform Jimmy Finn, one of Hannibal's drunkards and a model for Huck's Pap (*Autobiography* 74). The event is reported by Huck—it is related in what is recognizably his language—but Huck is not present, and so this episode must figure as an intrusion on Twain's part. It is, in effect, an intrusion by the narrator in the guise of the voice and perspective of the protagonist:

> When he [Pap] got out of jail the new judge said he was agoing to make a man of him. So he took him to his own house, and dressed him up clean and nice, and had him to breakfast and dinner and supper with the family, and was just old pie to him, so to speak. And after supper he talked to him about temperance and such

> things till the old man cried, and said he'd been a fool, and fooled
> away his life; but now he was agoing to turn over a new leaf and be
> a man nobody wouldn't be ashamed of. . . . And when it was bed
> time, the old man rose up and held out his hand, and says,
> "Look at it gentlemen, and ladies all; take ahold of it; shake it.
> There's a hand that was the hand of a hog; but it ain't so no more;
> it's the hand of a man that's started on a new life, and 'll die before
> he'll go back. You mark them words—don't forget I said them.
> It's a clean hand now; shake it—don't be afeard." (26–27)

More tears and more empty rhetoric surround the event, and
then, to no one's surprise except the new judge's and his wife's,
Pap backslides that very night.

Why is this event in the book? It is a jibe at John Clemens's
gullibility, certainly. The passage also allies Pap with all the other
masters of what Huck will later call "soul butter and hogwash"
(213): Emmeline Grangerford with her "sadful" poetry (140), the
King and Duke with their hard-luck stories of lost grandeur, the
King with his testimony at the Pokeville camp meeting and his
profession of grief at the Wilks's house, and Tom Sawyer with his
prisoner's inscriptions for Jim—all con artists moved to tears by
their own rhetoric. It would seem that Twain could have easily
contrived an event to demonstrate this side of Pap without violat-
ing the basic requirement of a first-person narrative that the narrator must be always present. But Twain's need to mock his father
evidently overrode artistic considerations. Further, Twain's viola-
tion of Huck's point of view also serves the purpose that interventions on the part of the narrator frequently serve in the boy
book: it provides a judgment on the protagonist—though in this
case, the judgment is not explicit and is only realized as the book
develops.

To explain this, I must return to the issue of Huck as protagonist. Whereas Huck is a sharp nay-sayer to Tom's pretensions
in the beginning of the book, he is most comfortable in a role that
allows for passive accommodation. Although he is forced to assert himself and escape, first from Pap and then from Jackson's
Island with Jim, he readily settles for a secondary role. When the
King and Duke enter the story, he soon recognizes them for what
they are. "But I never said nothing," he tells us, "never let on;
kept it to myself; it's the best way; then you don't have no quar-

rels, and don't get into no trouble." It is a principle of behavior he has learned from Pap: "If I never learnt nothing else out of pap, I learn't that the best way to get along with his kind of people is to let them have their own way" (165). Given what we have seen of Pap, it is likely that Huck learned this lesson both by his own experiences in dealing with Pap and by the example Pap set in his dealings with others. A psychologist would dispute Huck's claim that such passivity is "the best way." It may well protect Huck from Pap's brutality and the King's and Duke's meanness, but it exacts a cost, typically in the form of depression—that is, anger at what cannot be confronted turned safely inward. Huck's habitual somberness, his failure to show anger, his preoccupation with death and his periodically expressed wish to be dead, his low sense of self-worth, and his conviction that he is somehow responsible for everything that goes wrong are all symptoms of such repressed anger.[8] That Twain implicates Pap in his characterization of Huck suggests that he intuitively recognized a link between his self-doubt and his weak father. In so implicating his father, Twain takes a step beyond his presentation of his younger self in *Tom Sawyer*. Like Aldrich, he finds a father's failure to be the central experience of boyhood. It is a pattern we will see repeated and illuminated in subsequent boy books.

We would not expect a character of such passivity as Huck to emerge as hero of the story he tells. And we would not expect a character for whom a central function is to counter pretensions to grandeur to emerge as a hero. Yet *Huck Finn* forces Huck into a position where he must make a heroic choice on Jim's behalf. The role of hero is better suited to Tom Sawyer than Huck, and, appropriately, Huck is mistaken for Tom at the end of the book. Although Twain links Huck's passive demeanor to Pap, he cannot explicitly link the Tom Sawyer-like rhetoric and self-display that Huck exhibits near the end of the book to the same source. He could intuitively recognize the link between his own insecurity and his self-dramatizing in *Tom Sawyer*, but to go one step further and link both qualities with Pap would have been to repudiate both—something he must have been most reluctant to do. His theatrical side, after all, made *Adventures of Huckleberry Finn* the bravura performance it was. But his fiction said what he could not.

Henry Nash Smith does not treat the characters in *Huck Finn* as autobiographical surrogates, but he does see a link between Huck's rhetoric at the end of the book and Pap. He observes that Huck's analysis of his inability to pray after he writes to Miss Watson to reveal Jim's whereabouts is cast in a syntax that "takes on the rhythms of pulpit and rostrum" and is a "rather self-consciously theatrical gesture" (*Democracy* 113) on Huck's part. He quotes Huck's account of his problem: "I kneeled down. But the words wouldn't come. Why wouldn't they? It warn't no use to try and hide it from Him. Nor from *me,* neither. I knowed very well why they wouldn't come. It was because my heart warn't right; it was because I warn't square; it was because I was playing double. I was letting *on* to give up sin, but away inside of me I was holding on to the biggest one of all" (*Huck* 269). Smith then observes: "The boy who utters these pompous sentences is the legitimate heir of the Pap whom the 'new judge' in St. Petersburg had set about reclaiming from his drunkenness" (*Democracy* 114).[9] For Smith, whose concerns are formalistic rather than psychological, the change in Huck's behavior is explained in generic terms: Twain's desire to write a picaresque novel with a passive hero who merely observes is in conflict with his desire to write a bildungs-roman with a hero capable of growth in response to his experiences. Huck's empty rhetoric reflects Twain's surrender to these irreconcilable concerns in the form of a compromise in which Huck is relieved of his passivity only to have his heroism tainted by its self-consciousness (*Democracy* 116).

Huck's decision, like his analysis of his situation, can be considered in similar terms. The self-display we recognize in Huck's confession—"I was playing double"—infects the memories that lead to his decision. Again we hear the patterned rhetoric of the public speaker, here artfully translating private experience to the world at large. When Huck muses, "I see Jim before me, all the time, in the day, and in the night-time, sometimes moonlight, sometimes storms, and we a floating along, talking, and singing, and laughing" (270), we have come a long way from the seemingly artless descriptions of the storm on Jackson's Island and dawn on the Mississippi River that Huck delighted us with earlier. Harold Beaver, who also objects to the stylistic excesses here, brings an additional charge against Huck. He notes that Huck's memories end with a self-aggrandizing lie: "And at last I struck the time I saved him [Jim] by telling the men we had small-pox aboard, and he was so grateful, and said I was the best friend old Jim ever had in the world, and the *only* one he's got now" (*Huck* 270). In fact, Huck did not save Jim until Jim appealed to his friendship (Beaver 89–90). As was the case with Tom Sawyer, self-display emboldens Huck to more self-display, and this false memory is followed by Huck's announcement to a nonexistent audience, "'All right, then, I'll *go* to hell.'" "It was awful thoughts, and awful words" (271), Huck tells us, so caught up in the drama of the moment that he forgets that he once expressed a positive interest in going to hell because he wanted change and escape from Miss Watson (3–4). In this mood of excess, Huck readies himself for a life of crime: "I would go to work and steal Jim out of slavery again; and if I could think up anything worse, I would do that, too; because as long as I was in, and in for good, I might as well go the whole hog" (271). Huck's overstatement is another stylistic echo of Pap—even his "whole hog" recalls Pap's "hand of a hog."

Through Huck's rhetoric Twain tells us what he cannot articulate: the baseless sense of power Huck displays is complementary to his debilitating passivity; both are Pap's legacy. By extension *Huck Finn* acknowledges—indirectly, to be sure—that on some level Twain recognized that both his theatricality and his vulnerability were his father's legacy. Reading the book as autobiography enlarges our understanding of its author. It also enables us to understand why Twain is able to subvert Huck's original role of undercutting pretensions to grandeur with only a minimal but telling sign of compunction. After making his decision, Huck's immediate response is one of continued depression. He cannot be exhilarated at having finally shed his passive role, for his newly assertive role is no more authentic. When he arrives at the Phelps's plantation, the droning of insects suggests lonesomeness and death to him, and the spiritlike rustling of the leaves "makes a body wish *he* was dead, too, and done with it all" (276). But the depression is temporary; shortly thereafter Huck is "born again" (282) as Tom Sawyer when Aunt Sally misidentifies him.

But Huck has not really become Tom Sawyer by the end of the

book; in fact, Tom Sawyer is no longer Tom Sawyer either. Throughout the long Evasion at the end of the book, Huck plays the role of admiring acolyte that he will play in *Tom Sawyer, Detective* (1896); his objections to Tom's schemes are pro forma; they lack even the energy of the verbal sparring that he will muster in *Tom Sawyer Abroad* (1894). And Tom is the rather unattractive know-it-all of the later books; the insecurities that motivated him and won our indulgence earlier are gone now. Although the end of *Huck Finn* seems to return to the ground of the boy book—the setting recalled from childhood, the focus on boyish interaction—as Twain elaborates his conclusion, it is evident that having said what he can, he has now left the boy book and its autobiographical concerns for good and gone on to the mode of what will become an indifferent series of stories for boys. Even though he was drawn to Tom and Huck again and again in the years that followed, sensing perhaps that through them he had spoken an important truth about himself, he could not reanimate his protagonists. The adult needs that had given them life had changed; the period in which the problems of adulthood resonated with boyhood had passed. When Twain returned to autobiography, it was to the very different autobiography that he dictated in the confidence and bitterness of his old age.

4

# WILLIAM DEAN HOWELLS

That Howells himself should write a boy book was not inevitable. Although he had defined and celebrated the genre, it did not at first entice him as a writer. Twenty years elapsed between Aldrich's book and Howells's own first effort; Warner's and Twain's work provided pleasure but no more incentive than did Aldrich's. Then, in 1890, Howells published *A Boy's Town*, not only the first of his boy books (the second was *The Flight of Pony Baker* in 1902), but the first of a number of experiments in autobiography as well (Jacobson "Mask of Fiction"). What pushed Howells to write his first boy book was most likely the death of his oldest daughter Winifred in 1889, when he was fifty-two. Winny died of heart failure at twenty-six; she had suffered for years, her physical problems evidently a counterpart to severe psychological difficulties (Crowley, *Mask of Fiction* 90–91, 100) that arose in good part out of her conflicting desires to please and to escape her loving and demanding father.[1] Howells's letters—for years after, but especially in the year preceding *A Boy's Town*—reveal not only grief but guilt. He had failed as a father; he had lost his child. By writing a boy book, Howells found a way to escape from a burdensome present through a fictional return to the past and a way to confront the present by reexamining the sources of his character. Above all, he found a way to reexamine his relationship with his own father, the man who had taught him how to be a father.

In its central concern with the father-son relationship, *A Boy's Town* is typical of the boy book but unique among Howells's several autobiographies. In *Years of My Youth* (1916), the first of several projected volumes through which Howells sought to trace the lifelong development of the public figure he became, he observes that his mother "was not only the centre of home to me; she was home itself, and in the years before I made a home of my own, absence from her was the homesickness, or the fear of it, which was always haunting me" (20). Howells's biographers have explored this relationship in some depth. Kenneth S. Lynn observes that the numerous declarations of attachment to Mary Dean Howells in Will's autobiographies and letters have no counterpart in the letters by his brothers and sisters (31). Elizabeth Stevens Prioleau's and John W. Crowley's Freudian-informed works treat young Howells's closeness to his mother in the context of the conflict between her "extrarespectable standards" (Prioleau 147) and fiery temper and William Cooper Howells's idealistic but often impractical approach to life, which made him persist, in the face of his wife's mingled admiration and despair, in trying to establish himself as a radical newspaperman in one small Ohio town after another, and even made him try an ill-fated stint in a cooperative community with his brothers. *A Boy's Town,* however, goes back to the nine years the family spent in Hamilton, Ohio (a long period in one place for this family), a time before the tension between the parents had fully materialized and young Howells had identified with his mother's side of the conflict (Crowley, *Black Heart's Truth* 17). In turning to this time in his past life, Howells was choosing a time when he could look at his relationship with his father without the complicating factor of having to take into account his mother's unhappiness with the life William Cooper forced on her.

Following the precedent established by earlier boy books, Howells presented *A Boy's Town* as a story for children by serializing it in *Harper's Young People* before publishing it as a book. Of all the boy books, however, this one seems least likely to appeal to a child. It is deeply, even morbidly, introspective at times, and it is narrated in a manner that would probably try the patience of most children.[2] Percival Chubb tried to remedy matters in *Boy Life* (1909), a volume published by Harper's as a school text designed in part to introduce students to contemporary American writing. This book opens with a few lively chapters from *Pony Baker,* which is clearly aimed at a juvenile audience, and continues with a selection of lighter, less personal chapters from *A Boy's Town.* I am not sure that Chubb's production would have won converts to American literature, but it tells us that even Howells's own publisher recognized that *A Boy's Town* was not really juvenile literature.

Howells's adult perspective is ever present in *A Boy's Town* through a first-person narrator who convincingly recalls his childish view of events and at the same time reminds us by his manner of presentation that he sees very differently now. With his avuncular personality, he is the most definitively characterized of all the adult boy book narrators. He actually stands as a screen between us and his story by pointedly directing our attention to the fact that he speaks of manners and customs of a past time and by frequently using a past conditional form (this is what you could have done were you there) that at once involves us in and distances us from the life being recounted. Most important of Howells's distancing strategies is one that came to him only after he started writing. He began by referring to his younger self as "I" but quickly changed "I" to "my boy."[3] The effect of this shift is to ally him with a father's perspective. Unlike Aldrich, who begins, "I am, or rather I was, that boy myself," stressing his continuity with his past self, Howells insists by his narrative stance on the primacy of the present self. This in turn colors his narrative, for that present self who narrates the story is a father who owes much to the character of his own father. His view of the past is often judgmental and often ironic; seldom does he let himself go enough to indulge in the sort of lyrical immersion in the past that we have seen in earlier boy books.

The oddities of the memory at work engage the narrator at several points as he sets out to tell his story. Although Howells wrote to his father, "I am surprised, in delving in my childish past as I do in the Boy's Town, to find how much I can remember, and how clearly" (*Selected Letters* 3: 274), he could not recall what common sense told him must be the logical and chronological sequence of things: "There must have been a tedious time between the going down of the flood [of the Miami River] and the first days when the water was warm enough for swimming; but it left no trace. The boys are standing on the shore while the freshet rushes by, and then they are in the water, splashing, diving, ducking; it is like that; so that I do not know just how to get in that period of fishing which must always have come between" (29–30). Similarly, he could not recall the process of development that the autobiography of childhood records: "There was a time when he [his younger self] was afraid of getting in over his head; but he did not know just when he learned to swim, any more than he knew when he learned to read; he could not swim, and then he could swim; he could not read, and then he could read" (31). Memory, in fact, seems to hold individual pictures side by side without the need to rank or evaluate them. One of Howells's earliest memories is just such a picture, striking, disturbing, not integrated with the rest of the book. He recalls—or "seem[s] to remember"—"kneeling on the window-seat in the ladies' cabin" of an Ohio River steamboat, "watching the rain fall into the swirling yellow river and make the little men jump up from the water with its pelting drops" (8). The boat stops, and a yawl with a passenger approaches: "the passenger is a one-legged man, and he is standing in the yawl, with his crutch under his arm, and his cane in his other hand; his family must be watching him from the house. When the yawl comes alongside he tries to step aboard the steamboat, but he misses his footing and slips into the yellow river, and vanishes softly. It is all so smooth and easy, and it is as curious as the little men jumping up from the rain-drops" (9).

In writing *A Boy's Town,* Howells yielded to the power of a memory that recalled particular events without establishing causal relationships between them and let that memory shape much of his book. He begins with his narrator's explaining the book's title and announcing both his identification with the child's perspective from which the story will be told and his adult judgment on that perspective: "I call it a Boy's Town because I wish it to appear to the reader as a town appears to a boy from his third to his eleventh year, when he seldom, if ever, catches a glimpse of life much higher than the middle of a man, and has the most distorted and mistaken views of most things" (1). This opening sentence, which plays on the meanings of "appears," does not announce developmental concerns, but instead identifies a vantage point that conflates nine years into one unit. In so beginning,

Howells marks his book's affinity to other boy books: it is auto-biographical without being an autobiography of childhood, although it has been read as such.[4] Nor is it narrowly auto-biographical. The narrator continues, "For convenience, I shall call this boy, my boy; but I hope he might have been almost anybody's boy; and I mean him sometimes for a boy in general, as well as a boy in particular" (2). The combination of the generic or historic and the particular recalls Warner's *Being a Boy,* but unlike Warner who fails to distinguish between John and "I," Howells does not confuse "a boy in general" and "my boy."

In maintaining the distinction between the generic and the par-ticular boy, Howells further enlarges the possibilities of the boy book, for he has found a way to tell two stories at once. One is the collective biography of boys growing up in a small mid-western town in the 1840s. In accord with Howells's inability to think about his past in terms of causality, their story is presented topically rather than linearly or chronologically. In each of his chapters, the narrator details how "a boy" and, occasionally, "my boy," participates in the activity under discussion—school life, holidays, sports, and so on—with the book moving generally from discussion of less personal events to more private revela-tions. Loosely framing these chapters is the story of "my boy" that is the other story of *A Boy's Town.* The book opens with some of Howells's earliest memories, some even preceding the family's arrival in the Boy's Town, and closes with their removal to another town and "my boy"'s discovery that having left the Boy's Town and the mental state it implies, there is no going back. The two stories are curiously unintegrated. The various activities do not seem to have any effect on "my boy"'s develop-ment. Rather, they exist as timeless vignettes, like that instant when the boys "are in the water, splashing, diving, ducking" or when the one-legged man "misses his footing and slips into the yellow river."

Central to Howells's recollections of life in the Boy's Town is his acceptance of the notion of boyhood savagery. Whereas Warner gave passing mention to the subject, Howells explored the implications of the notion in some depth. It allowed him a way of explaining and accepting what he found repellent in boy behavior and what he remembered as disturbing in himself. He focused particularly on the distorted perspective on life and the erratic behavior exhibited by every boy:

> Like the savage, he dwells on an earth round which the whole solar system revolves, and he is himself the centre of all life on the earth. It has no meaning but as it relates to him; it is for his pleasure, his use; it is for his pain and his abuse. It is full of sights, sounds, sensations, for his delight alone, for his suffering alone. He lives under a law of favor or of fear, but never of justice, and the savage does not make a crueller idol than the child makes of the Power ruling over his world and having him for its chief concern. (6)

When Howells's narrator states at the beginning of his book that he wishes the Boy's Town "to appear to the reader as a town appears to a boy," he has in mind the perspective of the savagelike child who sees himself as the center of the universe.

The opening chapters of the book describe the town with its waterways, which supported a number of mills but "really" existed to provide the boys with opportunities for swimming and fishing and, in rare cold winters, skating. From here, the narrator goes on to describe the other pastimes of the boys. What emerges in the course of the book is a picture of a life lived in tune with the passing of the seasons like the life of primitive peoples:

> When the warm weather came on in April, and the boys got off their shoes for good, there came the races. (83)

> Kites came in just about the time of the greatest heat in summer. (88)

> Foot-ball was always played with a bladder, and it came in season with the cold weather when the putting up of beef began; the business was practically regarded by the boys as one undertaken to supply them with bladders for foot-balls. (83)

> The foraging began with the first relenting days of winter, which usually came in February. Then the boys began to go to the woods to get sugar-water, as they called the maple sap. (161)

The activities go on and on with no hint of an ending, for the cycle recurs year after year (to the extent that the topical organization of this book also makes it cyclical in structure, it again recalls Warner's book), and the various projects the boys undertake as the year passes—gathering nuts, making fluttermills, putting on a circus, and the like—are never successfully completed. In its depiction of the recurring and therefore timeless events in a boy's life and the eternal hopefulness with which he approaches them, *A Boy's Town,* like all boy books, is a restorative excursion into memory. Although darkened by its sober, judgmental narrator, it is a return to a time in which adult problems seem likely never to materialize because time does not pass and hopefulness is never disappointed by reality.

The recurrent games and pastimes give life in the Boy's Town stability and predictability. Similarly, the innumerable rules and superstitions that govern it give it a structure, although, as the adult narrator sees, those rules themselves express no inherent logic and are best explicable as an aspect of boyhood savagery:

> Everywhere and always the world of boys is outside of the laws that govern grown-up communities, and it has its unwritten usages, which are handed down from old to young, and perpetuated on the same level of years, and are lived into and lived out of, but are binding, through all personal vicissitudes, upon the great body of boys between six and twelve years old. No boy can violate them without losing his standing among the other boys, and he cannot enter into their world without coming under them. He must do this, and must not do that; he obeys, but he does not know why, any more than the far-off savages from whom his customs seem mostly to have come. His world is all in and through the world of men and women, but no man or woman can get into it any more than if it were a world of invisible beings. It has its own ideals and superstitions, and these are often of a ferocity, a depravity, scarcely credible in after-life. (67)

Entering (always with reservations) into the child's vision, the adult narrator devotes much of his book to the rules and superstitions that govern boy life. "My boy" is particularly susceptible to superstitions (most of which, as in Huck Finn's world, concern misfortune), and Howells is good naturedly ironic at his expense:

> ["My boy"] believed that warts came from playing with toads, but you could send them away by saying certain words over them; and he was sorry that he never had any warts, so that he could send

them away, and see them go; but he never could bear to touch a toad, and so of course he could not have warts. (199–200)

When you saw a lizard, you had to keep your mouth tight shut, or else the lizard would run down your throat before you knew it. That was what all the boys said, and my boy believed it, though he had never heard of anybody that it happened to. (201)

Rules are equally serious for the boys and are a cause for sober reflection for the adult narrator. Rules concern the way in which power is established and reallocated. They specify who can fight whom and who is obligated to fight whom; they permit some kinds of cruel practical jokes but forbid others; they account some kinds of theft honorable and condemn others. Adult logic does not govern such rules and there is no appeal from them. Like the games and pastimes that recur seasonally, the rules are an eternal feature of boy life: "I do not know where boys get some of the notions of morality that govern them. These notions are like the sports and plays that a boy leaves off as he gets older to the boys that are younger. He outgrows them, and other boys grow into them, and then outgrow them as he did" (98).

Within this context, in fact nearly hidden by it,[5] Howells depicts "my boy"'s singular life and character. Even though "my boy" evidently participated in the town's boy life—if he had not, the adult Howells would not have known it so well—he also stood aloof, and his distinction is central to the second story Howells has to tell. "My boy" is both shy and fearful; early in the book the narrator speaks of "the fear in which his days seem mostly to have been passed" (12). His gravity of manner prompts the printers at his father's newspaper to call him the "Old Man" "as soon as he began to come about the office, which he did almost as soon as he could walk" (238). His heightened moral scruples make him "rather a bother to his friends" (198), and his morbid fancies make him a ready prey to their teasing. He is an enthusiastic reader and a budding writer, though as a child he does not understand that being a writer is a possible future for himself. The narrator suggests, more defensively than convincingly, that "my boy" is no different from other boys: "All the boys may have been like my boy in the Boy's Town, in having each an inward being that was not the least like their outward being, but that somehow seemed to be their real self. . . . But I am certain that this was the case with him, and that while he was joyfully sharing the wild sports and conforming to the savage usages of the boy's world about him, he was dwelling in a wholly different world within him, whose wonders no one else knew" (171). No one else could know, for many of the furnishings of that inner world came from "my boy"'s reading and found expression only in his poetry and daydreams where he appeared "as this and that god and demigod and hero upon imagined occasions in the Boy's Town, to the fancied admiration of all the other fellows" (173). With a mixture of sympathy and harshness, the narrator sums up his existence: "Inwardly he was all thrones, principalities, and powers, the foe of tyrants, the friend of good emperors, and the intimate of magicians, and magnificently apparelled; outwardly he was an incorrigible little sloven, who suffered in all social exigencies from the direst bashfulness, and wished nothing so much as to shrink out of the sight of men if they spoke to him" (177). With a more assertive personality, "my boy" would be the self-dramatizing protagonist Tom Sawyer is; as is, the drama is merely imagined.

Howells never assigns blame for "my boy"'s difficulties. He allows himself to speculate that "my boy"'s morbid fancies "were, perhaps, projected over his narrow outlook from some former state of being, or from the gloomy minds of long-dead ancestors" (17–18). But he reveals more than a hereditary disposition at work in "my boy"'s case. He always speaks lovingly of "my boy"'s parents. His mother, Howells tells us, "was always the best and tenderest mother, and her love had the heavenly art of making each child feel himself the most important, while she was partial to none" (21).[6] He describes his father in more detail, emphasizing his gentleness and his decency, a dual emphasis that suggests that "my boy" was not getting as much affection from his mother as Howells claimed.[7] One of "my boy"'s earliest recollections is of meeting his father on his way home from work and continuing home beside him, sharing his cloak: "To get under its border, and hold by his father's hand in the warmth and dark it made around him was something that the boy thought a great privilege, and that brought him a sense of mystery and security at once that nothing else could ever give" (5). One of the most profound experiences of "my boy"'s childhood is his irrational fear that he will die at sixteen—a fear that is born when he is nine or ten and is not stilled until he passes his sixteenth birthday (we are beyond the Boy's Town years now, but this event was apparently too significant to omit). He finally confesses his fear to his father, and he is reassured by his understanding parent that he is now in his seventeenth year (204). "My boy"'s father also figures as an exemplar of "reason" (247). He encourages his son's literary development, teaches him to respect the rights and opinions of others and to side with the underdog, and seeks to govern his children by precept rather than by punishment: "Once, when their grandfather reported to him that the boys had been seen throwing stones on Sunday at the body of a dog lodged on some drift in the river, he rebuked them for the indecorum, and then ended the matter, as he often did, by saying, 'Boys, consider yourselves soundly thrashed'" (13). But these same parents, especially the father, whom Howells has been at such pains to exonerate, shame "my boy" repeatedly and instill in him an intense sense of guilt.

In part, that highly developed sense of guilt stemmed from the Howells family's religious practices (Olsen 16–18). Howells's father was a Swedenborgian, and Howells explains the doctrine by which they were governed through one of "my boy"'s recollections. Unlike Tom Sawyer's Presbyterianism, with its sporadically vindictive God and tedious doctrine of Election, "my boy"'s faith is a source of constant concern, for it places responsibility squarely on the individual:

> The boy once heard his father explain . . . that the New Church people believed in a hell, which each cast himself into if he loved the evil rather than the good, and that no mercy could keep him out of without destroying him, for a man's love was his very self. It made his blood run cold, and he resolved that rather than cast himself into hell, he would do his poor best to love the good. The children were taught when they teased one another that there was nothing the fiends so much delighted in as teasing. When they were angry and revengeful, they were told that now they were calling evil spirits about them, and that the good angels could not come near them if they wished while they were in that state. (12)

The Swedenborgianism of "my boy"'s father even compromises a crucial moment for the future writer. He discovers the rules of prosody in the back of one of his schoolbooks and figures out how to write poetry. When he shows his work to his father, the father "praised the child's work, and no doubt smiled at it with the mother; but he said that the poem spoke of heaven as a place in the sky, and he wished him always to realize that heaven was a *state* and not a *place,* and that we could have it in this world as well as the next." The boy tactfully keeps his rebellious response to himself, and the narrator refrains from passing overt judgment on the father: "Everybody else who made poetry spoke of heaven as a place; they even called it a land, and put it in the sky; and he ['my boy'] did not see how he was to do otherwise, no matter what Swedenborg said" (62).

"My boy"'s parents frequently intervene in his life to curtail (often by shaming their son) what they perceive as mean-spirited aggression. "My boy" believes his behavior is sanctioned because it conforms to accepted boyhood standards—the standards of the savage. In one instance "my boy" fights another boy and thereby establishes some degree of power and respect among the neighborhood boys. But his mother "witnessed the combat, and came out and shamed him for his behavior, and had in the other boy, and made them friends over some sugar-cakes" (69). More often it is his father who intervenes. I have already quoted Howells's account of his father's response to his stoning a dead dog; another time his father refuses "my boy" permission to buy a soldier's hat "because he would not have the child honor any semblance of soldiering, even such a feeble image of it as a boy's company could present" (125). Still another time he admonishes his son for wanton shooting. "My boy" has just learned how to shut his left eye and keep his right eye open, and the first result of his new-found ability to aim a gun is a successful shot at a sapsucker. But when he tells his father of his success, "His father asked him whether he had expected to eat this sap-sucker. . . . He said no, sap-suckers were not good to eat. 'Then you took its poor little life merely for the pleasure of killing it,' said the father, 'Was it a great pleasure to see it die?' The boy hung his head in shame and silence; it seemed to him that he would never go hunting again"

(155). Sensitized to this form of correction, "my boy" is frequently shamed by the comments of others outside his family as well. Toward the end of the book, Howells observes that "my boy"'s father "seldom forbade him anything explicitly" (233). Looking back over the book, we understand clearly why he did not have to.

An episode recounted early in the book shows how fully "my boy" internalized parental values. Here the narrator is talking about the sometimes arbitrary rules that govern boyhood behavior and that are severely enforced by the peer group:

> A boy was bound to defend them [his sisters and their girl friends] against anything that he thought slighting or insulting; and you did not have to verify the fact that anything had been said or done; you merely had to hear that it had. It once fell to my boy to avenge such a reported wrong from a boy who had not many friends in school, a timid creature whom the mere accusation frightened half out of his wits, and who wildly protested his innocence. He ran, and my boy followed with the other boys after him, till they overtook the culprit and brought him to bay against a high board fence; and there my boy struck him in his imploring face. He tried to feel like a righteous champion, but he felt like a brutal ruffian. He long had the sight of that terrified, weeping face, and with shame and sickness of heart he cowered before it. It was pretty nearly the last of his fighting; and though he came off victor, he felt that he would rather be beaten himself than do another such act of justice. (74)

The boy who cowers before his memory and "would rather be beaten himself" is the real victim here, although there is nothing in Howells's tone that suggests criticism of the parents who created such a strong internal policeman in their son.

Not surprisingly, "my boy," with his fantasy life and his heightened moral scruples, is a loner—a fact that stands out with special clarity when we recall the importance of the boys' gang in *Story of a Bad Boy* and *Tom Sawyer*. He does make friends with an apprentice in his father's print shop, a boy who shares his literary tastes and writes historical romances with him. But a more important relationship is poisoned by his father. "His closest friend," Howells tells us, "was a boy who was probably never willingly at school in his life, and who had no more relish of literature or learning in him than the open fields, or the warm air of an early spring day." It is the Huck Finn of *Tom Sawyer* come to life: "He was like a piece of the genial earth, with no more hint of toiling or spinning in him; willing for anything, but passive and without force or aim. . . . Socially, he was as low as the ground under foot, but morally he was as good as any boy in the Boy's Town, and he had no bad impulses. He had no impulses at all, in fact, and of his own motion he never did anything, or seemed to think anything" (191). In the company of such a boy, "my boy" could relax, secure in the knowledge that his friend accepted him unconditionally. Neither the self-dramatizing he fancied necessary to win the approval of "all the other fellows" nor the goodness he recognized as necessary to win the approval of his parents mattered to this companion:

> The two boys soaked themselves in the river together, and then they lay on the sandy shore, or under some tree, and talked; but my boy could not have talked to him about any of the things that were in his books, or the fume of dreams they sent up in his mind. He must rather have soothed against his soft, caressing ignorance the ache of his fantastic spirit, and reposed his intensity of purpose in that lax and easy aimlessness. Their friendship was not only more innocent than any other friendship my boy had, but it was wholly innocent; they loved each other and that was all. (192)

Boys in the Boy's Town seldom enter each other's houses—they call from outdoors, and they play outdoors. This custom is emphatically true with this boy: "His friend seldom entered my boy's gate, and never his door; for with all the toleration his father felt for every manner of human creature, he could not see what good the boy was to get from this queer companion" (191). "In a fatal hour" (192), "my boy" does what he must have believed would satisfy his father, though at this distance he has blocked out much of the painful memory: he cannot remember precisely how, but he induces his friend to wash and dress and come to school. But the experiment fails, and nothing is ever the same between the two boys again.

Lynn suggests that young Howells's accession to his father's wishes had far-reaching consequences in later life: "His youthful acceptance of traditional Howellsian snobbism eventually cost him dearly, for it inhibited him as a novelist from projecting himself into the lives of proletarian characters" (53). In the context of *A Boy's Town,* the event takes on importance as one in which "my boy" rejects himself in rejecting the one person who accepts him as he is and rejects the pleasurably sensual life he shares with his friend for the sterner values of the parental world (remember that his father "could not see what *good*" [my emphasis] was in the relationship). Yet the mature Howells remains slightly ambivalent. His stance throughout the book, as we have seen, commits him to siding with his father. Perhaps an unarticulated notion of manly behavior—such as we have seen in Warner—makes him willing to accept separation from a friend to whom he was emotionally drawn. Yet he seems to regret "my boy"'s behavior in this instance, not for his elitism, but for his denial of love. Redefining his father's criteria and hinting at an emptiness in his adult life, perhaps a diminished capacity to love, the narrator comments wistfully: "This friend of his must have had a great natural good in him; and if I could find a man of the make of that boy I am sure I should love him" (192). Still, on the whole, Howells does not regret the internalization of his father's values. Tellingly, he does not treat the younger self who struggles with his father's standards with his usual irony. Further, he positions the episode in which "my boy" tries to change his friend late in the book so that it acquires a kind of summary emphasis.

Looking back over *A Boy's Town,* we can find reason to regret "my boy"'s accommodation to the values of his parents: they heightened his sense of guilt, complicated his relationship to his peer group, and cost him a loving friendship. But with the exception of the instance I cite above, the adult Howells who narrates the story does not express misgivings. Instead, he sides defensively with his parents, in order, we must guess, to explain the man he himself became. In a late chapter called "The Nature of Boys," he suggests that he would have liked to see more accommodation in his younger self. This chapter opens with the narrator's seeming to generalize about boyhood on the strength of the memoir he has nearly completed by insisting, in contradiction to what his strategy of telling the stories of "a boy" and "my boy" suggests, that "one tiresome fact about boys is that they are all so much alike" (205). He continues the chapter by projecting many of the qualities of "my boy" onto "a boy" and by referring to his protagonist now as "a boy." This move allows him to criticize things he saw and regretted in himself all the more vehemently because he can claim they are widespread failings.

His narrator's tone in this chapter ranges from heavy-handed irony that masks anger to a degree of outright anger that seems excessive. He comments ironically: "I do not pretend that what I say of the boys of forty years ago is true of boys nowadays, especially the boys who read *Harper's Young People*. I understand that these boys always like to go tidily dressed and to keep themselves neat. . . . They would rather go to school than fish, or hunt, or swim, any day. . . . They never laugh at a fellow when he hurts himself or tears his clothes. They are noble and self-sacrificing friends." More antagonistically, he castigates boys for the thoughtlessness that leads them to harm others, the selfishness that forbids sympathy with others and courage on behalf of principle, and the lack of "moral strength" (212) that would permit them to defy peer pressure. The root cause of their failings of course is their innate savagery. Most reprehensible of all is the boy who should be able to but cannot master this savagery, not "a boy" as Howells pretends, but recognizably "my boy":

> The spirit of the boy's world is not wicked, but merely savage, as I have often said in this book; it is the spirit of not knowing better. That is, the prevailing spirit is so. Here and there a boy does know better, but he is seldom a leader among boys; and usually he is ashamed of knowing better, and rarely tries to do better than the rest. He would like to please his father and mother, but he dreads the other boys and what they will say; and so the light of home fades from his ignorant soul, and leaves him in the outer darkness of the street. (213)

The excessive feeling is surprising. The narrator would be more forgiving—more willing to recognize that if the boy is a savage, he cannot help himself—if he did not need to convince himself of what he has to say. But he cannot forgive. The adult Howells finally looks back on his younger self and sides with his strongly directive parents.

Howells's respectful treatment of his father in *A Boy's Town* was colored not only by his need to defend himself as his father's son,

but also by the fact that William Cooper Howells was still living, and Howells, well into middle age, was still negotiating his
relationship to him. In a move recalling "my boy"'s behavior,
Howells sent his father proofs of *A Boy's Town* and invited revision, and then rejoiced in his father's approval of the book (*Selected
Letters* 3: 274, 280). He had a brief moment of misgiving—Lynn
quotes him as writing to his father: "I see now, with more thought
and time I could have made it ever so much better. But it's too late
now; it must go" (38). Perhaps this was merely a self-protective
gesture in anticipation of criticism, perhaps a recognition that he
really had not done all he could—his text, as I have noted, just
barely hints at his ambivalent feelings toward his father. Still, he
had good reason to feel satisfied with his accomplishment. He had
recalled the past with a facility that surprised him as it evoked both
past happinesses and terrors. More important, in devising the
stories of "my boy" and "a boy," he had found a way to express
the feeling of inadequacy that, in his unhappy present, seemed to
have existed since childhood. At the same time, in subjugating his
protagonist to a judgmental narrator, he had found a way to express the values he had learned from his father and carried into
adulthood. But there was one additional step that Howells could
not take in *A Boy's Town*. Because the past and present do not come
together at the end of a boy book, Howells was not forced to draw
the logical conclusion his picture of his boyhood relationship with
his father suggests. He shows us how much pressure his demanding father exerted and how much of his father he internalized, but
his form frees him from having to acknowledge explicitly that as a
father himself, he must have been an equally difficult parent. Given
the timing of the book in Howells's life, it is tempting to believe
that he knew this on an intuitive level.

Howells's second boy book came out of an only slightly less
despondent mood than his first. As Cady notes, Howells never
really recovered from Winny's death (*Realist at War* 98). By the late
1890s, when he began publishing parts of what was to be *The
Flight of Pony Baker: A Boy's Town Story,* he was in ill health (as
was his wife) and, now in his early sixties, felt himself to be an
old man. The death of his father in 1894 "aged me as nothing else
could have done," he wrote to Charles Eliot Norton (*Selected*

*Letters* 4: 78). In March 1902 because, as he wrote Aldrich, "I am tired out, and have lost the trick of sleeping" (*Selected Letters* 5: 16), he took a ten-day trip down the Ohio River from Pittsburgh to Cincinnati with his older brother. *Pony Baker* must have been well under way at this point (it was published in September), but perhaps the glimpse of "a vanished epoch in the life of the shores, where the type of Americanism, for good and for bad, of fifty years ago, still prevails" (*Selected Letters* 5: 17; to Norton) helped sharpen the memories that went into this second Boy's Town book.

Howells's brooding on old age, which surfaces again and again in his correspondence, seems to have had a particular relevance to *Pony Baker*. The deaths of several contemporaries near the turn of the century, along with his own ill health, provoked questions about himself. When Bret Harte died in May 1902, Howells saw the death as implicating his literary generation: "He belonged to our youth which was glad, and knew it" (*Life in Letters* 2: 156; *Selected Letters* 5: 24), he told Aldrich. Aldrich agreed and commented on the impact of age on himself: "The older I grow the less positive I get concerning the state of affairs beyond those 'gates ajar'—very much 'ajar' for a fellow after he has past sixty. I envy my old grand-father his unquestioning faith. He used to read a big bible covered with rough green baize, and believe every word he read, even the typographical errors" (*Life in Letters* 2: 158). In response to this confession of doubt, Howells expressed his own worry:

> I should not mind being old, so much, if I always had the young, sure grip of myself. What I hate is this dreamy fumbling about my own identity, in which I detect myself at odd times. It seems sometimes as if it were somebody else, and I sometimes wish it were. But it will have to go on, and I must get what help I can out of the fact that it always *has* gone on. I think I could deal with the present, bad and bothering as it is, if it were not for visions of the past in which I appear to be mostly running about, full of sound and fury signifying nothing. Once I thought that I meant something by everything I did; but now I don't know. (*Life in Letters* 2: 158–59; *Selected Letters* 5: 32)

It is not clear which past Howells is remembering here; the image he presents of himself suggests young adulthood. But the mood of this letter, dismay at the discovery that present confusion about the self also extends backward to undermine the seemingly secure past, is the same mood that is felt in *Pony Baker*. In the book Howells examines his youngest self and sees him equally confused about his identity. But in the guise of fiction, so often therapeutic to Howells, he is able to explore paths he might have taken and come to a happier conclusion than he does in his letter.

Unlike *A Boy's Town, Pony Baker* was not written as a continuous whole. The book tells the story of Pony's abortive attempts to run away from home (the flight of the title) to get back at his overly protective mother and strongly directive father. He is encouraged by his schoolmates, by one Jim Leonard in particular, a boy who is full of wild schemes that get other people in trouble. Pony vacillates between what he knows to be right and what Jim and his schoolmates urge on him. He is an incarnation of "my boy" who "does know better, but . . . is seldom a leader among boys." Pony's wavering is highlighted by contrast with his cousin Frank Baker, a paragon among boys, one "who does know better" and is able to act on his knowledge. Pony's story follows a simple linear form beginning near the end of the school year in June and running on into October. Pony entertains a series of ideas about running away: he might join the Indians, or a circus, or take a raft down the Ohio River—fantasies that rework material from *A Boy's Town* and pay implicit homage to James Otis's popular children's book, *Toby Tyler or Ten Weeks with a Circus* (1880 with continual reprintings) and to Twain's *Huck Finn*. Each of these schemes occupies a couple of chapters, and each is separated by a chapter or two on either Jim or Frank. These four intervening chapters were written and published before Pony's story, with Pony appearing as a minor character in three of them. By interleaving Pony's linear story with the earlier published material, Howells blurs the passage of time since three of the four intervening chapters are flashbacks and the fourth can be read as such. Like all boy books, *Pony Baker* is about a particular point in the protagonist's life that resonates in the life of the author/narrator; it is not about growth.

*Pony Baker* also differs from *A Boy's Town* in its putative audience. With the exception of one chapter, *Pony Baker* is clearly aimed at a young audience. It is a shorter book than *A Boy's*

*Town,* its language is simpler, and the events it details are more fully developed and more concretely presented. Nevertheless, *Pony Baker* also speaks to adults. Its first-person narrator rarely calls attention to himself. He intervenes only occasionally to set the scene, and he does so with an excessive precision suitable to a child reader: "Before I go the least bit further with the story of Pony Baker's running away, I have got to tell about Jim Leonard, and what kind of boy he was" (30). But we feel the narrator's presence constantly as he recaptures the child's perspective and subjects it to the adult's irony: "She was not exactly a bad mother, and she was not exactly a good mother. If she had been really a good mother she would have let him do whatever he wanted, and never made any trouble, and if she had been a bad mother she would not have let him do anything; and then he could have done it without her letting him" (7). It is a gentle irony. Of course a good mother would not be completely permissive as young Pony thinks, but a bad mother would be absolutely restrictive. We laugh at the rigidity of Pony's categories, but not at his understanding that a mother who cannot trust her child at all will not get trust in return. This ironic voice, present in all of Pony's adventures, is what we would expect given his status as a version of "my boy." It is not present in the chapters devoted to Jim and Frank. In fact, one of these chapters, "How Frank Baker Spent the Fourth at Pawpaw Bottom, and Saw the Fourth of July Boy," rises to lyrical heights.

The chapter on the Fourth of July is the one that seems aimed primarily at adults. It was published in *Harper's Weekly* in the 5 July 1902 issue; the other chapters that preceded the book appeared in *Youth's Companion.* In this chapter Frank spends the Fourth with his friend Jake at another boy's farm instead of in town. In town they might have set off fireworks and shot pistols and watched others doing the same—a grand holiday for a boy on the evidence of *A Boy's Town* (and *Story of a Bad Boy,* for that matter). Instead, Frank agrees to call on a boy he does not know—and ends up helping with the onerous chore of distributing wood rails in piles so that a fence can be built. But they are rewarded by a joyous afternoon of berrying, playing Indians in the rain, rafting on the creek, and eating heartily. In all their activities, they seem to be accompanied by another boy, a spirit boy who can be seen by only one of them at a time. Howells's description of the ride home at the end of the day summarizes the sensual feast the day has been and recalls some of the pleasures of his own childhood in rural Ohio. In its attention to both the details of the natural setting and the preoccupations of boyhood, the passage recalls Warner's celebration of the New England countryside and Twain's account of daybreak on Jackson's Island:

> It was almost sundown now, and they heard the turtle-doves cooing in the woods, and the bob-whites whistling from the stubble, and there were so many squirrels among the trees in the woods-pastures, and on the fences, that Frank could hardly get Jake along [Jake is pretending to hunt quail]; and if it had not been for Jake's horse, that ran whenever Frank whipped up his pony, they would not have got home till dark. They smelt ham frying in some of the houses they passed, and that made them awfully hungry; one place there was coffee, too. (131–32)

Boylike, they delight in retelling their adventures. One of the neighbors remarks that her recently dead son "was always such a Fourth-of-July boy. . . . I know he'd give anything to been here with the boys to-day. . . . And he's been here, *too;* I just know he has" (137–38). After she leaves, Frank recalls the spirit boy and is surprised at the way the adults seize on his story. Howells closes with the adults speculating on what they have heard. Too precious for our tastes, certainly, but the turn of the century saw a widespread interest in spiritualism (Henry James and Edith Wharton, for example, found a ready market for their ghost stories in this period), and the story does reveal Howells's customary psychological acumen, perhaps whetted now by his thinking about aging: he recognizes that adults, not boys, hunger for some reassurance of immortality.

Whereas *Pony Baker* is similar to other boy books in its range of tones, it is unique in its handling of its protagonist. Like Twain, Howells multiplies his protagonist, here into three characters—Pony, Jim, and Frank. Twain, as we have seen, dramatized his adult need to judge his child self in the characters of Huck and Tom. Howells's characters are even more closely related, all being variations of one another, dramatizations of the "dreamy fumbling about my own identity" that Howells complained of to

Aldrich. Their basic affinity and the composition of the book do not bring these characters into conflict with one another; instead, Jim and Frank exist as options, paths Will/Pony might have followed but happily does not.

Pony, as I have noted, is a fictionalized version of "my boy." Family circumstances have been altered for this book: instead of having an idealized (and sometimes resented) older brother, Pony is the only boy in a family of girls; a brother died in infancy, and his mother is understandably protective of her son. It is a recasting of Howells's own life that allows him both to relish and to criticize remembered maternal attention. Pony's mother is expecting another baby, though he does not understand this until a little brother arrives at the end of the book, and she is nervous and emotional. Pony's usually impossible task is to reconcile the demands of his peer group with his mother's solicitude and his father's right-mindedness. We are back on the same ground as *A Boy's Town,* but now Howells looks at his protagonist's relationship with both parents and devotes slightly more space to the relationship with the mother.

In response to this emphasis on Pony's relationship with his mother, both Prioleau and Crowley discuss *Pony Baker* in terms of Howells's treatment of the Oedipal theme. Prioleau claims that "this deceptively slight book reaches into the maternal matrix of his [Howells's] childhood and divines the heart of his neurosis" (139)—his excessive attachment to this mother. Crowley stresses the resolution of the attachment (the birth of the new baby permits mother and son a new independence from each other) to conclude that "Howells shows an intuitive knowledge not only of 'Oedipal' fears and desires, but of the psychological process by which a boy moves beyond them into the 'latency period.'" He outlines the process for us: "a boy's dread of his father's power . . . leads him eventually to repress his sexual desire for the mother and to identify himself with the father, in part by incorporating paternal 'authority' as the kernel of his own developing 'super ego'" (*Mask of Fiction* 167, 169). To illustrate this, Crowley examines the fears dramatized in Pony's nightmare the evening he expects to run off with the circus and notes that Pony eventually rejects Jim Leonard's leadership for the values of the parental world. This is what we also saw happen to "my boy," though in that case the relationship with the mother was omitted. Prioleau, who sees Howells's autobiographical writing as leading him ever inward, would say he was not ready for such depth when he wrote the earlier book. As I have indicated, I am more inclined to give credit to Howells's need to examine a father-child relationship in shaping that earlier book.

I would also stress Howells's need to continue thinking about that relationship in *Pony Baker*. Although Prioleau and Crowley are correct in identifying the mother-son relationship as the emotional center of the book, it is not the intellectual center. Here, in his second boy book, Howells's concern with his identity as he approaches old age leads him to think more directly than he has previously about how fathers shape sons and about how he was shaped by his father. He considers Pony in relation to the two other boys. Pony's friend Jim, whom Prioleau identifies as "the projection of Howells's bad-boy self" (140), is presented as a negative counterpart to Pony. Jim's mother, in Pony's eyes, "was a very good mother to Jim"; unlike his own protective parent, Jim's mother let her son "do whatever he pleased—go in swimming as much as he wanted to, stay out of school, or anything" (196). She is a gruff, lower-class woman who smokes a pipe—a rather androgynous figure who is both mother and father to Jim. She is always on the verge of whipping her son for some misdeed (a contradiction to her supposed permissiveness that Pony does not perceive) that Pony's gentle and rational father would have talked over with his son. If Jim is an aspect of Pony or young Howells, then Jim's androgynous mother stands in for Howells's own parents—disguised by class and manner so as to permit expression of the animosity Howells could not otherwise allow himself.

Without parents to show the way, significantly, without a father at all, Jim's behavior is not bad so much as it is asocial and wildly erratic. Although Howells does not use the word "savage" in this book, Jim is kin to the boys described in *A Boy's Town*: "Sometimes he was so good to you that you could not help thinking he was one of the cleverest fellows in town, and then all of a sudden he would do something mean. He acted the perfect coward at times, and at other times he was not afraid of anything" (70). With his tenuous hold on reality, he is also highly imaginative, believing that "he did all kinds of things that he would like to have done" (35–36). His mind is stocked with ideas from his reading. As a joke for adult readers, Howells notes that Jim had even read a novel, though "he could not tell the boys exactly what a novel was, but that was what it said on the back" (195). He is the one who tells Pony how to run away and join the Indians or the circus or journey down the river. Pony's mother dislikes Jim and worries about his influence on her son. "'He's so low down,'" she complains. Pony's father, with a generosity of spirit that "my boy"'s father could not muster—Howells is wistfully rewriting history—rightly reassures her, "'I don't believe there's any harm in the fellow'" (197). In "Jim Leonard's Hair-breadth Escape," Jim finds himself floating down a flood-swollen river on the roof of his mother's stable: "He could see the top of Pony Baker's house, and he thought what a good, kind man Pony's father was. Surely *he* would try to save him; and Jim Leonard began to yell. . . . 'Save me, Mr. Baker, save me!'" (42). Luck and another townsman save him, but Jim's cry for help echoes: it is a plea for what is missing in the boy's life—and to the extent that Howells identifies with Jim, it is a wish for a "good, kind" father.

While Jim is a negative counterpart to Pony, Frank is a positive one. Not surprisingly, given what we know of Howells from *A Boy's Town,* he feels a greater affinity for his good-boy self than for his bad-boy self. Frank is a cousin, not just a friend; he shares Pony's given name; and his parents are characterized in much the same way Pony's are. But whereas Pony is easily swayed by peer pressure, Frank, who is a little older, is "one of those fellows that every mother would feel her boy was safe with. She would be sure that no crowd he was in was going to do any harm or come to any, for he would have an anxious eye out for everybody, and he would stand between the crowd and the mischief that a crowd of boys nearly always wants to do" (166). As a result, Frank is much put upon to help his mother as well as neighbors who "got him to do a good many things that they would not have got other boys to do" (169). His origin lies, not in some abstract notion of virtue on Howells's part, but in Howell's memories of "my boy"'s idealized older brother whom we met in *A Boy's Town:* "My boy would as soon have thought of his father's doing a wrong thing as of his brother's doing it; and his brother was a calm light of common-sense, of justice, of truth, while he was a fantastic flicker of gaudy purposes" (185). As the comparison with the father makes clear, this boy is the embodiment of parental values. In Prioleau's scheme Frank is Pony's "tyrannical conscience" or "superego" (139–40).

Yet Howells does not allow Frank any influence over Pony. "The Adventures that Pony's Cousin, Frank Baker, Had with a Pocketful of Money" is a story related by Pony's father (significantly) about "how splendidly Frank had behaved" (166) when he was asked to carry a large sum of money for a local merchant from a nearby town back to the Boy's Town. Frank did so without taking or losing any of the money in spite of a number of difficulties encountered on the journey. Because Frank is held up to Pony as an example, Pony cannot bring himself to ask Frank about the wisdom of running away, and the two boys have no contact with each other.

In addition, the narrator hints that incorporation of the values Frank represents might not be desirable. Here Howells has moved beyond *A Boy's Town,* where, as we have seen, he labors to convince himself that his parents' values are indeed more important than the claims of the boys' world. Frank, who represents those values, is described as "the worrying kind of boy" who is so "used . . . to having care put upon him . . . [that] he would even borrow trouble when he had none." His face is "a little more careworn than it ought to be at his age" (169). And his experience with the money is a nightmare of anxiety. The complications that arise before he can give the money to its rightful owner—a carriage ride with a runaway horse, a night in a strange inn with a thunderstorm raging outside, and a walk through a covered bridge—might have given Tom Sawyer or Jim Leonard pleasure. Instead, they heighten Frank's already-present worries for the safety of the money; for the well-being of his younger brother, who is with him; for his father, who expects his speedy return home. When the money has been safely delivered, Frank "felt light, light as cotton, and gladder than he almost ever was in his life before" (189)—a short-lived happiness that is dashed when his father immediately plunges him into confusion by catechizing him on the real importance (or lack of importance, as this idealistic father would have it) of money. We might wish to argue that the overburdened boy has his reward in seeing the spirit boy on the Fourth of July, but Howells makes no such suggestion. In fact, the original version of this chapter (in which Frank, who has the symbolic name of many heroes of stories for boys, had the more suggestive name of Luke Willing), unlike the novel version, concluded with a glimpse of this too-responsible boy's future:

> All this was a great while ago. Luke is now a grey, elderly man. He has never since had so much money in his pocket as Mr. Bushnell stuffed into it that afternoon in the city, when he was a boy of eleven years.
>
> He sometimes thinks he would like to have a little more money than he earns, but perhaps he would not enjoy it. He is a care-worn man as he was a care-worn boy, doing always for others and not doing much for himself; but in spite of all his care, he has the light heart of a child for innocent pleasure, and I do not think he could have had anything better if he had always had a pocketful of money. ("A Pocketful of Money" 618)

The last two phrases are clearly a sop to the young reader; in context of the boy's story, they carry little conviction. This boy has been damaged by his well-meaning father.

Pony's story ends with his rejection of Jim Leonard. Somehow the scheme for Pony and Jim to take a raft down the local tributary to the Ohio River has changed. Now Pony will walk to the river and Jim will, perhaps, catch up with him later on a raft; and Pony will spend his last night in the family barn and Jim will, perhaps, come to see him off in the morning. Only the fear of Jim's telling "all the fellows" (212) that Pony is a coward holds Pony to the plan, but for the first time he "felt that he did not like Jim Leonard very much himself. It seemed to him that Jim Leonard had not used him very well, but he could not have told how" (210). He spends part of a wretched night in the barn, and then his father finds him and brings him home. Jim and his values are rejected, but Frank's are not embraced in their stead, and the book ends on a satisfyingly open note. Pony's confusion about his relationship to Jim and his peer group remains one of the mysteries of boyhood—he cannot tell his father why he wanted to run away from a loving home, and his father, displaying a greater degree of understanding than Frank's earnest father, does not press him. In the guise of fiction, Howells has found a way to reject what he finally recognized as excessive in his father while acknowledging what was admirable in him. Pony seems likely to have a happier future than Frank: with a new baby in the house, his parents back off a bit and let him "do more things" (223). He is granted freedom not only to run barefoot and go swimming when the other boys do, but also to grow in his own way. Through his fiction Howells gives his protagonist a second chance and, vicariously, rewrites his own past. Whereas all boy books provide writer and reader alike a therapeutic but temporary release from the present in those moments of lyrical celebration of the past, *Pony Baker* has the distinction of permitting its author a real reconception of the past.

Despite their origin in his feelings of inadequacy as a father and his uncertainty about himself as he aged, Howells's boy books transcend the personal. They evoke mundane life in pre–Civil War America with a memorable clarity, and they present the savage code that enshrines a boy's peer group and sets him, to his confusion, in opposition to his parents with more directness than any of the other boy books to this point. Howells recalls one acknowledgment of the appeal of his work. In *Literary Friends and Acquaintance* (1900), the autobiography–cum–literary memoir Howells wrote commemorating his early days in New England, he describes a visit from the aging historian Francis Parkman, who, with considerable effort, "came to me during my final year in Boston for nothing apparently but to tell me of his liking for a book of mine describing boy-life in Southern Ohio a half century ago [this would have been *A Boy's Town*]. He wished to talk about many points of this, which he found the same as his own boy life in the neighborhood of Boston; and we could agree that the life of the Anglosaxon boy was pretty much the same every-where" (121–22). They could agree on this despite the fact that Parkman's past, in contrast to Howells's, was a very privileged one. Mark Twain also found something familiar in the books. After reading *Pony Baker*, he wrote Howells, "It is a charming book, & perfectly true"—a comment that seems at first glance to be simply the flattery of a friend and a misreading of the book, with "charming" and "true" standing in apposition. But as Twain continues, it becomes apparent that he finds the book to be "perfectly true," not because it is charming, but because it captures the confusions and frustrations of childhood: "I ran away twice. . . . There is not much satisfaction in it, even as a recollection. . . . The heroics squish out of such things so promptly" (*Mark Twain-Howells Letters* 2: 746). He was less expansive in his praise of *A Boy's Town* because the book came to him in the midst of a variety of family troubles, and he could only comment briefly on it: "'A Boy's Town' is perfect," he wrote, "perfect as the perfectest photograph the sun ever made" (*Mark Twain-Howells Letters* 2: 633). His bright metaphor reminds us that these books were important to their readers not only as history, but also as an escape from history.

# 5

# HAMLIN GARLAND

Garland's title—*Boy Life on the Prairie*—announces an innovation in the boy book. Warner's and Howells's titles, *Being a Boy* and *A Boy's Town,* point to the authors' wishes to generalize about boyhood and boy nature. Although both authors refer to a particular time and place, as Parkman's appreciation of Howells's work reminds us, the particular place is subordinate to the author's general concerns. Garland's book, in contrast, evokes a specific time and place in both its author's life and in the life of the country. Its counterparts are such books as Joel Chandler Harris's *On the Plantation* (1892) and Edward Everett Hale's *A New England Boyhood* (1893). It is a better book than either of these: it is less rambling than Harris's and less plodding than Hale's. In its placing of the personal story, again a generational conflict of father and son, in the context of late nineteenth-century industrialism as it impinges on farm life on the midwestern frontier, *Boy Life on the Prairie* brings together public and private issues in a more direct way than any of the other boy books I have considered.

*Boy Life on the Prairie* had its origins in Garland's nostalgia for his childhood and in his efforts to define himself as a writer. In the late 1880s he was living in Boston, having sought out that "storied city" (425) for the same reasons Howells did about thirty years earlier. In 1887, when Garland was twenty-seven, he returned to the Midwest, homesick and deliberately seeking material that could be worked up for publication. His mother's stroke and another visit to the Midwest the next year seem to have intensified his desire to preserve his boyhood experience and his need to assuage his guilt at having left the family. Later that same year, he published a series of six articles in the *American Magazine* under the title "Boy Life on the Prairie." These articles presented a year's life on a midwestern farm as a boy would have experienced it in the 1870s. After this Garland's career flourished until the end of the 1890s, when he seemed to have exhausted his ideas for fiction. He took a trip to the Midwest in 1897 (he was still living the in East, in Washington, at this point) and to the Yukon in 1898, again looking for literary material and, to some extent, seeking the vanished western world of his youth. He had some notion of developing his early sketches and outlined a story of boy life in the Midwest before he left for the Yukon. On his return, apparently at the suggestion of his publisher, he began work on what became *Boy Life on the Prairie* in 1899. The book developed the story he had outlined before his trip and incorporated and expanded the 1888 sketches: new events were added, others were developed at greater length, and material was rearranged; poems from Garland's *Prairie Songs* (1893) were included and sometimes rewritten to fit the new context; and, most significant for our purposes, the nameless, uncharacterized boy whose point of view informs the sketches was replaced by a boy protagonist, Lincoln Stewart, a boy with a definite personality, a family, and a circle of friends.[1] A group of essays became a boy book that spoke to Garland's needs to preserve his past, justify his break with his family, and revive his literary career.

In his first Preface to *Boy Life on the Prairie,* Garland outlined the publication history of his book and identified his narrative stance in relation to his subject matter and his protagonist. He presented himself with some exaggeration as an aging historian (he was thirty-nine), emphasizing his distance from his material: "The life I intended to depict was passing. The machinery of that day is already gone. The methods of haying, harvesting, threshing, are quite changed, and the boys of my generation are already middle-aged men with poor memories; therefore I have taken a slice out of the year 1899 in order to put into shape my recollection of the life we led in northern Iowa thirty years ago. I trust the reader will permit my assumption of the airs of an old man for a single volume" (xix). Perhaps feeling that the role of historian was incompatible with that of autobiographer, he denied what he had come close to acknowledging: "It is not my intention to present in *Lincoln Stewart* the details of my own life and character, though I lived substantially the life of the boys herein depicted. I have used *Lincoln* merely as a connecting life-thread to bind the chapters together. . . . All of the incidents. . . . are typical of the time and place. In short, I have aimed to depict boy life, not boys" (xx).

Later readers who turned to *Boy Life on the Prairie* after reading Garland's autobiography of childhood, *A Son of the Middle Border,* would recognize that the earlier book in fact was autobiographical,[2] and they would see that, as with the autobiography, the life story did not compromise the history. Howells, who seems to have missed *Boy Life on the Prairie,* greatly admired *A Son of the Middle Border* and praised it as "a precious contribution to human knowledge," for it offered its readers "a psychological synthesis of personal and general conditions in a new country" (Review of *Son* 309). As Garland came to recognize, *Boy Life on the Prairie* provided the same synthesis. He asserted his role as historian in "To My Young Readers," an introduction prepared for a 1926 school edition of *Boy Life on the Prairie.* Now he more accurately appraised his relation to his material by recalling its origin: "I wrote this book while still a young man. It is therefore not an old man's dream of the past; it is the recorded recollection of a writer of thirty years of age [his age when he wrote the first sketches]" (427). He identified the places and people referred to in his book and admitted that "this book is substantially made up of the doings of my own family" (426–27). And he expressed the idea, evidenced in all the boy books, that fictionalizing was a means of presenting the truth: "All of the events, even those in fictional form, are actual, although in some cases I have combined experiences of other boys with my own" (427).

Although Garland's title does not commit him to a single boy's experience, his autobiographical concerns keep him reasonably consistent in focusing on one boy's experience—that of his autobiographical counterpart, Lincoln Stewart—with an occasional look at that of a friend or brother. Lincoln never emerges as vividly as Tom Sawyer, with his self-centered fantasies and his irrepressible thirst for 'life, or "my boy," with his equally self-centered world view and his morbid fears. Perhaps Garland lacked the insight or skill to render boyhood as realistically as Twain and Howells had. He may also have lacked the courage to probe too deeply. His decision to subordinate his story to the history of life on the prairie ensures that, as narrator, he will remain at some distance from his protagonist. Lincoln will be more a case study for him, less a repository of ambivalent memories. Garland assigns Lincoln experiences and feelings appropriate to his childhood self and so distinguishes that restive, uncertain self from the confident figure who looks back, but he does so in the voice of the historian; he makes no attempt to evoke the child's voice. The result is a book that conveys the dual perspectives of child protagonist and adult narrator in a style that tends to mask the child's point of view. Appropriate to his role as historian, the narrator rarely calls attention to himself by referring to himself as "I," preferring instead to disappear behind his narrative. I refer to him as Garland as a matter of convenience, as I have referred to other narrators by their authors' names, but this self-effacing narrator is properly one of Garland's adult personae.

A second adult persona appears in the poems interspersed throughout the text. The inclusion of poetry allows Garland to split his narrator into two characters—the poet and the historian. At times it seems that Garland is using the poet to voice the elegiac mood and the historian to present the picaresque vision that we see elsewhere combined in one narrator. But more often the two perspectives are similar, for the historian, like the poet, broods longingly over the vanished past. Nineteenth-century notions of what constitutes poetry, however, permit Garland as poet an extravagance denied to the historian. He often speaks in personal terms, using "I" and "you," and he is emotional, italicizing lines and using exclamation points for emphasis.[3]

The poems appear throughout the text, sometimes offering a lyrical celebration—both literally and figuratively—of something that has already been referred to in the prose text, sometimes reaching beyond the events of the story to the situation of the adult writer. Typically, the city-dwelling poet muses on the distance between his past and present lives. In "Corn Shadows" the sight of some corn, oddly flourishing in the city, transfixes then overwhelms him with memories of his childhood and a feeling of loss. He bursts out:

> *Oh wide, sweet wilderness of leaves!*
> *O playmates far away! Over thee*
> *The slow wind like a mourner grieves.*
> *And stirs the plumed ears fitfully.*
> *Would we could sound the signal horn*
> *And meet once more in walls of corn!* (134)

The movement in these poems is not always toward the past. In "In Stacking Time" a daydream of the past is abruptly shattered and the poet recalled to the present. Garland imagines himself lying in the shadow of a haystack, reveling in the sensations of a bygone autumn day. He concludes:

> As I muse, the shadows wheel and lengthen
> Across the stubble-land, which glows,
> A mat of gold inlaid with green.
> The sun sinks. Sighing, I rise to go—
> The noise of near-by street car breaks the spell
> Of cloud and sun and rustling sheaves,
> Drowning the call of the mystical wind—
> And overhead I hear the jar and throb
> Of giant presses; and the grinding roar
> Of ceaseless tumult in the street below
> Comes back and welters all my world
> As the grey sea returns to sweep
> In sullen surges where the roses bloomed.[4] (179)

Taken together, these poems, with their opposing movements, suggest that Garland's concern is not merely a sentimental longing for the past but a strongly felt discontinuity between past and present, a sharp sense of the contrast between the beauty of the rural past and the bleakness of industrialized contemporary life.

More than anything else, this concern with discontinuity distinguishes *Boy Life on the Prairie* from Garland's autobiography of childhood, *A Son of the Middle Border*. The autobiography deals with the development of the protagonist into the author; its theme is continuity. The boy book, too, traces a boy's development. Unlike the other boy books I have examined, however, *Boy Life on the Prairie* looks back to a period of change that has relevance to the author's present life instead of to what seems like a timeless state of boyhood. But the changes recorded do not culminate in a merging of protagonist and narrator; in this regard *Boy Life on the Prairie* is entirely typical of the boy book. Furthermore, the protagonist's growth is finally meaningless, for the skills Garland's younger self learns are rapidly outmoded by the advent of new farm machinery. An author could treat his childhood miseducation ironically, as does Henry Adams in the *Education* (1907), but Garland's nostalgia made the past the subject of elegy with little room for the irony that we typically find in the boy book. His elegiac poems function like Warner's rhapsodies on the glories of the New England countryside and Twain's loving reconstruction of the coming day on Jackson's Island. And his complex formal structure enhances the elegiac mood.[5] Twain and Howells worked variations on the boy book by multiplying the number of protagonists; Garland does something similar in structural terms: he takes the simple cyclical form appropriate to farm life, just as Warner did, and repeats it with variations in Parts 1 and 2 of his book. The proliferation of cycles results in a work in which remembered boyhood experience is emphatically distanced from the present. Part 1 of *Boy Life on the Prairie* simultaneously describes a year of farm life and several years of Lincoln's life. The book begins with the arrival of the Stewart family in northern Iowa in 1868. It is time for fall plowing, and Lincoln, "a small edition of his father" (1), is ten years old. Part 1 continues through the cycle of the year describing seasonal farm activities and holidays that highlight the passage of time. Garland is careful to mention Lincoln's age periodically: he is ten when he starts school in the winter, twelve when he seeds wheat in the spring, thirteen when he stacks late summer hay. The scheme falters a bit when Garland makes Lincoln fourteen a couple of chapters previous to "Lincoln's First Stack," but because Lincoln behaves like a child in spite of his age—he makes himself sick by eating too many sweets at the Fourth of July celebration and gets into a fight with a group of town boys ("such were the ways of boys," the adult Garland moralizes [150])—we do not feel that this is a serious problem. Part 1 ends with an account of corn husking interrupted and spurred on by Thanksgiving dinner—and a return to the chronology of the opening: Lincoln is eleven. The framing of one chronology with another is both an economical way of linking an account of how things were with a life history and a way of intimating what it is that constitutes maturity. For a boy like Lincoln, this structure suggests, one year is like all others: growth comes not through encountering new challenges, but through meeting the same tasks year after year and gaining increasing mastery of them.

We are made aware from the beginning of the book that this mastery of farm tasks allows a boy to develop his male identity— an identity, as we will come to see, that Lincoln at first embraces and then, with some difficulty, rejects. When ten-year-old Lincoln is told to run the plow team, he is excited, for "this seemed a very fine and manly commission" (9). But like most of the farm work Garland describes, the job soon becomes drudgery because it is arduous as well as monotonous. Furthermore, it is too taxing for a small child. I quote Garland's description at length because it is typical of what occurs throughout the book:

> The task soon became exceedingly tiresome and the field lonely. It meant moving toward and fro, hour after hour, with no one to talk to and nothing to break the monotony. It meant walking eight or nine miles in the forenoon and as many more in the afternoon, with less than an hour off at dinner. It meant care of the share,— holding it steadily and properly. It meant dragging the heavy implement around the corners, and it meant also many mishaps where thick stubble or wild buckwheat rolled up around the standard and threw the share completely out of the ground.
>
> Lincoln, although strong and active, was rather short, and to reach the plough handles he was obliged to lift his hands above his shoulders. He made, indeed, a comical but rather pathetic figure, with the guiding lines crossed over his small back, plodding along the furrows, his worn straw hat bobbing just above the cross-brace. Nothing like him had been seen in the neighborhood; and the people on the roadway, looking across the field, laughed and said, "That's a little too young a boy to work like that." (10)

Although the narrator remembers the boredom and fatigue such labor engendered, he docs not even temporarily limit his perspective to that of his protagonist. His repetition of "it meant" conveys the tediousness of the work and at the same time reminds us of the presence of the interpreting adult narrator. The narrator further distances himself from his subject when he describes him as "a comical but rather pathetic figure." There is no place for indulgence; Lincoln must persevere in his work. There is not enough money to hire another hand, and, equally compelling to Mr. Stewart, "it seemed a natural and necessary thing to have his sons work. He himself had been bound out at nine years of age, and had never known a week's release from toil" (12). Through such an apprenticeship, the "small edition of his father" will in time become a duplicate.

As will his brothers. While Lincoln struggles to fill a man's place, his younger brothers Owen and Tommy also serve their apprenticeships, gradually moving up into more adult roles. This is particularly evident in the chapters on threshing. The first of these is a flashback to the days in Wisconsin before the Stewart family moved to the Iowa prairie. Then grain was stacked in the barn until late fall, when it was threshed with the help of family and friends. Again, boyhood feelings are recalled but held at a distance, this time by the narrator's interpretive metaphors. For Owen, two years Lincoln's junior, the arrival of the threshing machine and the gathering of the folks was "the keenest joy" (199) and "all drama" (201), for he was too young to have any responsibilities. For Lincoln, who was old enough to hold the sacks to collect grain, "it was a bad play. He had now become a part of the machine—of the crew. His liberty to come and go was gone" (201). A year later the family has moved to Iowa, where threshing is adapted to larger fields: wheat is threshed from the shock in the fields in the early fall, and the hands are nomadic workmen instead of family and friends. There is a decline in "the old-time neighborliness and charm" (211) that troubles the narrator, but the principal change for the boys is that each moves into a new stage of his apprenticeship: "The first year Lincoln left the position of sack-holder to Owen, and moved up to hauling away the straw. The third season Owen took his place at the stacker, and Lincoln became a band-cutter, while Tommy took his turn at holding sacks for the measurer" (211). It is worth noting that while Owen had a real-life counterpart, Tommy did not. His presence, which emphasizes the apprenticeship theme, is an instance of the fictionalizing that enhances the truthfulness of the story.

Despite the difficulties of work and the lure of the open prairie, the boys are not unwilling apprentices. Their problem, as they see it, is not that they are expected to work, but that they cannot stop work when they are ready to. Throughout Part 1 Lincoln enthusiastically embraces task after task, only to tire quickly of his labor because of its monotony or because it asks too much of him. The narrator offers an explanation of this restlessness: "A boy wants to do everything, but he doesn't want to do anything long. No matter how enjoyable a job may be for a time, it soon grows old to him. He is an experimenter. That is his trade. To do one thing long cuts him off from acquiring a complete education. Moreover, he wants to do a man's work. Set him to turning bundles, he longs to pitch in the field, or some other job for which he is not fitted" (181). We have seen this boy before: he is the restless, erratically behaved savage that Warner and Howells have described, "anxious to be a man," as Warner said, but not yet able.

As Part 1 draws to a close, however, Lincoln is able to respond to the tasks set before him as a man, not a boy. The task that Garland uses to dramatize this new maturity is hay stacking. This is a job that must be done carefully so that any rain that sinks into the egg-shaped stack will work its way out. Like other farm skills, it requires an apprenticeship: "For several years Lincoln had been instructed by his father in the rudiments of stacking, and had been allowed to 'start the bottom,' and even to lay a course or two of the 'bulge.' To stack well was considered a nice job, requiring skill and judgment, and the privilege of doing even an occasional 'inside course' was of great value to ambitious boys" (184). Lincoln is such a boy, and he gets a special opportunity when his father slips and sprains his arm. Mr. Stewart hands his job over to Lincoln—"'I guess you are the boss stacker from this on'"—and Lincoln responds enthusiastically, feeling that "his father's words made a man of him" (185).

What follows is a classic story. The work, as always, is taxing, "but after all, it was a man's work, and he [Lincoln] had no mind to complain" (186). With "wilful pride" (188) he determines to make a giant oat stack to impress his father, who immediately perceives the challenge and comments, "'Trying to beat your old dad, are you?'" (189). But Lincoln succeeds and the next day moves on to stacking the more slippery wheat. Now he is not so fortunate, and he has a "slide out" (191), an accident made all the more painful because his father appears before he is able to fix it. Mr. Stewart says nothing, however, and Lincoln responds to his implicit trust: "His father considered him quite equal even to a disaster, capable of taking care of himself and a crew. By nightfall he had repaired all mistakes; thereafter, he was the stacker of the crew" (191). Of course success at one task does not mean automatic success at others. Although the threshing that follows the stacking overtaxes Lincoln's strength, he endures the work without complaint. He is moving gradually into maturity as it is defined in the context of prairie life.

As Garland details Lincoln's growth, he notes changes in every aspect of prairie life. Always central are the technological changes connected with farming itself. Such changes make the farmer's life easier, but they are not without cost, for they are at the heart of the discontinuity between past and present that along with the generational conflict of father and son will become increasingly central concerns in Part 2. The first instance I quote is one of the rare places where Garland calls attention to himself as the historian narrator; the second is a more emotional account in which the historian abandons reportage for metaphor and so reminds us that he is not so very different from the poet who appears in this book:

> Raking, in the olden times, was a long and hard task. I can just remember seeing a row of men using hand-rakes as they gathered the hay on a valley farm in Wisconsin, but at the same time, on the Iowan prairies they were using a revolving rake drawn by a horse and operated by a man walking behind. A year or two later came the riding horse-rake; and by the time Lincoln was able to take an important part in the haying-field, the rake had been improved so that a boy could run it. (108–09)

> It was not long before the "mounted power" gave way to the stationary engine, and the separator surrendered its "apron" and its bell-metal cog-wheels, its superb voice diminished to a husky roar and loose rattle. It was as if some splendid insect had become silent. The engine made a stern master, and work around the thresher became one steady, relentless drive from dawn to dusk;

the black monster seemed always yelling for coal and water, and occasionally uttered cries of hate and anger. (211–12)

It is evident from such descriptions that fathers and sons did not have quite the same experience in Lincoln's time. Nevertheless, Lincoln and his father could think in terms of a boy's apprenticeship as long as the essentials of their experiences were the same. But the changes these passages record point to a time in which farming will be a very different matter, and the stamina and skill Lincoln had to develop will be irrelevant. The elegiac note sounded in the last few chapters of Part 1 follows from this recognition. "The spirit which made the old-time threshing a festival, the circumstances which made of it a meeting together of neighbors, is now largely a memory," Garland observes; "The passing of the wheat-field, the growth of stock-farms, the increase in machinery, have removed many of the old-time customs. Lincoln Stewart walks no more in the red dawn of October, his fork on his shoulder, while the landscape palpitates in ecstasy, waiting the coming of the sun" (217). The palpitating landscape recalls the "jar and throb / Of giant presses" in the poem I quote above; the fecund land that signified the past has been replaced by the barren reproductivity of industrial life.

These observations prepare us for Part 2 of *Boy Life on the Prairie*. Like Part 1, Part 2 (with the exception of the concluding chapter) follows the cycle of the year, beginning this time with late spring. Instead of one chronology framing another as is the case in Part 1, Part 2 tells two stories concurrently: one is of the disappearance of the prairie, alluded to above; the other is the continued story of Lincoln's growth. Occasionally, some of the stages in this growth are a bit obscured by flashbacks necessary to show the changes in prairie life, but the combination of the two stories results in a moving account of Lincoln's last three years on the prairie. The final chapter, in which an adult Lincoln returns to the prairie, brings the two stories together and provides an effective conclusion to the work as a whole and a variant method for a boy book author to conclude a cyclical story.

The disappearance of the prairie is spelled out in greatest detail in the chapters of Part 2 that deal with summer and fall cattle herding. As the number of farms multiplied in consequence of improved farming technology, grazing cattle became an increasing nuisance. After the Stewarts had been on the prairie for three years, a law was passed making cattlemen responsible for what their animals did but not requiring farmers to build fences. This meant that the cattle that had formerly been "free commoners" (296) on the land now had to be driven west to unfarmed grazing land. For Lincoln and his friends, this creates a new task: herding the cattle to open range land and then staying with them for weeks at a time. The boys are delighted, for they have long fantasized about the West. They find that it does live up to their expectations in many ways: it is beautiful country, with enough danger and excitement (in the forms of wild horses, angry bulls, and treacherous rattlesnakes—massasaugas) to give life the edge the boys seek and to evoke in them a feeling of kinship with savage Indians. But it is not the untouched West of their dreams, as they discover once they start to move westward: "For a couple of hours the ground was familiar, but at last they came to the Cedar River, beyond which all was unknown. They were deeply disappointed to find houses there, but toward noon they came to a long, low swell of wild land, reaching far to right and to left. It seemed to be the beginning of wild country. It was a wet and swampy country; for that reason it was yet unclaimed, but there were herds of cattle already feeding there" (298–99). And so they move on. It is clear that as civilization spreads westward, herding will soon become impossible for the Iowa farmer. For Lincoln and his companions, the experience lasts only a year. Then the Stewarts, like many others, become dairy farmers instead of beef farmers, reserving a small amount of pasture land out of their farms for their animals. With this change, Garland notes: "On every side the tame was driving out the wild. The sickle soon swept every acre of meadow, and the reign of the Massasauga was ended" (327).

As the prairie changes, Lincoln continues to grow. In Part 2 Garland remains faithful to the ideas illustrated in Part 1: for a farm boy, growth comes through repeated encounters with the same tasks; he serves an apprenticeship until he can fill a man's role. The long chapter on the harvesting of spring wheat, in fact, recapitulates the chapter in Part 1 on stacking and threshing. The first part of the chapter details Lincoln's apprenticeship, from carrying food and water to the hands, to riding the lead horse for the man who drives the thresher, to carrying sheaves, to his success at the age of fifteen at the most difficult of tasks: binding wheat on an appointed station.

The second part of the chapter describes the impact of technological change on harvesting. The year after Lincoln proves himself by binding on a station, his father buys a harvester that cuts the wheat and allows the men riding on the machine to bind it. The harvester eliminates the task of gathering the grain and allows two men to bind as much as four formerly could. Still, binding is hard work, and Lincoln can take pride in his accomplishments. But the prairie farmers live in an age of rapid change: "Harvesting was enormously facilitated by this reaper, but invention was already busy on something far more wonderful. Already there were rumors that a machine had been invented which cut and bound grain entirely of its own motion" (290). With the introduction of the self-binder, "the blinding toil of binding by hand was gone, and the work of shocking [piling sheaves] was greatly lightened by the bundle-carrier attachment, which dropped the sheaves in windrows" (291). With this change, the apprenticeship Lincoln served is no longer meaningful. Garland's sentimental summary is barely adequate to the loss the chapter describes, for it does not address Lincoln's need for a new definition of manhood: "But with all these gains there was a loss—the inexorable change from old to new forever drops and leaves behind pleasant associations of human emotion—the poetry of the familiar and the simpler forms of life" (291). The effect of a comment like this, along with the discussion of change in the chapter itself and in the chapters on herding that immediately follow, is to elegize the past by putting Part 1 of the book at a distance. The period it covers seems locked in an increasingly irretrievable past.

The Lincoln who will leave the prairie also emerges in Part 2. We caught glimpses of him in Part 1, where he revealed an imaginative nature excited by the books he read, a play he saw, and the magnificence of the prairie landscape and showed himself covertly envious of city boys. The conflict between this boy and the apprentice to farm life is barely explored in Part 1 of *Boy Life on the Prairie,* though it is a central issue in Garland's treatment of those same years in *A Son of the Middle Border* where he is seeking early evidence of his literary bent. In *Boy Life on the Prairie* Garland is careful to give full attention to the prairie boy's apprenticeship in a changing world before he gently introduces conflict with it at the beginning of Part 2. Part 2 begins with an account of a circus that brings "the splendors of the great outside world" (231) to the farm boys.[6] The numerous animals and the dazzling performers impress Lincoln strongly. He is overwhelmed and numbed at first, but ultimately is able to see his own life in a new perspective and to recognize that manhood for him can be different from what he prepared for. In the days that follow the circus:

> One by one the splendid acts, the specially beautiful women, and the most wonderful men were recalled and named and admired. . . . But deeper down, more impalpable, more intangible, subtler,—so subtle they ran like aromatic wine throughout his very blood and bone,—were other impressions which threw the prairie into new relief and enhanced the significance of the growing corn as well as the splendor of the pageant which had come and gone like the gold and crimson clouds at sunset.
>
> Lincoln had a dream now, that the world was wide, and filled with graceful men and wondrous women, as well as with innumerable monsters and glittering, harsh-throated birds and slumberous serpents. Some day, when he was a man, he would go forth and look upon the realities of his dream. (250–51)

The lack of specificity in this passage makes it seem false to the boy mind, but it allows the historian narrator to claim that the circus entices without making prairie life look poor by comparison. So described, the event is an appropriate introduction to Part 2 of *Boy Life on the Prairie,* which commemorates prairie life and announces Lincoln's break with it.

In the chapters toward the end of *Boy Life on the Prairie,* Garland presents Lincoln as increasingly restless and discontented with farm life. His aesthetic sensibilities are stirred by the improvements in prairie homes, his ambitions fanned by his local success in "speak[ing] pieces" (377), and he listens eagerly when his closest friend talks about his plans to go to college and leave farming. The event that enables Lincoln to leave is a pure fiction:

a fall from a horse during a winter wolf hunt leads to a long illness in which "the hearty, noisy boy became as weak and dependent and querulous as a teething child" (403). But while Lincoln's hard-won maturity, already threatened by the changes in farm life, is undone by his illness, the hours he spends alone give birth to new ambitions: "His brain was very active. . . . Hopes, aspirations, plans, hardly articulate heretofore, now took shape in his mind. He was sixteen years of age . . . and the question of an education had come to dominate all others. He did not like farm work. The mud and grime and lonely toil connected with it made each year more irksome, while the town and other trades and professions grew correspondingly more alluring" (404).

It is the changing nature of prairie life we have seen documented in *Boy Life on the Prairie* that separates father and son, but Garland uses the related secondary issue of Lincoln's education to divide them irrevocably. Lincoln's father complains to his son, "'You have all the education you need . . . if you're going to farm, and I don't intend to fit you to be a shyster lawyer in a small town'" (404). There are other sons in the family who could carry on the farm; what Mr. Stewart feels and vaguely articulates in his complaint is that his son's choice of a different life will negate his achievement as a farmer and as a father. But rather than portray the intense and ongoing struggle he had with his father over his vocation as he does in his autobiographies, rather than acknowledge how much like his father he is in his determination to have his way,[7] Garland localizes the father-son conflict in the discussion of education that comes about as a result of Lincoln's illness. He uses the conventional literary device of a life-changing illness to highlight the conflict and contain it at the same time so that the historian's concern with prairie life will remain the dominant focus of the book. Garland's stance as historian, in short, enables him to evade full recognition that, for all his hostility to his father's way of life, in character he is indeed his father's son—a recognition that, as we have seen, was similarly troublesome for both Twain and Howells.

Garland allows Lincoln an easier break with his family than he himself had: the boy enlists an uncle's aid, and the family agrees to let him move to Wisconsin to work as a carpenter with his uncle and continue his schooling. With a new life to look forward to, perhaps because there is a new life to look forward to, Lincoln regains his health:

> At last when the sun of March had melted the snow from the chip-pile, he crawled forth into the open air for the first time, the ghost of his old-time self, a pale, sad boy on crutches, with big, wistful brown eyes sweeping the horizon. . . . It was all so beautiful, so good to see and hear and feel, that the boy was dumb with ecstasy. It was as if the world were new, as if no spring had ever before passed over his head, so sweet and awesome and thrillingly glorious was the good old earth. The boy lifted his thin face and big sombre eyes to the sky, his nerves quivering beneath the touch of the wind, the downpour of the sun, and the vibrant voices of flying fowl. Life at that moment ceased to be simple and confined—at that moment he entered his young manhood. (408–09)

Helpless as a child, literally (if temporarily) crippled, he now looks forward to his "young manhood." The boy who became a man in the wheat fields of a prairie farm must enter a new apprenticeship. Lincoln's changed view of himself in effect juvenilizes him, and from this perspective, the world before him seems like a new country. The placement of this event in *Boy Life on the Prairie* legitimizes Lincoln's new ambitions by suggesting that a space was created for them once the changing conditions of prairie life robbed his first apprenticeship of much of its meaning. Private concerns and broad social change come together here.

In the concluding chapter of *Boy Life on the Prairie*, an episode that has no exact counterpart in Garland's life, a twenty-four-year-old Lincoln returns to Iowa for the first time in eight years. At this point Lincoln has not yet found an adult role to replace the one he had prepared for as a boy growing up on the prairie, and there is no suggestion that he has become the adult narrator—this, we remember, is not an autobiography of childhood. Nevertheless, his perspective is that of an adult, and the dual perspective of adult and child, present throughout the book, now vanishes. We are not told why Lincoln returns, but he seeks contact with his own past, as if to recheck its relationship with the present. With a friend he revisits his old home: "As they approached the old place, Lincoln's heart beat distinctly faster. It was like re-discovering a part of himself to retrace his steps" (417–18). But contact with the past proves impossible: "When he came opposite the house, it was less familiar than he had hoped. . . . Something mystical had gone out of it all. It was not so important as his imagination had made it. It was simpler, thinner of texture some way, and he drove on with a feeling of disappointment" (418). Every adult visiting his childhood home after a long absence feels something of this disappointment, but for Lincoln the feeling is intensified by the fact that the world in which he grew up has completely vanished. Everywhere he looks he sees that "it was a changed world, a land of lanes and fields and houses hid in groves of trees which he had seen set out. No one rode horseback any more. Where the cattle had roamed and the boys had raced the prairie wolves, fields of corn and oats waved. No open prairie could be found. Every quarter-section, every acre, was ploughed. The wild flowers were gone. . . . The very air seemed tamed and set to work at the windmills which rose high above every barn, like great sunflowers" (416). Even had Lincoln stayed in Iowa, he would have found himself in a new country, unlike that in which he grew up. But his return after eight years makes the changes that separate his boyhood from his adulthood especially vivid.

The concluding chapter of *Boy Life on the Prairie* is to the book as a whole as Part 2 is to Part 1. It distances and elegizes what has gone before, firmly reminding us that it is history now. At the beginning of the book Garland described Lincoln's first view of the Iowa prairie: "The scene made an indelible impression on him. It was as though he had suddenly been transported into another world, a world where time did not exist; where snow never fell, and the grass waved forever under a cloudless sky" (2). But timelessness is an illusion in this book. Garland's interlocking cycles effectively convey that illusion by recording change but containing it within the single years depicted in Parts 1 and 2. In his concluding chapter Garland moves outside the cycles he has been describing and accepts the passage of time. The voices of the historian, the poet, and the adult Lincoln come together as the book ends with a celebration and a letting go. With an old friend Lincoln seeks out "a slip of prairie sod" (422): "Carefully, minutely, the prairie boys studied the flowers and grasses of the sloping banks, as they recalled the days of cattle-herding, berry-ing, hazel-nutting, and all the now vanished pleasures of boy life on the prairies, and on them both fell a sudden realization of the inexorable march of civilization. They shivered under the passing of the wind, as though it were the stream of time, bearing them swiftly away ever farther from their life on the flowering prairies" (423). Leland Krauth speaks of Garland's "wondrous repossession" of the past to make it suitable as literary material, "a reclamation of it in memory," made possible only by his leaving it and its limitations behind (26). But Garland has done more than turn history into art. Like all boy book writers, he has reconsidered his relationship with his father in the process of writing about the past. The "inexorable march of civilization" that is finally Garland's subject allows him to set aside his father by consigning him and his way of life to the past.

# 6

## STEPHEN CRANE

Crane's Whilomville stories began appearing in *Harper's Monthly* in August 1899, the same year in which his mentor's boy book, *Boy Life on the Prairie,* was published. Like Garland's work, Crane's was an excursion into new subject matter for its author. But whereas Garland's book was the end result of a long genesis and careful reshaping, Crane's work was the hastily written product of desperation. Garland's book appeared in the middle of his life and initiated a series of autobiographical volumes, but Crane's work marked the end of his young life. The last two of the thirteen Whilomville stories were published in July and August of 1900 after his death at twenty-eight, and the volume entitled *Whilomville Stories* appeared later that same year. Its form—a loosely connected group of short stories, a result of the unhappy conditions of its inception—along with a perspective on life that marks Crane as the only literary naturalist in the group of realistic writers I have been considering, make *Whilomville Stories* another innovation in the history of the boy book.

*Whilomville Stories* was not Crane's first evocation of life once upon a time; "The Monster" and "His New Mittens," also set in Whilomville, were written more than a year earlier. "The Monster" unsparingly sketched the cruelty of small town life and made clear that the town's sentimental name was an ironic joke. "His New Mittens" examined the tension between an overly protective mother and her dependent but rebellious son and revealed Crane's insight as each character manipulates the other. Together the stories formed the provocative beginning of a critical examination of one version of America's idealization of the past. But there is no evidence that Crane intended to pursue this subject. He continued to do a variety of other kinds of writing, and he responded with alacrity to the opportunity to go to Cuba and eventually Puerto Rico, hoping at first to fight in the Spanish-American War and then settling for work as a newspaper correspondent.[1] Perhaps he was courting death—he was not well when he left England, where he had settled with Cora Taylor, his common-law wife, and he took incredible risks. Perhaps he was fleeing the life he had been leading—he stayed on in Havana, nearly incommunicado, for several months before returning first to New York and then to England and to Cora at the end of 1898.

In England the end came rapidly for Crane. He and Cora moved to Brede Place, an ancient manor house that provided a setting for their aristocratic pretensions and extravagances and for the lavish hospitality that they could ill afford. In addition to servants, animals, and guests, the household also included two of Harold Frederic's young children, who had been taken in by Cora after their father's death. The Cranes were in debt even before they settled at Brede. Cora complained, using a chilling metaphor, that Crane lacked "that machine-like application which makes a man work steadily" (*Correspondence* 2: 413). She hoped that Brede would provide a quiet setting in which he could work. As always, she was fooling herself about their ability to lead a quiet life. But the financial demands of paying off old debts and maintaining the Brede establishment did provoke Crane to "machine-like" labor. The letters that he and Cora wrote during this year are appalling to read. The two were always in need, appealing to Crane's agent for advances to pay the bills (yesterday's and today's) and to pay off previous advances, dealing on occasion with one agent behind another's back, promising more and more fiction, translating each story into a word count and computing its monetary equivalent. There is more than a little truth to A. J. Liebling's claim that Crane "died . . . of the cause most common among American middle-class males—anxiety about money" (18).

Much in Crane's life seems overdetermined—a point I will return to in connection with *Whilomville Stories*. His death was no exception. When he left for Cuba he had probably already contracted the tuberculosis that was the proximate cause of his death; after he returned he suffered recurrent bouts of fever, probably malaria. He evidently knew he was dying. In August 1899 (a point at which half the Whilomville stories were written) he wrote a friend: "Please have the kindness to keep your mouth shut about my health in front of Mrs. Crane hereafter. She can do nothing for me and I am too old to be nursed. It is all up with me but I will not have her scared" (*Correspondence* 2: 504). Between this letter and the end of the year, when he suffered his first tubercular hemorrhage, he wrote steadily and rapidly—war stories, western stories, and the second half of the Whilomville stories. At very nearly the same time that he was confessing his life a lost cause, he was assuring his agent that he would earn a much-needed advance "mainly, in Whilomville Stories for they are sure and quick money" (*Correspondence* 2: 494). The current group of Whilomville stories were "sure and quick" because they were shorter and simpler than the earlier Whilomville stories and because nearly all of them followed "His New Mittens" in focusing on childhood and thereby securing for themselves a ready market among readers of boy books and children's classics. Additionally, they gained impetus because they were written with a dying man's felt need to review his past to find some explanation for the insecure present.

Given the conditions of Crane's last year and a half of life, it is astonishing that he wrote as much as he did and wrote as well as he did. But the same conditions that forced him to constant production also worked against the production of an extended piece of fiction. There simply was not time to think out and shape and reshape a long book. Some of Crane's critics, arguing in accord with earlier critical tastes, have maintained that *Whilomville Stories* is in fact a unified whole. Noting that the stories follow the chronology of two and a half years, both Eric Solomon and Milne Holton argue that the stories taken together depict the melancholy education of Jimmie Trescott, the protagonist of seven of the thirteen stories and a participant in five of the others (Solomon 205–28; Holton 214–24). In Solomon's words, "The narratives grow more bleak until at the end Jimmie Trescott displays all the hypocrisies of the adult world" (207). But the chronology is lightly sketched at best. Many of the stories do not indicate the time of year, and those that do are separated from one another by many months. Further, both Solomon and Holton assume that the child is an innocent creature who is corrupted by society and that the passage of time must denote change. These assumptions are not borne out by the text.[2] Nor do they tally with what we know of Crane's own sense of his emerging text. How little notion he had of the work as a finished whole is revealed by his regret that contractual obligations prevented his publishing the 1899–1900 group of stories with his earlier and different Whilomville stories (*Correspondence* 2: 425, 463–64) and by his desire, if a letter from Cora really speaks for Crane, to add some more stories to the current group in order to make a longer book and generate some more money (*Correspondence* 2: 542). The closest Crane came to defining a shape to his stories is an inaccurate reference to both the old and new ones as "stories of Jimmie Trescott" (*Correspondence* 2: 463), a description that points not to a developmental scheme, but to an emotional center—an autobiographical core, I will argue—in the stories.

Before turning to *Whilomville Stories,* or more precisely, to the Jimmie Trescott stories, it is worth considering them in the contexts of Crane's other writing and of the developing genre of the boy book. As I have observed, *Whilomville Stories* seems over-determined. From the perspective of Crane's earlier work, the book is clearly the product of a naturalistic writer: war is the central metaphor of child and adult life in Whilomville, as each member of the community constantly jockeys to achieve and maintain a desired position of power; characters barely exist except as embodiments of force and desire; and throughout, the narrator's voice mocks the pretensions that obscure and dignify the basic struggle. From the perspective of the boy book, *Whilomville Stories* is surprisingly conventional. Familiar situations abound—Jimmie shows off to impress a would-be girlfriend, Jimmie fails as a schoolroom orator, Jimmie is embarrassed at a picnic by local sophisticates, Jimmie is rescued by friends who are playing pirates and cowboys, Jimmie is misled by a Sunday school teacher. Boyhood savagery prevails—lies, taunts, and fights are the outward expressions of a strict code that governs boy life. Typical of the boy book, the narrator's voice varies: irony is his most frequent expression, but anger and indulgence also result from his backward glance at childhood. The coincidence of the two contexts has significant implications. In terms of the history of the boy book, Crane's work foreshadows the ideological death of the genre, because it accepts the notion of boyhood savagery as helpfully explaining boyhood behavior but at the same time insists that such savagery does not distinguish boyish behavior from adult (or, for that matter, girlish) behavior. Twain, of course, would have agreed with Crane's evaluation of adult life, but because Twain's boy books foreground boyish perspective, his response to adult behavior, unlike Crane's, is necessarily muted. In terms of autobiography, Crane's work raises a new set of difficulties because it seeks to combine a conventional genre that is nonetheless hospitable to the personal with naturalistic assumptions about character—that is, the absence of character—that would seem to make autobiography impossible. *Whilomville Stories*—by which I mean the Jimmie Trescott stories in particular—commends our attention as it grapples with these issues.

I will begin with autobiography and return to the death of the boy book at the end of this chapter. I am not claiming that the Jimmie Trescott stories are a factually dense autobiographical record. In fact, I make the claim that these stories are autobiographical with some caution. All of Crane's biographers note parallels between the events of *Whilomville Stories* and Jimmie's experiences in particular and Crane's young life, but much of this information is based on letters whose originals have not surfaced, interviews that cannot be verified, and imaginative conjectures by biographers (Cady, *Crane* 15–26; Katz 227–31). John Northern Hilliard, who met Crane when Crane was twenty-two, wrote Thomas Beer in 1922, when Beer was collecting material for his biography of the writer, that Crane "was exactly as he delineated Jimmie Trescott in the Whilomville Stories. He was Jimmie Trescott. That book comes pretty near to being autobiography" (*Letters* 325)—a statement that may mean only that Hilliard remembered his adult friend as being similar to the child Jimmie, not that Crane ever spoke of his autobiographical intentions.

Crane himself deflects our attention from his book as autobiography. He privately acknowledged that the Whilomville setting was based on Port Jervis, New Jersey, the town in which he lived for the four years—from seven to eleven—before his father died. "I suppose that Port Jervis entered my head," he wrote his brother Will and worried that townspeople might see themselves in "The Monster" and take offense (*Correspondence* 2: 446). He never identifies himself overtly with his young protagonist in his text or in an introduction or afterword, as do all of the other boy book writers I have examined (with the exception of Howells in *Pony Baker,* a book whose autobiographical basis is made plain by its similarities to the books Howells identifies as autobiographies). And if Jimmie is the surrogate for young Stephen Crane, his creator took disguising and wish-fulfilling liberties with the facts of his own early life. While Crane was the youngest of fourteen children (eight living at the time of his birth) born to a Methodist preacher and his even more austerely devout wife, Jimmie is the only child of genially philosophical Dr. Trescott and his socially conscious wife.[3] While Crane's family moved frequently and lived in genteel poverty, the Trescott family is comfortably ensconced in Whilomville (Crane having forgotten the loss of professional and social standing the Trescotts suffered at the end of "The Monster"), and we are told that Jimmie and his friends "were all born in whatever purple there was to be had in the vicinity" (130). But perhaps Crane has not gone as far afield as he seems to have. Nearly all of the boy book writers recast family life to some extent. Although Crane's omission of the religiosity of his family life and the beloved older sister who virtually raised him are striking, his position as the last child of older parents whose other children are grown would have made him the same focal point of hope and concern as an only child.

Although fidelity to fact puts *Whilomville Stories* on the margin of autobiography, we see in this work the emotional reinvestment in the past that reveals itself in the presence of both lyrical and ironic passages that we have seen in the other boy books. At one point, Crane uncritically, if a little patronizingly, adopts the perspective of his boy protagonist. "Lynx-Hunting" elaborates on an event described in one of those unverifiable letters from Crane to Beer: "Will, one of my brothers, gave me a toy gun and I tried to shoot a cow with it over at Middletown when father was preaching there and that upset him wonderfully" (Beer 40; *Correspondence* 2: 690). In the story Jimmie and his friends go lynx hunting: like Tom Sawyer, they are playing out an idea acquired from a book. The narrator stands apart from the boys; his "I am sure" directs our attention to the sophistication of the adult who has grown beyond boyhood fantasies. But that same narrator sympathetically recalls and therefore emphasizes the boys' sense that they are attuned to the wondrous secrets of nature:

> They passed along a maple-lined avenue, a highway common to boys bound for the freeland of hills and woods in which they lived in some part their romance of the moment—whether it was of Indians, miners, smugglers, soldiers or outlaws. The paths were their paths and much was known to them of the secrets of the dark-green hemlock thickets, the wastes of sweet-fern and huckle-berry, the cliffs of gaunt blue-stone with the sumach burning red at their feet. Each boy had, I am sure, a conviction that some day the wilderness was to give forth to them a marvelous secret. They felt that the hills and the forest knew much and they heard a voice of it in the silence. It was vague, thrilling, and altogether fabulous. (139)

At another point, the narrator's voice becomes bitterly ironic in the extreme. "Making an Orator" is the only one of the stories that looks beyond the time of its telling. The story concludes with the narrator's observation that Jimmie's humiliating experience in oral recitation cripples him for life: "Jimmie of course did not know that on this day there had been laid for him the foundation of a finished incapacity for public speaking which would be his until he died" (163). It was an incapacity the adult Crane suffered from, and it is evident that still-painful memories inform the anger with which the narrator intrudes to introduce the story: "By process of school law unfortunate boys and girls were dragged up to address their fellow-scholars in the literature of the mid-century. Probably the children who were most capable of expressing themselves, the children who were most sensitive to the power of speech, suffered the most wrong. Little block-heads who could learn eight lines of conventional poetry and could get up and spin it rapidly at their class-mates did not undergo a single pang" (158). Years after the event, the expressive, sensitive, unconventional man/child gets back at "school law."

The Jimmie Trescott stories not only convey the remembered

texture of boy life, but, as always with the boy book, are also the means by which the narrator confronts that period in his past that seems to resonate with his adult life and examines his relationship with his father as he seeks to understand his present difficulties. The Whilomville stories in which Jimmie plays the role of acolyte to another child illuminate by contrast the stories in which he is the central character. In one such set of stories, including "The Angel-Child" and "The Stove," an imperious little girl named Cora (a rather cruel joke at the expense of Cora Taylor) leads her devoted followers, including Jimmie, into several sorts of mischief, only to be fussed over and petted by her devoted mother instead of punished.[4] In the other set, two boys, Homer Phelps, in "The Trial, Execution, and Burial of Homer Phelps," and Johnnie Hedge, in the linked stories, "The Fight" and "The City Urchin and the Chaste Villagers," are obligated to conform to set boy rituals in order to secure a place in the hierarchy of the "tribe" (227) headed by Willie Dalzel. Jimmie's role here is secondary, for it is Willie who controls the encounter with the outsider and Jimmie who assists him. ("The Knife," the remaining story that is not a Jimmie Trescott story, concerns Whilomville's Negro community and does not involve children at all.) In his own stories, Jimmie's role is never so well defined or so secure.

"Lynx-Hunting," the first-written of the Jimmie Trescott *Whilomville Stories* (Levenson xliii), sounds the keynote of these stories. The temporary possession of a gun inspires Jimmie, Willie, and an unnamed third boy to go hunting. Willie and the third boy take their turns with the gun, and then it is Jimmie's turn: "The two others had of course some thought of cheating him out of this chance but, of a truth, he was timid to explode such a thunderous weapon and, as soon as they detected this fear, they simply over-bore him and made it clearly understood that if he refused to shoot he would lose his caste, his scalp-lock, his girdle, his honor" (141). Such a precarious situation is very nearly always Jimmie's lot. He is never able to dictate terms as Cora and Willie are, nor are the rules that govern his life so clearly laid out before him as they are for Homer or Johnnie. There is a sort of ad hoc quality to his life: at one moment one thing is required of him; at another, something else. He can never anticipate what will happen, and the result is that his experience is a roller-coaster ride, with achievement coming unexpectedly and loss of caste following every achievement.

Crane rationalizes the notion of boyhood savagery by making clear that Jimmie's affinity for violent behavior is both an expression of his desire to achieve and maintain status and an expression of his frustration at being continually challenged. In "Lynx-Hunting" he rises to the occasion and fires the gun: "To him, there was a frightful roar, his cheek and his shoulder took a stunning blow, his face felt a hot flush of fire and, opening his two eyes, he found that he was still alive. He was not too dazed to instantly adopt a becoming egotism." In the next instant, it becomes apparent that he has shot someone's cow, and his pride dissolves: "The first evidence of this fact [that Jimmie hit the cow] was in the celerity with which he returned the discharged gun to Willie Dalzel." Denials, accusations, and confessions follow, further wiping out Jimmie's pride in "the first shot of his life" (142).

Jimmie's experiences do not always end unhappily. In "The Carriage-Lamps" the disgrace he incurs for hiding a small pistol and for throwing stones inexplicably vanishes; in "Making an Orator" the agony of classroom recitation is temporarily ended when the frustrated teacher sends Jimmie to his seat. But most often Jimmie's moments of glory come early in the story and are short-lived. In "The Lover and the Tell-Tale"[5] Rose Goldege, a classmate, taunts Jimmie for writing a letter to "his girl" (146) Cora at recess. The presence of the teacher keeps Jimmie from turning on his female adversary in the classroom, but Rose's taunts excite the other boys in the class. The playground becomes a battlefield as Jimmie takes on the little "barbarians . . . excited . . . by the actual appearance of human woe" (147). He is triumphant: "When they came to form into line for the march into the school-room it was curious that Jimmie had many admirers. It was not his prowess; it was the soul he had infused into his gymnastics; and he, still panting, looked about him with a stern and challenging glare." An instant later all is reversed: "And yet when the long tramping line had entered the school-room his status had again changed. The other children then began to regard him as a boy in disrepair and boys in disrepair were always accosted ominously from the throne" (148). In "Shame" the changes in status are equally rapid. Jimmie is disconsolate because he does not have a lunch to take to the picnic that everyone is attending. He succeeds in cajoling the cook into making him a lunch: "A few minutes previously his soul had been gloomed in despair; now he was happy" (166). But when he arrives at the picnic, Minnie Phelps mocks him for carrying his lunch in a pail instead of a more genteel basket. The other children join in the derision, and "in a moment he had been made a social leper" (167). A young woman, one of the mothers' friends, befriends Jimmie, and he blossoms under her attention: "Their gentle intimacy was ineffable to the boy. He thought he had a friend, a beautiful lady, who liked him more than she did anybody at the picnic, to say the least" (170). He fantasizes all the way home that "she would like him more and more—more and more. And he—he would be a little god." Then the fall comes: "As he was entering his father's grounds an appalling recollection came to him. He was returning with the bread-and-butter and the salmon untouched in the pail! He could imagine the cook, nine feet tall, waving her fist" (171). "'Showing Off'" and "A Little Pilgrimage" offer similar but briefer versions of the same dizzying shifts in status.

The repetitive pattern of Jimmie's experience—enhanced by the short story format—recalls Tom Sawyer's experience of constant deflation, but the differences are instructive. Tom wins a moment of glory by conscious and deliberate exertion: he barters tickets in order to be awarded a Bible in Sunday school; he talks his friends into prolonging their stay on Jackson's Island in order to return in time for their own funeral. He is robbed of his glory by Twain's or Huck Finn's intervention: Twain undercuts Tom's ploy to win public acclaim by making him appear foolish, and Huck adds a discordant note to the resurrection of the "dead" boys. Unlike Tom, Jimmie is a victim of circumstance, not seizer of opportunity; he is a creature of instinct, not a master of imagination. Significantly, Crane as narrator, unlike Twain and his surrogate Huck, does not judge or chastise his boy protagonist from a distance, but instead implicates himself in his protagonist's experience.

Consider two instances in which Crane interprets boy behavior. In "Lynx-Hunting" Jimmie and his friends try to run away after he shoots the cow, but they are intercepted by a farm hand who marches them off to see the farmer who owns the cow. The boys, including Jimmie, deny their guilt and blame each other. The narrator understands that the denials and accusations are not what they seem:

> The boyish view belongs to boys alone, and if this tall and knotted laborer [the farm hand] was needlessly without charity, none of the three lads questioned it. Usually when they were punished they decided that they deserved it and the more they were punished the more they were convinced that they were criminals of a most subterranean type. As to the hitting of the cow being a pure accident and therefore not of necessity a criminal matter, such reading never entered their heads. When things happened and they were caught, they commonly paid dire consequences and they were accustomed to measure the probabilities of woe utterly by the damage done and not in any way by the culpability. The shooting of a cow was plainly heinous and undoubtedly their dungeons would be knee-deep in water. (142–43)

In the passage, the narrator both speaks from a distance and adopts the boys' perspective. When he begins by commenting on "the boyish view," he is clearly speaking from a distance. He understands the limits of boyish thinking; he is beyond such limits. Yet when he notes, "When things happened and they were caught, they commonly paid dire consequences," he has moved closer to the boy mind: theirs is not a foolish view; it is based on real experience. Then he withdraws again with the exaggerated language of his last sentence, which in effect pokes fun at the boys for their misestimation of what has happened.

In "The Carriage-Lamps" the narrator lets us see directly into the boy mind. In disgrace for throwing stones at Peter Washington, the handyman who reported that Jimmie had a pistol, Jimmie broods on his fate while he awaits his father and punishment. He believes that if a stone had not gone astray and broken some carriage lamps on the carriage-house shelf, he would not have been found out. He feels betrayed:

> He had not intended to destroy the carriage lamps. He had been merely hurling stones at a creature whose perfidy deserved such action, and the hitting of the lamps had been merely another move

of the great conspirator Fate to force one Jimmie Trescott into dark and troublous ways. The boy was beginning to find the world a bitter place. . . . Everything was an enemy. Now there were those silly old lamps—what were they doing up on that shelf, anyhow? It would have been just as easy for them at the time to have been in some other place. . . . Furthermore, the flight of that stone had been perfectly unreasonable. It had been a sort of freak in physical law. Jimmie understood that he might have thrown stones from the same fatal spot for an hour without hitting a single lamp. He was a victim—that was it. Fate had conspired with the detail of his environment to simply hound him into a grave or into a cell. (177–78)

The language is not that of a child, but the perspective certainly is. Jimmie's sublime egotism assures him that fate and the environment have combined to torture him—and once again, he melodramatically envisions incarceration as a possibility. The stones and carriage lamps are slightly personified in keeping with his vision of them as antagonists, and his own behavior—"merely hurling stones"—is quickly justified and passed over. But in this story, too, child and adult perspectives overlap. The narrator's account of the event precedes Jimmie's lengthy meditation: "With diabolic ingenuity, one of Jimmie's pebbles had entered the carriage-house and had landed among a row of carriage-lamps on a shelf, creating havoc which was apparently beyond all reason of physical law" (175–76). As in Jimmie's thinking, the stones have a life of their own. In context the child's interpretation is not an egotistical misinterpretation but an elaboration of the adult's perception, fleshed out by fear and anger.

The mingling of the narrator's perspective and that of the protagonist is not unique to Crane's Jimmie Trescott stories. Max Westbrook looks at several other Whilomville stories—"The Monster," "His Mittens," and "The Trial, Execution, and Burial of Homer Phelps"—and notes that Crane's perspective typically encompasses both that of "the removed and ironic observer" and that of "the intimate and sympathetic observer" (91). This dual approach allows Crane to present what Westbrook calls a character's "personal atmosphere" (90), the combination of limitations and conceits that a character presents unawares to the world. This characterization of Crane's perspective accurately describes the passages I have been examining. But Westbrook goes on to note a point in the stories under discussion when the protagonists embrace "an ineluctable duty," and the authorial voice "becomes straight, and hard, and affirmative" (104)—a situation that does not apply to Jimmie. His enthrallment to circumstance and instinct and the roller-coaster ride that characterizes his experience make it impossible for him to grasp "an ineluctable duty." Although Westbrook does not recognize the fact, his discussion of the Jimmie Trescott stories is tellingly cursory. A second critic, who is skeptical of any reading of Crane that focuses on individual autonomy, is more helpful. Lee Clark Mitchell notes that the narrative voice of *The Red Badge of Courage,* the text he chooses to examine, "slides back and forth between the free indirect discourse of Henry's atomized perspective and an omniscient third person" (113) with the result that Henry "gradually becomes absorbed into the larger discursive world" of the novel so that we see him finally as a character "constructed through a pattern of conflicting voices" (115) and not as an autonomous individual. In the case of the Jimmie Trescott stories, the narrator is not strictly an omniscient third person. He identifies himself as "I" occasionally, and, as we have seen, we have good reason to think of him as a surrogate of the author and an intimate of the protagonist. Yet Mitchell's point that the mingling of perspectives denies autonomy to the protagonist does apply to Jimmie Trescott. While Twain steps back from Tom to judge the boy, Crane remains a part of his presentation of Jimmie. In autobiographical terms, childhood and adulthood merge in Crane's art as the precariousness of the author's present evokes an equally precarious past.

Like other boy book authors, Crane intuitively looks to his father as the source of difficulty. *Whilomville Stories* is replete with fathers and father figures who are in a position to provide some guidance that might enable the boy to cope with the precariousness of experience but who repeatedly fail to do so. In the Jimmie Trescott stories, we have the anomaly of a father who is in fact present but in reality absent, something that is best illustrated by comparison of Jimmie's situation to that of a boy with a particularly conspicuous father—Howells's "my boy." "My boy" was chastised by his father for, among other things, throwing stones at a dead dog and shooting a bird merely to demonstrate his prowess with a gun. The equivalent incidents for Jimmie are his breaking the carriage lamps in "The Carriage-Lamps" and his shooting a farmer's cow in "Lynx-Hunting." In neither case is he reproved for his behavior; in both, the father figure is disarmed by the author and rendered harmless. In "The Carriage-Lamps" Dr. Trescott sends his son indoors to await punishment. He complains to his wife that it is the stone throwing, not the lamp breaking, that concerns him. She leaps to her son's defense, sounding like Tom's Aunt Polly—" 'Of course much of it is pure animal spirits. Jimmie is not naturally vicious'" (176)—and proposes (erroneously in this case) that the real troublemaker is Willie Dalzel, who leads Jimmie on. Her suggestion succeeds in deflecting Dr. Trescott's anger. When the doctor does seek out his son, Jimmie is at a window about to be rescued from his captivity by his friends who, except for one dissenter playing cowboy, are playing pirates under Willie's leadership. Dr. Trescott is enchanted and sits back in hiding to enjoy the boys' play and Jimmie's discomfort when he becomes aware of his father's presence. The episode ends when Jimmie discovers his father doubled over with laughter. The boy is dismissed with no word about his behavior—his notion that the perverse carriage lamps were the real cause of the trouble apparently still intact.[6] This episode recalls the end of "Lynx-Hunting," where the terrified Jimmie confesses that he shot the farmer's cow believing it was a lynx (a confession of fear rather than fact, since he did not even aim at the cow), only to see the farmer, an adult and therefore an authority figure in the child's eyes, and his farm hand, like Dr. Trescott, laugh themselves "helpless" (143). A father lurks behind the farmer, for this episode, we recall, is apparently based on young Stephen Crane's real-life attempt to shoot a cow, a move that upset his father "wonderfully."

The father figure incapacitated through laughter is one form of ineffectual father; others appear throughout *Whilomville Stories*. There is Peter Washington, the Trescotts' Negro handyman, who actually has more contact with Jimmie than his own father does. His repeated threats to report Jimmie's misdeeds to his father are defused by the friendly contempt of the boy, who knows Peter is not a serious threat: " 'Go soak your head, Pete'" (232) is Jimmie's typical response. And there are other father figures who might plausibly be read as avatars of Crane's own father, an elderly minister who, Beer quotes Crane as saying, was "so simple and good that I often think he didn't know much of anything about humanity" (40; *Correspondence* 2: 690). This category includes Cora's father, a man "never energetic enough to be irritable unless some one broke through into that place where he lived with the desires of his life" (130), a place that excludes his wife and child. Lost in his dream world, he is indirectly responsible for the outrageous behavior of his Angel Child. And it includes the Sunday school superintendent, an "ideal" superintendent because he is "one who had never felt hunger or thirst or the wound of the challenge of dishonor" (237). Both John Berryman and Stanley Wertheim cite hostility to father figures as the central motif of Crane's work, but note the degree of restraint with which he referred to his real-life father (Berryman 304, 309; Wertheim 43, 46). Significantly, the father figures in the autobiographical Whilomville stories are accorded the same restraint. Crane's attitude toward them is one of distant amusement or irony, as if to say that these men are irrelevant to the real facts of life. It is a self-protective attitude that spared Crane the kind of anger Twain's ineffectual father provoked in him.

In a world where fathers are ineffectual (and mothers too, although they impinge less directly on Jimmie's life), where the narrator himself does not stand in judgment on the boy life he is rendering, it is not surprising that children are not very different from adults. The savagery that characterizes boyhood (and girlhood) for Crane extends to the adult world as well. Or, to consider this idea from a slightly different angle, the savagery that put boys in a separate and in some ways privileged world in the previous boy books is not restricted to boys alone in Whilomville. In *Whilomville Stories* Crane repeatedly alludes to the universal savagery that boys and men, children and adults, share and have always shared:

> Yes, they were all most excellent children, but loosened upon this candy-shop with five dollars, they resembled, in a tiny way, drunken revelling soldiers within the walls of a stormed city. (131)

> Commonly he [Jimmie on the school playground] was of the worst hoodlums, preying upon his weaker brethren with all the cruel disregard of a grown man. (144)

The class was a-rustle with delight at this cruel display [the teacher's snapping at Jimmie after his blundering attempt to recite "The Charge of the Light Brigade"]. They were no better than a Roman populace in Nero's time. (162)

Jimmie's crowd, sizing up Johnie Hedge, might have been savages observing the first white man or white men observing the first savage. (217)

In so linking childhood and adulthood, Crane's metaphors express the same perspective on human experience as his merging of child and adult points of view: this is emphatically a book in which adults and children are very much alike.

In discussing *Whilomville Stories,* Solomon argues that "Crane both mocks the familiar boyhood idylls and uses the form to disguise his savage attacks on his society" (202). He notes that Crane's work not only counters the "earlier syrupy tradition of childhood stories that called for a good-good hero or heroine" (203), but also counters books like Aldrich's *Story of a Bad Boy,* which sought to replace those earlier books with realistic pictures of boyhood but then did so in idyllic terms. Solomon appropriately introduces his chapter on *Whilomville Stories* by quoting from a letter Beer attributes to Crane: "If the Whilomville stories seem like Little Lord Fauntleroy to you you are demented and I know that you are joking, besides" (201; Beer 112; *Correspondence* 2: 688)—a remark that nicely captures the toughmindedness of *Whilomville Stories.* Solomon is correct, too, in noting that the criticism of society in Crane's work is not new to the genre but exceeds that of earlier boy book writers. He cites Howells's *A Boy's Town* as a precursor, but *Tom Sawyer* and *Huck Finn* are much better examples. To Solomon's appraisal of Crane's achievement, I would add that Crane extends the possibilities of autobiography. Jimmie Trescott is a naturalistic protagonist, a product of environment and desire, lacking the complexity of a Tom Sawyer or "my boy," who is put through the conventional situations of the boy book. But then he is given substance by the narrator's involvement with him. His thoughts live; his freedom from criticism or guidance becomes convincing; his tumultuous life fills the space that the delineation of personality might fill in a boy book by another writer.

Further, as I suggested early in this chapter, Crane's book foreshadowed the ideological death of the boy book. A year before *Whilomville Stories* was published, William Allen White published *The Court of Boyville*. The book includes some autobiographical elements, it is a collection of loosely related short stories, its title has an antique flavor, it evokes the often savage rules and customs of boyhood, and it plays out some of the conventional situations of the boy book. But it is worlds away from *Whilomville Stories*. Despite its depiction of boyhood savagery, *The Court of Boyville* is ultimately a sentimental book. It includes touching incidents, poems mourning the passage of time and the loss of childhood, a narrator who is rather smug at the expense of the boys whose adventures he is recounting, and a Prologue that begins: "We who are passing 'through the wilderness of this world' find it difficult to realize what an impenetrable wall there is around the town of Boyville. Storm it as we may with the simulation of light-heartedness . . . the walls remain. If once the clanging gates of the town shut upon a youth, he is banished forever" (xvii–viii). The burden of the book is a vicarious return to Boyville. In Crane's book boyville and whilomville and, by implication, nowville are all the same; one is never excluded from boyville because one never grows beyond it. *Whilomville Stories* denies the central premise of the boy book by refusing to treat boyhood savagery as a transitional stage in the evolution of man. This is a view that should have made later authors and readers attracted to the boy book hesitant. It makes the beliefs that set boyhood apart as an excitingly dangerous but nevertheless comfortingly temporary time appear to be mere fantasy. But it is also a view, as I have argued, that took its urgency from Crane's personal experience. As it turned out, more than the chaos of Crane's life was needed to sound the death knell of a genre that produced so many bright and entertaining works. There was room for one more notable contribution, in the form of Tarkington's Penrod books, before Sigmund Freud and World War I sounded that knell.

# 7

# BOOTH TARKINGTON

In 1911 Tarkington returned to Indianapolis, his boyhood home, and took up residence in the house in which he had grown up.[1] He had spent the last half dozen years in Paris and New York trying his hand at writing plays and achieving only the most moderate success. Now, at forty-two, his personal life was a shambles. Although his first success had been with the novel, he had not written a novel in years, pursuing instead the gaudier rewards of play writing, as had Twain and Howells before him; he was drinking heavily; and his marriage was failing. In November he was divorced; in January of the next year, he suffered a heart attack. Despite all these adversities, he was able to reclaim his private life and his career. With the encouragement of his father and sister, who lived nearby, and Susanah Robinson, whom he was to marry that November, he stopped drinking and returned to the work he was best equipped to do. By September he was able to claim: "Now I'm in condition as I was ten years ago, with a very piquant realization of wasted time. . . . I want to make up for that time & have the energy to do it, & the 'stuff' stored. I don't want to lose any *more* time" (quoted by Woodress 166). The ten years that Tarkington would eradicate were the years of his first marriage and the years as a playwright. He would return to his life as a novelist.

Booth and Susanah Tarkington settled in Indianapolis in the old Tarkington house, a pleasant Victorian in a fashionable neighborhood. But the city was changing. In his loosely autobiographical account of early twentieth-century life, *The World Does Move*

(1928), Tarkington broods about the changes that struck him on his return to Indianapolis: "For, although most things 'looked about the same' to the returned native, and the same old people and houses and trees and lawns and saloons appeared to be but slightly altered, principally by seeming a little older, there were tokens of a stirring, of something moving underneath, of unknown powers at work to produce a new kind of growing; but at first these hints were faint and not insistent" (124–25). The tokens were the omnipresent dirt from the soft coal that had replaced natural gas and anthracite; the small but real increase in the number of new office buildings and apartments; the emphatic presence of cars and with them asphalt paving, traffic officers, and rules of the road; the citified aspect of country people who came to town on the new interurban trains; and the increased number of immigrants who had come, as "everybody knows" (130), to make money and who, in the process, were changing American values. (These last tokens of change are voiced in the person of a fictitious judge, as if Tarkington knows there is something not quite seemly in complaining about immigrants.) Few complained—"If the business men worried about the increasing smoke—for there was visibly more of it almost from day to day—they worried for fear some other city should have even more of it than we did" (132)—but Tarkington notes uneasily that "the easy-going old days were gone forever" (125).

At this point we are on familiar ground: the writer facing a personal crisis—in this case a return to his original calling and a new marriage—in a nostalgia-evoking situation. These are the conditions that, as we have seen, provided the impetus for each of the boy books we have examined. It is no surprise then to discover that *Penrod* (1914) was the first book Tarkington wrote after his marriage. The circumstances surrounding this book suggest that it functioned for Tarkington as a means of returning to his origins to assess the vulnerability that had led him astray and to exorcise it by turning it into fiction, although his awareness of this function must have been largely intuitive. But *Penrod* comes late in the history of the boy book, and its immediate origin is literary. The result is a book in which Tarkington's consciousness of the genre in which he is writing blurs his autobiographical effort. If Crane's *Whilomville Stories* looks to the death of the boy

book by calling into question the assumptions about human development on which it is based, Tarkington's *Penrod,* in a complementary manner, looks to the end of the boy book by reminding
us how stiflingly conventional it became.

Susanah Tarkington recalled the immediate origin of *Penrod* for
James Woodress, Tarkington's biographer. She had been reading a
book about life in an English boys' school; moved by its account
of boyhood suffering, she gave it to Tarkington to read and was
surprised at his response that the book did not ring true. She
challenged him to write a realistic account of boy life.[2] The result
was, in Woodress's words, "the first of the Penrod adventures and
Tarkington's first real bid for a permanent place in American
literature" (174). In the book that grew out of this first adventure,
Tarkington draws an implicit contrast between his work and that
of earlier writers when he introduces a chapter detailing a particularly lawless fight between the two Negro boys who are companions to Penrod and a bully who has recently made an appearance
in the neighborhood: "How neat and pure is the task of the
chronicler who has the tale to tell of a 'good rousing fight' between boys or men who fight in the 'good old English way,'
according to a model set for fights in books long before Tom
Brown went to Rugby" (213). That Tarkington's bully is characterized by his Irish name and lower-class manners and the
Negroes by their lack of restraint in consequence of their low
stage of evolution reminds us that although Tarkington was a
literary realist, his realism was tempered by the fact, of which he
was unaware, that he observed life through the prejudices of his
time and place. In this sense he was not so very different from
Thomas Hughes and his compeers in their devotion to a traditional formula.

Tarkington must have been aware, however, that his invoking
the school of Hughes was somewhat disingenuous. Although a
Hughes-like book was the immediate inspiration for *Penrod,* Tarkington knew that the pertinent context for his book was the
American boy story with its more familiar concerns. In response
to a 1937 appeal for some words on Crane's *Whilomville Stories*
from Alexander Woollcott, who thought "the immortal Penrod"
to be "Jimmie Trescott seen through eyes as honest and observant
but more genially philosophic," Tarkington recalled the "ap-

plause and pleasure" Crane's stories had evoked when they appeared in magazine form. He then went on to add: "The sequence seems to me: *Tom Sawyer, Helen's Babies, Whilomville Stories,* Owen Johnson's *Lawrenceville Stories, The Tennessee Shad,* etc. No doubt there were 'realistic children' before Mark Twain—bits in Dickens and elsewhere—and, of course, Tom and Huck are realistic only in character. He gave 'em what boys don't get, when it came to 'plot.' All that the boy, Sam, had wished to happen, he made happen" (Woollcott 966). Two observations are in order. First, Tarkington did not distinguish an autobiographical strain that set some of the books he cites apart from others. This may not have seemed a salient distinction to him: his claim in his introduction to *Huck Finn* that fidelity to the remembered boy mind, despite a fantastic plot, was enough to make a book autobiographical suggests that traditional generic distinctions did not carry much weight with him. Second, he most likely knew all of the books he cites at the time he wrote *Penrod*.[3]

*Penrod* itself encourages the supposition that Tarkington was working with these and similar models in mind. *Penrod* includes such well-established character types as the pretty girl (Marjorie Jones), the rich kid (Maurice Levy, whose name suggests an additional stereotype), the model boy (Georgie Bassett), the snob (Roderick Magsworth Bitts, Junior), the bully (Rupe Collins, whose ethnic background I have already commented on), and the boy pal (Sam Williams). Many of the events that take place in the book are equally conventional: Penrod and his friends put on a show, fight a bully, and con a friend, and in the end, Penrod finally gets a long-sought declaration of affection from Marjorie when she sends him a note announcing, "'Your my Bow'" (306). Echoes of *Tom Sawyer* suggest that Tarkington wrote with that book in particular in mind. Sam, like Huck, questions marriage: "'What you want to get married for? What do married people do, except just come home tired, and worry around and kind of scold?'" (256). The Reverend Mr. Kinosling, like Twain's minister, fatuously praises boyish innocence and decency only to be upstaged by a couple of examples of authentic boy behavior. My aim, however, is not to trace the many sources or the specific influences that helped create *Penrod*; I want simply to note that

Tarkington wrote within what had become a well-established tradition and was evidently aware that he was doing so.

What, in such circumstances, is the place of autobiography? Tarkington deflected attention from the autobiographical element in his book. In "As I Seem to Me" (1941), the uncollected series of articles he wrote recounting his life from childhood to the acceptance of his first book, he remembers his twelve-year-old self writing a note to a girl he did not want to escort to a dance. In the note he excused himself from his social obligation because he had fallen off the barn roof. Happily, the girl's mother thought the note funny enough to save and show to the adult Tarkington, who was equally amused. It became a part of Penrod's story. Tarkington explains, "When I was writing a story about a boy who was not at all myself, though of course, here and there, in scattered spots, a slight reflection of bits of me, I printed the note as his" (*Saturday Evening Post* 2 August 1941, 25). Hamlin Garland recalled a meeting with Tarkington a year after the publication of *Penrod:* "When I spoke in high praise of his Penrod stories, he remarked with a chuckle, 'The material came directly from my nephews. All I had to do was to watch their antics and report!'" (*My Friendly Contemporaries* 82–83). And *Penrod* is dedicated to those nephews "FROM A GRATEFUL UNCLE" (v).

In making such disclaimers, Tarkington was as disingenuous as he was in invoking the school of Hughes. His nephews could hardly have been his models. Although he had always taken a keen interest in them—perhaps they provided some compensation for the fact that his only child was a daughter whom he saw for one month a year after his divorce—only one of them, the youngest (who, in a happy coincidence, was Tarkington's namesake) was near Penrod's age. The other two were young men, eleven and thirteen years older than their little brother.

And Penrod Schofield is more than a "slight reflection" of his creator. He bears many similarities to young Booth as he appears in "As I Seem to Me." True, Booth is more bookish and more self-aware than Penrod, but Booth is the central character in an autobiography of childhood by an author seeking to link past and present by emphasizing the personal qualities that made him a writer, whereas Penrod is the central character in a boy book.

Nevertheless, Penrod shares Booth's imagination (like his creator, he writes a novel and puts on a show), his tendency to escapist and self-glorifying reverie, and his need for attention. Like Tom Sawyer, he personifies the performer within his creator that made the creator think he could be a successful dramatist. He also shares Booth's family, with minor modifications. There are the two strong women: an older sister (nineteen to Penrod's twelve; Booth's sister was eleven years older than he) and a socially and culturally conscious mother. There is also a rather put-upon father, like Booth's own, but one who responds to his frustrations with compliance accompanied by temperamental outbursts rather than with the easygoing accommodation that characterized Booth's father.[4] Many of Penrod's experiences are taken from Booth's life, existing alongside adventures suggested by earlier fiction or blending with those conventional adventures to result in something fresh. Where Penrod's story diverges most from the life of its creator is in its temporal setting: *Penrod* is not set in the past. The present in the novel is not the Indianapolis of the late nineteenth century whose disappearance Tarkington mourned in *The World Does Move* but the present in which Tarkington was writing.

The physical setting of *Penrod* is only lightly sketched. Tarkington may have been thinking of both the Indianapolis in which he grew up and the Indianapolis in which he lived when he wrote the book and so created a world vague enough to accommodate memory and observation. He may also have deliberately contrived a vague setting to enable his readers to imagine that the events of the book were occurring in a familiar place. We know few specific details. The Schofield house is a large one—it has both a front and back staircase—and is on a piece of property large enough to include a barn. Herman and Verman, Penrod's Negro companions, live in a little cottage at the back of a nearby house on a similar piece of property. The story takes place in a town larger than that of any of the other boy books I have considered, for Rupe Collins is from a different school district than Penrod. But we know little beyond these things.

In contrast to the physical setting, the temporal setting is explicit. Tarkington firmly, if unobtrusively, locates the events of his story in the present. The most specific temporal marker is an allusion to Mrs. Schofield's coming-out party in 1886 (20); since she is now the mother of a nineteen-year-old daughter, we can date the events of the book to within a few years of its writing. Throughout the book there are allusions to some of the changes Tarkington notes in *The World Does Move*. Mr. Schofield is "thinking" (6) of an automobile; Penrod enjoys movies; the ethnic mix of Penrod's companions (in addition to those cited above, there are some "wistful Polack children" [175] sitting near Penrod at a dog and pony show) suggests the increasing number of immigrants; and the sexy dance that Fanchon Gelbraith (herself a new phenomenon, "one of those grown-up little girls, wonderful product of the winter apartment and summer hotel" [284]) teaches the children is the new rage, the turkey trot. And of course the illustrations help fix the time for an alert reader.

With its substantial incorporation of material from its author's boyhood and its setting in its author's adulthood, *Penrod* is an anomaly among boy books. A significant result of this combination of subject and setting is that *Penrod* lacks those lyrical or elegiac moments in which the boy book narrator fully invests himself in his young protagonist in order to recall his pleasure in a long-lost time and place. There is nothing in *Penrod* like Warner's John recalling the sensual delights of the New England hills, or Twain's Tom awakening on Jackson's Island and watching the day dawn, or Howells's Frank and Jake returning home from a day in the Ohio countryside. Tarkington had such feelings about the time and place in which he grew up. "As I Seem to Me" includes a memorable description of the "Golden Age" of Hoosier life, when Tarkington was close to Penrod's age, when life was slow-paced and secure, when summer evenings at home were transfigured by his sister's singing, her beautiful voice arresting even strangers, who paused in the wide, tree-shaded street to listen (*Saturday Evening Post* 2 August 1941, 47).[5] But the present-day setting of *Penrod* made such nostalgia and the elegiac or lyrical mood that goes with it impossible.

Because Tarkington's decision to set his book in the present denied him an elegiac indulgence in the past, it ensured that *Penrod* would always be subject to the ironic perspective of the adult narrator who necessarily understands more than the child can. We might suspect, in fact, that Tarkington turned to this setting because he had an intuitive sense that his story of boy life was more self-revealing than he found comfortable and sought distance from his protagonist. Tarkington's narrator does adopt the perspective of the child protagonist at times, but such identification is always partial because the narrator's softer emotions are never touched as they are in the boy books set in the past. This narrator is necessarily an active presence in *Penrod,* though an occasional "we" is as close as he comes to identifying himself; rather, he is present through his tone, which is ironic, arch, coy, and never fully sympathetic. At the same time, this narrator is not fully sympathetic to the adults who govern Penrod's life either. It is a stance that is explicable in autobiographical terms, which is to say that although Tarkington's book is set in the present, the drama he plays out in it has its roots in the past. The present-day setting, by preventing Tarkington full identification with his child self, freed him from his childhood hesitancy in passing judgment on his elders.

The circumstances under which *Penrod* was written and published created many opportunities for Tarkington's ironic backward glance. Like many boy books, *Penrod* was serialized before it was published as a book; unlike others, it was not serialized in one place with a single chapter developing a complete episode. Instead, Tarkington devoted several chapters to each episode and placed these episodes in a handful of different family magazines. These were printed between June 1913 and April 1914. When Tarkington assembled the chapters for his book, he added material to develop some of the episodes and reordered them so that they would take Penrod from the end of a school year through much of the summer and tell a loose but coherent story.[6] For all of his care in presenting his story, Tarkington made an interesting slip: Penrod is twelve in the opening episode, and he celebrates his twelfth birthday in the concluding episode. (And in the sequel, *Penrod and Sam* [1916], which carries on the seasonal sequence and implies knowledge of the events of the first book, he is ten or eleven.) Like all of the boy books, *Penrod* is an account of boyhood, not an account of growth. Like *Story of a Bad Boy* and *Tom Sawyer,* it is a potentially unending series of adventures presented in simple linear fashion. The difference is that each episode is punctuated by the lesser climaxes of the chapters that make it up and topped by the grand climax of the concluding chapter. The grand climaxes typically provide an ironic comment—often by virtue of both what the narrator says about his protagonist and what the author does to him—on the episode as a whole.

The typical *Penrod* episode involves the unexpected playing out of a given situation to Penrod's disadvantage. The difficulty arises because of Penrod's trouble in conforming to the domestic and social rituals that adults, usually women, wish to impress upon him. To some extent this is true of Tom Sawyer as well, but Tom is also granted a life apart from the world governed by adult expectations. Penrod, in this first book and in its sequels, must make his way in a world that is not congenial to him and that he does not understand—or, as he would see it, a world that does not understand him: "One of the hardest conditions of boyhood is the almost continuous strain put upon the powers of invention by the constant and harassing necessity for explanations of every natural act" (47). We recognize in Penrod's struggles what Tarkington will articulate at the end of his book: that Penrod's condition evidences the recapitulation theory of human development. Tarkington's white boys are simply at a lower stage of evolution than the adults they will become. (His Negro boys, in accord with his prejudices, will remain at the lower stage.) His emphasis is less on savagery than on confusion and restiveness. This situation is, of course, one in which Penrod's inability to understand and to do what is expected of him makes him an easy target for Tarkington's irony.

But Tarkington is also critical of the adults who do not understand that their expectations are inappropriate for a boy. That these adults are most often women certainly tells us something about the realities of a young boy's life in the early years of the twentieth century, as well as something about Tarkington's own remembered difficulties and present insecurities. The focus on women also makes *Penrod* look superficially like an exception to my claim that at the heart of the boy book is the author's confrontation with his father, but as we will see, in the end, *Penrod* is no exception.

Conflict between the uncivilized boy and the feminized world is most fully illustrated in the first six chapters of *Penrod,* the first-written and first-published episode of the novel (in *Everybody's*

*Magazine,* June 1913). This episode, originally published under the title "Penrod and the Pageant," is the longest of the episodes that make up the book and is the most in debt to Tarkington's childhood experience in its details (Woodress 174–75). It recounts Penrod's enforced participation in "The Children's Pageant of the Table Round" (4), a charity event staged by a group of literary ladies whose sentimentalization and domestication of the Arthurian legend characterize them as touchstones of popular taste. In the role of Child Sir Lancelot, Penrod must say lines that embarrass him because they call attention to his childish state, and he must wear a costume that humiliates him because it is constructed from an old dress and some discarded undergarments. He would much prefer to spend his time in the large sawdust box in the barn, writing a story of adventure in the wild West. He retaliates by borrowing the janitor's overalls and "protected and sheltered in the human garment of a man" (38) appears on stage to both the "dismay and incredulous joy" (39) of the audience. Some of the other child actors, as harassed as Penrod, understand what is really at stake: "A few precocious geniuses perceived that the overalls were the Child Lancelot's own comment on maternal intentions; and these were profoundly impressed" (40). Nascent masculinity is granted a temporary victory over the female guardians of charity and culture: "Strong women and brave girls in the audience went out into the lobby, shrieking and clinging to one another" (41); Penrod's girl Marjorie, on whose behalf he earlier sought to ruin the performance of a rival child actor, tells him never to speak to her again; Penrod's mother and sister are tactfully avoided by their friends. But that evening Penrod's father plays the role dictated to him by a culture in which female values rule the home: "There was put into practice an old patriarchal custom. It is a custom of inconceivable antiquity: probably primordial, certainly prehistoric, but still in vogue in some remaining citadels of the ancient simplicities of the Republic" (43). Tarkington's description of Penrod's punishment is unpleasantly coy. His circumlocutions and his distancing himself from the event suggest discomfort with the image of masculinity represented by the conventional Victorian paterfamilias he has substituted for his own more tolerant father who he says never resorted to corporal punishment (*Your Amiable Uncle* 159), as well as uneasiness with the strong women who instruct this stern father as easily as they instruct his son.

Tarkington's irony, as I suggested earlier, is directed against both his hapless protagonist and, to a lesser extent, the adults who governed his life. The narrator summarizes the events of the first six chapters of the book:

> His [Penrod's] case is comparable to that of an adult who could have survived a similar experience. Looking back to the sawdust-box, fancy pictures this comparable adult a serious and inventive writer engaged in congenial literary activities in a private retreat. We see this period marked by the creation of some of the most virile passages of a Work dealing exclusively in red corpuscles and huge primal impulses. We see this thoughtful man dragged from his calm seclusion to a horrifying publicity; forced to adopt the stage and, himself a writer, compelled to exploit the repulsive sentiments of an author not only personally distasteful to him but whose whole method and school in *belles lettres* he despises.
>
> We see him reduced by desperation and modesty to stealing a pair of overalls. We conceive him to have ruined, then, his own reputation, and to have utterly disgraced his family; next, to have engaged in the *duello* and to have been spurned by his lady-love, thus lost to him (according to her own declaration) forever. Finally, we must behold: imprisonment by the authorities; the third degree—and flagellation. (43–44)

The narrator distances himself from his protagonist by objectifying him as "fancy pictures" the boy. His repetitive "we see," "we see," "we see," "we conceive," "we must behold" involve us by making us spectators along with himself rather than participants. The overstated descriptions of the boy as a "comparable adult" and a "thoughtful man" ironically underline the fact that he is clearly neither, for his "virile" impulses have been denied and he is "dragged," "forced," and "compelled" to turn against himself. Nor is his resistance successful: the narrator again overstates his case. His description of Penrod's engaging in "the *duello*" and suffering "imprisonment by the authorities" and "flagellation" recall Tom Sawyer's book-fed imagination and even Jimmie Trescott's melodramatic fear of incarceration, but *"duello"* and "flagellation" are not a child's words, and this is not the child's interpretation of events. Rather than adopt his boy protagonist's perspective, the narrator in this passage has subtly shifted his focus, and we come away from it laughing less at Penrod than at the adults and girlfriend whose expectations are inappropriate to a young boy and who mete out punishment that is disproportionate to the offense.

The conflict between a boy's needs and the female authorities' demands remains a central theme in the remaining episodes in *Penrod*. Again and again victory turns to defeat for Penrod, and defeat is modified, not by the narrator's sympathy for his protagonist, but by his undercutting female authority. In "A Boy in the Air" (Chapters 7 through 11, originally in *Cosmopolitan*, October 1913), Tarkington draws on his remembered unhappiness in school and his difficulties with his fourth-grade teacher. "The nervous monotony of the schoolroom inspires a sometimes unbearable longing for something astonishing to happen . . . every boy's fundamental desire is to do something astonishing himself, so as to be the centre of all human interest and awe" (57), the narrator says authoritatively. His comment becomes ironic as he recounts an event in which Penrod finds himself the center of attention in an unexpected way. Penrod sasses his teacher when she interrupts his daydream of attention-inspiring self-levitation. When she reproves him, he wins a real audience: "The school shivered in ecstatic horror, every fascinated eye upon him; yet there was not a soul in the room but was profoundly grateful to him for the sensation—including the offended teacher herself" (63). He finally extricates himself from his predicament by inventing a movie-inspired story of a family crisis that has called forth heroic behavior on his part and left him too tired to pay attention in class. His victory is temporary, however, for his family learns of the lie, and the inevitable punishment follows, once again administered by his father. It seems as if the joke is on Penrod, who becomes the "centre of all human interest" in a manner he does not want, yet Tarkington's remark about the gratitude of the offended teacher also makes the episode a jibe at the hypocrisy of (female) authority.

"An Overwhelming Saturday" (Chapters 15 through 17, originally in *Cosmopolitan*, November 1913) provides yet another example of a victory turned to defeat at the hands of female authority and defeat compromised. Inspired again by childhood memories, in this case by his own remembered pleasure in putting on a show, as well as by the fact that a show is by now a standard feature of the boy book, Tarkington has Penrod and his friend Sam Williams put on a show along with Herman and Verman. Young Booth Tarkington put on a puppet show; his fictional boys do something more extravagant. Their prize attraction is Roderick Magsworth Bitts, Junior, who happens to share the name Magsworth with a convicted murderess. Roddy is unaware of his family's fury over "the sacrilegious coincidence of the name" (144) and is eager for acceptance by Penrod and his friends; he willingly consents to his role. The show is successful beyond the boys' most hopeful fantasies: the crowd includes both children and adults. Alarmed, Mrs. Magsworth Bitts breaks up the performance and complains to Mrs. Schofield and Mrs. Williams about the bad influence of their "common" (154) sons on her child. A meeting of the accused parents ensues. The two mothers speak with hypocritical sympathy of Mrs. Magsworth Bitts's troubles and then send their husbands out to do the "'one thing to be done'" (154) to the boys. The narrator generalizes: "This is a boy's lot: anything he does, anything whatever, may afterward turn out to have been a crime—he never knows. And punishment and clemency are alike inexplicable" (155). With this hint, we assume—as does Penrod—that once again he will be whipped, his father as usual carrying out the wishes of his mother. But now, surprisingly, behavior offensive to the authorities is rewarded: Penrod is given a quarter by his father, as is Sam by his. We laugh, as we are surely meant to, at the boys for not understanding why what they have done is forgivable. But we also recognize an unarticulated criticism of the hypocritical mothers and cowardly fathers who will not speak out.

I suggested earlier in this chapter that, despite the dominance of female values in *Penrod,* consideration of the father is nevertheless central to the book as it is to all the other boy books. As *Penrod* draws to a close, Tarkington looks more closely at the father who has repeatedly failed his son by not being a strong presence in his life. Whereas Mr. Schofield differs in character from Tarkington's own father, he is as compliant in regard to female will as his real-life counterpart, and in the last episode of the book (Chapters 28 through 31, originally in *Cosmopolitan,* March 1914; no episode title), Tarkington seems to turn a critical eye on that compliance. But now, at this crucial point in the book, that criticism is muted by the way in which literary convention blurs autobiographical needs. The occasion is Penrod's twelfth birthday, a birthday to be especially celebrated: "Thirteen is embarrassed by the beginnings of a new colthood; the child becomes a youth. But twelve is the very top of boyhood" (273). Penrod's family fusses over him at breakfast, and his father greets him optimistically with, "'Well, well! How's the *man?*'" (274). He is then taken to see Sarah Crim, his ninety-year-old great aunt. Later in the day, a dance in his honor will take place. Aunt Sarah is a wise matriarch, old enough to be beyond the need for social acceptance that governs the younger women who have charge of Penrod. She gives him an appropriate present for a boy, "a superb, intricate, and very modern machine of destructive capacities almost limitless. She called it a pocket-knife" (276). She also gives him his father's old slingshot, the destructive toy of his boyhood. She tells Penrod what his father did with the slingshot and observes, "'He doesn't look like a person who's ever done things of that sort, and I suppose he's forgotten it so well that he believes he never *did,* but if you give it to him from me I think he'll remember'" (275). The slingshot does indeed jar Mr. Schofield's repressed memory when Penrod breaks a window with it. His first response is his typical bluster; when he recognizes what Aunt Sarah meant him to, he responds mildly, "'Never mind, little boy. A broken window isn't much harm'" (304).

This seems like a moment of real rapport between father and son that separates them from the female domestic world, but Penrod is oblivious to the gesture his father has made, and the gesture seems to make most sense in reference to the father himself. On the level of syntax, Mr. Schofield's "little boy" seems to deny the "man" he earlier saw in Penrod. But he speaks so gently and "thoughtfully" (the word is reiterated twice [304]) that it seems that his expression is a recognition of the little boy in himself rather than a denial of the "man" he earlier saw in his son. Tarkington seems to be reminding the compliant father of what he once was and what his adult life denies—at a cost to himself, evident in his manifest discomfort with his paternal role, and to his son, evident in the father's acquiescence to female authorities.

That this is another instance of a boy book author who finally finds in his father's failures the source of his own trouble is not quite as clear as my discussion suggests. The ending of *Penrod* strays farthest from the facts of Tarkington's life in the events it depicts and recalls its fictional predecessors in the issues it raises. As a result Tarkington's intentions, even his unconscious wishes, become an indistinguishable part of the familiar tale he tells. Tarkington uses the visit to Aunt Sarah to make explicit the assumptions that we have seen govern all boy books, including *Penrod.* Aunt Sarah frankly observes that what distinguishes boys is their lack of the social hypocrisy we call civilized manners: "'Boys are just like people, really. . . . Only they're not quite so awful, because they haven't learned to cover themselves all over with little pretenses'" (276). Their honesty is to be explained by the recapitulation theory—in Aunt Sarah's words: "'He's [Penrod's] had to repeat the history of the race and go through all the stages from the primordial to barbarism. You don't expect boys to be civilized, do you? . . . You might as well expect eggs to crow'" (278). Against this background the coming together of father and son over the slingshot looks like another aspect of the recapitulation theory—namely, that a rambunctious boyhood is the heritage of every man. We read the encounter without particular reference to Mr. Schofield's failings, or to the implied failings of Tarkington's own father, unless we also bring to the novel a knowledge of Tarkington's own life and an awareness of the real-life tension between father and son that typically lies behind the boy book.

The final chapters of *Penrod,* in which the romance between Penrod and Marjorie Jones is brought to a happy conclusion (that will last only until the next book), reveal a similar blurring of autobiographical needs by literary convention. Remembering Tom Sawyer and Becky Thatcher, we might expect Penrod to have to prove himself to win Marjorie. But oddly, he does not. John D. Seelye examines the ethnic and social prejudices at work in *Penrod* and concludes that the book dramatizes a kind of American fairy tale in which the protagonist need only represent plain American virtue to merit a nice girl (603)—an explanation that might well account for some of the enthusiasm with which Tarkington's book was received, but one that only partly explains what happens at the book's conclusion. Not only is Penrod exempt from having to prove himself, but it is Marjorie who claims him. Penrod has admired her since the beginning of the book, but she has repeatedly rejected him, sometimes preferring Maurice Levy and the amenities his family's money can provide, more often—rehearsing the role she will play as an adult—rejecting him as a sign of her disapproval of his conduct. At his birthday dance, Fanchon Gelbraith, the intriguing visitor—"In years she was eleven, in manner about sixty-five, and evidently had lived much at court" (283)—flirts with all the boys, regrets the lack of champagne, and teaches the children a new dance in which "the word 'step' is somewhat misleading, nothing done with the feet being vital to the evolutions introduced by Fanchon" (294). Penrod, like all the boys, is captivated, and he forgets Marjorie. Enraged, she drags him off the dance floor, shouting, "'You BEHAVE yourself!'" And Penrod does: "He was stunned; obeyed automatically, without question, and had very little realization of what was happening to him. Altogether, and without reason; he was in precisely the condition of an elderly spouse detected in flagrant misbehaviour" (297). He is rewarded by parental approval for not participating in the dance and by Marjorie's declaration at the end of the book that he is now her beau. But the narrator's language is chilling: at the "very top of boyhood," Penrod is a male ready to be managed like a misbehaving "elderly spouse." Mr. Schofield was once as uncivilized as his son; his son, correspondingly, will be as compliant as his father.

Again, our knowledge of Tarkington's life fleshes out the significance of this event: in tracing Penrod's and Mr. Schofield's stories, Tarkington is commenting on both his own need to be managed and his father's failure because of that same need. But his adept handling of his genre spared him direct confrontation with what he on some level knew and prevents us from dwelling on what he has revealed. The conventional happy conclusion to Penrod's romance, here working hand in hand with the narrator's distance from his protagonist, obscures the somber implications of the narrator's imagery. When Marjorie sends Penrod her note announcing her affection for him, Penrod's world is transfigured. He is happy because Marjorie has saved him from his usual disgrace, and his father has forgiven him the broken window. The narrator concludes, "The last shaft of sunshine of that day fell graciously and like a blessing upon the boy sitting on the fence" (305). When Marjorie's affectionate note sails over the fence, he adds, "The sun sent forth a final amazing glory" (306). Amidst language of redemption, the cost of Penrod's victory recedes into the background.

With its adventures spun out of the material of everyday life, its humorous portrayal of a boy harassed by domestic values and manners, and its ultimate allegiance to those virtues, *Penrod* struck a responsive chord with the public. Tarkington was wrong in claiming that the book would appeal to any man "unless he lived in the east side of New York or went yachting out of Newport" (quoted by Woodress 178) only in limiting the appeal of the book to male readers. *Penrod* became a best-seller (Mott 313), joining Twain's two boy books in that distinction. More Penrod stories followed over the next several years and were collected as *Penrod and Sam* (1916) and *Penrod Jashber* (1929; the last-published material for this collection appeared in 1918).

Like many sequels, neither of these quite lives up to the original. Each is governed, to its detriment, by Tarkington's ideas about the nature of boys, which is also to say each is less indebted to Tarkington's own boyhood than *Penrod*. We learn again that "Penrod and Sam were not 'bad'; they were never that. They were something which was not their fault; they were historic" (74) as the boy pals proceed to get into one sort of mischief after another in *Penrod and Sam*. We are reminded again that "the thing that a boy most shrinks from . . . [is] having his private affairs exposed, and himself involved in the mysteries of grown-up jurisprudence, where intentions go for nothing and all is incalculable and ominous" (198) as Penrod sees the elaborate game of detective that unifies *Penrod Jashber* entangle him ever more deeply. Still, the sequels are entertaining books. *Penrod and Sam* has the further distinction of presenting, in the quarrels that are "the very texture" (85) of the boys' friendship, an interesting domestication of a facet of boyhood savagery and a juvenile version of one of those competitive alliances that mark male friendship in our culture (Fasteau 6–19; Tannen 245–79).

Tarkington became a sort of spokesman on boyhood, with his studies of adolescence, *Seventeen* (1916) and *Alice Adams* (1921), adding to his authority on preadult life. He published an essay called "What I Have Learned from Boys" in *The American Magazine* in January 1925; he wrote introductions to *Tom Sawyer* and *Huck Finn* for the Limited Editions Club (1923, 1933); his opinion was cited by Alexander Woollcott in his own Foreword to *Whilomville Stories* in *Woollcott's Second Reader* (1937). To some extent he took up the role of definer and champion of the boy book that Howells had abandoned after his generation had written its own boy books. But the boy book no longer needed a champion. It was a readily recognized and well-received genre. In "What I Have Learned from Boys," Tarkington does not tell us what he learned from experience with boys; instead, he tells us once again how his culture taught him to think about boys. He makes his point by describing several Penrod-aged boys, boys he claims to know, but boys who conveniently illustrate what Aldrich, Warner, Twain, Howells, Garland, and Crane have already told us: "From eight to fourteen is a period of life piquantly interesting to the congenial observer; for in studying it he may perceive unconcealed in the boy not only what is later to be found coated over in the man but something also of the history of all mankind" (6). That Tarkington found a ready audience for this familiar idea is testimony to both the liveliness of his writing and the profound attraction of the recapitulation theory.

# 8

# THE END OF THE BOY BOOK

The boy book is an impressive and poignant contribution to our literature. Focusing on a limited period of time and deemphasizing the passage of time, the boy book is not about growing up, but is instead about the meaning of boyhood for the adult author. Motivated to write by particular pressures in his adult life, he draws on autobiographical fact but imaginatively reorders, elaborates, and colors—in essence, fictionalizes—remembered experience so that his book becomes an account of the essential truth about his childhood as he understands it. These books are formally complex, for their authors are engaged in their work on the levels of both remembering adult and experiencing child, of narrator and protagonist. Such an author is critical one moment and celebratory the next as he shifts his perspectives on the past. He is wonderfully inventive in exploiting his different perspectives: he interrupts the story he is telling to comment fondly or critically on people and events, he adopts the child's limited point of view to savor past pleasures or to expose childish ignorance, he splits his child protagonist into several characters to examine different recollections of himself, he incorporates lyric poems to celebrate the past, he frames his story to distance it, he blurs the distinction between child and adult perceptions to confound our expectation of adult superiority. The result is a book whose uneven tone bespeaks its author's investment in presenting his past as he reviews it in light of his present condition.

The social and personal contexts of the boy book help to explain the mixed feelings the boy book authors bring to their

work. At the beginning of this study, I spoke of the social disloca-
tion occasioned by the changes in American life between the Civil
War and World War I, citing in particular the transformation of
the United States into an industrialized, urbanized nation and
the changed national values and experiential gulf between generations that developed as a result. These changes, as I noted,
impinged on the lives of each of the boy book authors I have
discussed. The immediate impetus for writing, however, was the
personal crisis each experienced, a crisis of male adulthood. Confronted with the difficulties of being a man, each reverts to being
a boy again. Ray Raphael, writing from a perspective of a late
twentieth-century social critic, describes contemporary male
problems in a way that illuminates the formative years of our
culture as well. He argues that as a result of its emphasis on
diversity and competitiveness, American culture, unlike more
traditional cultures, provides no definitive rite of passage that
publicly, irrevocably confers manhood on a boy and so separates
men from boys. The result is that manhood is a precarious state,
vulnerable to even the normal crises of adulthood (xii, 3–23). In
reverting to childhood in their boy books, the boy book authors
yielded to their vulnerability without understanding that their
need to turn to the past was symptomatic of a failure inherent in
their culture.

Although the reversion to boyhood began as a simple desire to
turn away from a difficult present and to seek consolation and
restoration in a vicarious return to the past, it typically became
something more complex. Despite the celebratory gestures, despite the humor (indeed, the humor is often at the expense of the
younger self), the very form of the boy book with its dual perspectives of narrator and protagonist accommodates a critical
stance toward the author's past. In this frame of mind, the boy
book author is inevitably drawn to confront what he intuits (for
the recognition is seldom directly acknowledged) to be the source
of his difficulties as an adult: the father who failed him, who
was not present when his growing son needed him, who sapped
his son's self-confidence, who demanded too much of his son,
who failed to recognize his son's own needs, or who was merely
ineffectual—the father, in short, who did not give his son what he
needed to be a man. Given the experiential gulf between fathers

and sons, and given the absence of significant rites of passage in American culture, it is doubtful that any father could have been good enough—or could have been perceived as good enough. Freudian-oriented psychologists and Marxist-oriented social historians would agree with this assessment and would locate the difficulty not in the immediate particularities of the authors' individual lives but in human nature or history. The psychologists would see the father-son conflict as the working out of the Oedipal drama; the historians would see it as the consequence of industrial life, which removes the father from the emotive life of the home and consigns him to the workplace (Demos, *Past* 41–67; Osherson 1–43).

Of course, no nineteenth-century writer could have conceptualized his experience in such terms, though, as we have seen, he typically presented his story as a representative one. Nevertheless, these books live for us because of the particular stories they tell and the imaginative ways in which they tell them. In emphasizing the imaginative handling of the past, I have implicitly advanced the claim that the boy book enlarges the territory we as readers and critics can legitimately claim for autobiography. It has been customary to recognize that nineteenth-century autobiography is rather public in nature, that the autobiographer is typically a man—or, less often, a woman—whose significant achievements legitimize and circumscribe the kind of claim he or she makes on our attention. Susanna Egan, noting that these autobiographers commonly emphasize their role in national history, speaks of the nineteenth century as a time "when the private autobiographer is so frequently representative or serviceably public" (76). We see this understanding of the nature and function of autobiography in Twain's dictated autobiography and in Howells's *Years of My Youth*, autobiographies that are products of their authors' old age, shaped with their subjects' full consciousness of having grown up with the country to enjoy conspicuous public roles as adults. Perhaps this same understanding is one component of the hesitancy with which the authors I have considered acknowledge their boy books as autobiographical, if they do so at all.

The absence of public reference and the creative freedom that characterize the boy book make it, in fact, closer to modern autobiography than to what the nineteenth century recognized as autobiography. Critics of twentieth-century autobiography have observed that modern autobiography is a democratic form in its hospitality to all sorts and conditions of writers and that it is a creative form in its preference for psychological truth over factual truth. Such critics rejoice particularly in the inventiveness modern authors bring to the telling of their life stories and celebrate the author's role as a maker of truth-revealing fictions. Paul John Eakin notes the change modern practice has brought to our thinking about the form: "Adventurous twentieth-century autobiographers have shifted the ground of our thinking about autobiographical truth because they readily accept the proposition that fictions and the fiction-making process are a central constituent of the truth of any life as it is lived and of any art devoted to the presentation of that life" (5). Timothy Dow Adams reiterates this point and notes the therapeutic value of the form for the writer and the aesthetic appeal that is an intrinsic part of the imaginative autobiography: "This form of writing . . . possesses a peculiar kind of truth through a narrative composed of the author's metaphors of self that attempt to reconcile the individual events of a lifetime by using a combination of memory and imagination—all performed in a unique act that partakes of a therapeutic fiction making, rooted in what really happened, and judged [by the reader] both by the standards of truth and falsity and by the standards of success as an artistic creation" (3). The very fact that the boy book authors chose to write about boyhood instead of manhood freed them from the conventional expectations that attached to autobiography as a genre and permitted the imaginative forms and fictions we see in the boy books. That they wrote in a time in which there was a ready market for fiction for and about children clearly pointed them in a fruitful direction. As a result they might justly be considered the true precursors of the modern autobiographers Eakin and Adams celebrate.

Yet the boy book did not survive past World War I. The paradigm on which it depended, the recapitulation theory, was supplanted by another, seemingly more cogent, description of growth and development: that offered by Freud. The recapitulation theory had proved serviceable in providing a conceptual basis for the variety of needs the boy book addressed. It served an educative function by explaining bad boy behavior as a part of natural development and by reassuring parents and teachers that the uncivil behavior that characterized boys would in time give way to something better. It served an escapist and therapeutic function by allowing the reader a vicarious indulgence in antisocial behavior while at the same time assuring him that what was or had been troublesome in himself was not a permanent part of himself. The recapitulation theory was so comforting in its implications that writers and readers clung to it despite its manifest failure to accord with reality. It flourished in the wake of the Civil War and persisted through half a century of brutal conflict with Indians and violent labor strikes. Twain and Crane both recognized the savagery of adult life in their boy books, but the popularity of Tarkington's books reminds us how much the reading public had invested in a theory that comforted, flattered, and diverted them.

But the social changes of the late nineteenth and early twentieth centuries finally demanded a new paradigm to explain human experience. What emerged to meet this need and to become a governing idea in autobiography was the concept of adolescence. This was not a totally new idea. It had been conceptualized and popularized by G. Stanley Hall as a refinement of the recapitulation theory, for it postulated a further state in the step-by-step evolution of the human being toward maturity: "The child comes from and harks back to a remoter past; the adolescent is neo-atavistic, and in him the later acquisitions of the race slowly become prepotent." Adolescence is a period of "storm and stress" (xiii) in which the individual struggles with conflicting emotions and impulses, feeling powerful and secure one moment, uncertain and helpless the next, a period in which developing sexuality seeks appropriate forms of expression and sublimation, and a period in which one is particularly vulnerable to social pressure (Hall, Kett 217–21, Ross 325–40). It all sounds familiar. Yet as John and Virginia Demos have noted, Hall's reputation was short-lived; his work, with its emphasis on distinct states of development, seemed outmoded by the mid-1920s ("Adolescence" 215–16). Nevertheless, shorn of its evolutionary trappings, Hall's description of adolescence was congenial to the increasingly industrialized and impersonal world that took shape after World War I (Hays; Leuchtenburg 140–273), and it lives on into the present, a fact that suggests that it served and continues to serve some real social needs. David Bakan suggests that the idea of adolescence was developed by industrial society to impose a "second childhood" (980) on its young members as a way of keeping them out of a labor market that could not absorb them. Kenneth Keniston suggests that the free-floating quality and the lack of focus that characterize the behavior of American adolescents (the term he uses is "youth," by which he means late adolescence) is in fact an adaptation to a rapidly changing culture (209–40).

Hall's description of adolescence survived his conceptual framework, additionally, because it merged so nicely with Freud's notion of human development and so complemented the interest in Freud that began before World War I and became a popular enthusiasm in the twenties (Hoffman 44–86, Leuchtenburg 163–67, May 232–36). Hall himself played a central role in promoting Freud's ideas by inviting Freud to speak at Clark College in 1909 when Hall was president and by his own receptivity to Freud's work (Ross 381–94). Freud's scheme of human development, which acknowledged childhood sexuality and the learned repression of it and presented adolescence as a time in which the individual's latent sexuality reemerged and sought acceptable forms of expression, did not contradict Hall's memory and observation of the experience of adolescence; instead, it removed a constricting framework and presented human development as a continuum. Further, it fit both male and female experience more easily than did the recapitulation theory, and it did not lend itself to the kind of racial discrimination we saw in Tarkington's work. Freud's scheme was also blunter in identifying sexuality as one of life's central themes than Hall could have been, although Hall found Freud's emphasis congenial (Ross 384–85). A definition of adolescence that emphasizes sexuality also serves the needs of industrial society. Peter N. Stearns discusses the impact of nineteenth- and twentieth-century social change on male identity and observes, "The necessity of compensating for the decline of patriarchy imposed new emphasis on special male characteristics, which serve functions in themselves, in reasserting gender identities, quite apart from economic utility" (63). Adolescence was the time in which those identifying male characteristics were exhibited and tested.

Freudian ideas ensured the end of the boy book in several ways. Not only did the concern with adolescence more effectively speak to contemporary social needs than the recapitulation theory, but the emphasis on sexuality—both childhood and adolescent sexuality—also made a scheme that disregarded it look naive. After Freud it would be impossible for a writer to say unselfconsciously of a boyhood friend what Howells said of his relationship to his Huck Finn–like companion: "Their friendship was not only more innocent than any other friendship my boy had, but it was wholly innocent; they loved each other and that was all; and why people love one another there is never any satisfactory telling" (*Boy's Town* 192). All childhood and adolescent friendships, whether with the same or the opposite sex, would come under an increased scrutiny on the part of writers and readers. Similarly, boyhood savagery could no longer be innocently invoked as a metaphor for naughtiness that would be outgrown. After Freud asocial behavior was seen to be deeply rooted in all of us and to include sexuality (as suggested by "desires" and "passions" in the genteel example I offer below). In Chapter 1 I cited Trowbridge's claim that "the man is an enlightened being, the boy is a barbarian. He inherits not only the mild parental possibilities, but also the cat-like or tigerish traits which enabled his progenitors . . . to make the struggle for existence." In his account of the acceptance of Freudian thought in the twenties, Frederick J. Hoffman quotes Arthur E. J. Legge's description of the unconscious as typifying contemporary understanding. Legge extends the metaphor of savagery and so destroys the particularity of boyhood created by the recapitulation theory: "The unconscious would appear to be a region resembling the Zoological gardens, with all the keepers on strike. A host of unnoticed and unsuspected desires and passions are constantly roaring and raging in their cages" (69). The Freudian paradigm thus provided an acceptable explanation of Twain's and Crane's intuition that boys and men are fundamentally alike.

In addition to its vulnerability because of the outmoded paradigm on which it was based, the boy book was vulnerable on another score: it addressed an increasingly narrow segment of the American public. We have seen that many of the boy book writers knew each other, read each other's work, and saw their own books as a part of a shared conversation. This was possible because these writers came from similar backgrounds. All were white; all were beneficiaries of the high degree of social mobility available to the ambitious middle-class man in the nineteenth century. The late years of the nineteenth century and the early years of the twentieth saw an unprecedented number of immigrants coming to the United States and saw women enjoying increased mobility and new social and economic power (Degler 8–9, 179–83; Hays 95–104, 156; Leuchtenburg 141–42, 159–62). We have seen Tarkington's uneasiness in the face of these changes. But the people he would marginalize refused to be silent; like middle-class white men, they too had their stories to tell, and the developmental paradigm was readily accommodating.

The book that emerged to take the place of the boy book—the coming-of-age book—is necessarily quite different from its predecessors. In embodying the Freudian paradigm, whether explicitly or implicitly, it treats childhood as a part of the passage to adulthood. It focuses more often on adolescence than on childhood with the protagonist's developing sexuality a major theme and the parents less central in the fuller world the protagonist inhabits. With the emphasis on adolescence, the adult narrator is less distant from the young protagonist and is often scarcely visible. And the putative audience is clearly one of other adults. Sherwood Anderson's *Winesburg, Ohio* (1919) and Ernest Hemingway's Nick Adams stories (1925–1933) are representative. So too are Katherine Anne Porter's Miranda stories (1930s), Henry Roth's *Call It Sleep* (1934), and Richard Wright's *Black Boy* (1945), and a host of others. The coming-of-age book continues to be written and deserves a closer and finer analysis than is appropriate here. We can note in general that the coming-of-age book is congenial to us because its emphasis on the continuity of the different periods of life and its interest in adolescent sexuality strike us as a convincing account of human development. Further, the coming-of-age book records a more diverse range of experience than the boy book and so offers us a richer picture of American experience.

But with these gains there is a corresponding loss. The boy book was based on a now outmoded paradigm, but that paradigm rationalized the exclusive concentration on childhood. That concentration, in turn, recovered boyhood as an enduring, revitalizing memory that provided a respite from the difficult world of manhood for the authors I have examined. It also permitted exploration of their intuition that their adult lives made sense when understood as a result of childhood experience and that, within this experience, their relationships to their fathers were crucial in determining the kind of men they became. In writing their accounts of boyhood at pressure points in their adult lives, they acknowledged that a man never finishes being a boy. Recognizing this, we sense that in a parallel but doubtlessly different way, childhood lives into adulthood for a woman as well. Paradoxically, what we see as a naive and fanciful theory of human development informed an autobiographical genre that today strikes us as psychologically astute. In re-creating the events and patterns of childhood that resonated into their adult lives, the boy book authors present us with a view of human experience that complicates our tendency—often our wish—to believe that development is simply linear, that as we grow up, we grow away from the past and into a fresh start. By reminding us that the child lives on in the adult, the boy book continues to engage our imaginations and command our assent.

# 1. The Boy Book

1. Edwin H. Cady speaks of the *"boy-book"* as "a book written not so much for the entertainment of boys as for the purpose of exploring and defining the experience—and its significance—of the American boy" (*The Light of Common Day* 89). I do not know who first used the term.

2. In "Novel-Reading and Novel-Writing" Howells lists the auto-biographical as one of the shapes of "the inward life of the novel," to him "the most perfect literary form after the drama" because of its realism, a term that for Howells always means more than a superficial rendering of experience (*Norton* 2: 279–80).

3. For accounts of the late nineteenth- and early twentieth-century best-seller, see James D. Hart (140–223), Marcia Jacobson (*James* 3–8), and Frank Luther Mott (136–240).

4. Cady extends this definition in *The Light of Common Day* (96–101). Other discussions of the boy book typically inventory their contents and/or discuss their relationship to Twain's work. See Alan Gribben, Joseph Hinz, J. Hunter, Henry R. Sparapani, Albert E. Stone (24–32), and Anne Trensky. Alfred Habegger limits his discussion to the role of the boys' gang and looks particularly at Howells's contributions (206–19). Steven Mailloux considers books about bad boys, including Twain's books, in the context of contemporary fears that such books were a cause of juvenile delinquency (110–29).

5. The phrase is from a letter by Henry David Thoreau: "The *great west* and *north west* stretching on infinitely far and grand and wild, qualifying all our thoughts. That is the only America I know. I prize this western reserve chiefly for its intellectual value. That is the road to new life and freedom . . . and knowing this, one need not travel it" (20 October 1856, to Thomas Cholmondeley, *Norton* 1: 1864).

6. There are many discussions of this subject. Some helpful introduc-

tions are Carl Degler's, Samuel P. Hays's, and William E. Leuchtenburg's work.

7. Quoted in Henry Steele Commager (138). For other discussions of the feeling of foreclosure, see Randolph S. Bourne (594–96) and Joseph F. Kett (160–61).

8. Howells remarks on this in *A Traveler from Altruria*. One of his characters comments:

> I should say that within a generation our ideal had changed twice. Before the war, and during all the time from the revolution onward, it was undoubtedly the great politician, the publicist, the statesman. As we grew older and began to have an intellectual life of our own, I think the literary fellows had a pretty good share of the honors that were going; that is, such a man as Longfellow was popularly considered a type of greatness. When the war came, it brought the soldier to the front, and there was a period of ten or fifteen years when he dominated the national imagination. That period passed, and the era of material prosperity set in. The big fortunes began to tower up, and heroes of another sort began to appeal to our admiration. I don't think there is any doubt but the millionaire is now the American ideal. It isn't very pleasant to think so, even for people who have got on, but it can't very hopefully be denied. It is the man with the most money who now takes the prize in our national cake-walk. (119–20)

Also see John Tomsich for a discussion of the ineffectual role of the man of letters in post–Civil War America.

9. Slater argues that American history is a series of circumstances in which "an experiential chasm between parent and child" developed and "eroded the authoritarian family pattern prevailing in Europe" (54). He further suggests that an authoritarian family pattern never existed on a large scale here (55). What this meant, among other things, was that a man had to compete for authority not only in the marketplace, but also in the family.

10. Beard's passions were pioneer-style activities and woodcraft for boys. In 1905 he founded the Sons of Daniel Boone and five years later became involved in bringing the Boy Scouts to America (Macleod 132–33, 239). He was also a writer and illustrator, known today to Twain scholars as the man who did the original illustrations for *A Connecticut Yankee in King Arthur's Court* (1889). Ernest Thompson Seton was also attracted to outdoor activities for boys. In 1902 he founded the Tribe of Woodcraft Indians; like Beard's organization, this one was eventually subsumed under the Boy Scouts (Dubbert 148–53, Macleod 130–32). Seton also wrote a number of books for boys, including one that com-

bines the autobiographical elements of the boy book with the nature lore and woodcraft he was so interested in: *Two Little Savages* (1903).

11. Another explanation of woman's exemption from savagery appears in Harold Frederic's *The Damnation of Theron Ware* (1896), a fact that reminds us that the whole topic was very much a part of popular discourse. Frederic's misogynist Dr. Ledsmar outlines the recapitulation theory of boyhood development and then concludes: "'But the woman is totally different. She is infinitely more precocious as a girl. At an age when her slow brother is still stumbling along somewhere in the neolithic period, she has flown way ahead to a kind of mediæval stage, or dawn of mediævalism, which is peculiarly her own. Having got there, she stays there; she dies there. The boy passes her, as the tortoise did the hare'" (219). Also see Lears's discussion of the parallel the late nineteenth century saw between the childhood of both sexes and the medieval period (142–49).

12. Louisa May Alcott's *Little Women* (1868), Susan Coolidge's *What Katy Did* (1873), Lucy Larcom's *A New England Girlhood* (1889), Kate Douglas Wiggin's *Rebecca of Sunnybrook Farm* (1903), and Eleanor Porter's *Pollyanna* (1913) are representative girl books. Although they are auto-biographically based, they do not parallel the boy book in purpose or content. They appeal specifically to a child audience, include a strain of piety (without being as heavily didactic as Martha Finley's popular *Elsie Dinsmore* [1867]), and are centrally concerned with growing up. This group of books would merit serious scholarly discussion.

13. Barbara Ehrenreich and Deirdre English also note the twofold response to the child: "Thus the turn-of-the-century exaltation of the child was both romantic and rationalist, conservative and progressive. The child was 'primitive' but this meant it was also malleable, hence really more 'modern' than anyone else. . . . The child was the 'founder of the family,' the foundation of the home; it was also the only member of the family truly prepared (by virtue of its very inexperience) for the technological turmoil of the outside world" (170). This formulation stresses the teachableness of the child more than I do. As Trowbridge makes clear, one of the attractions of the recapitulation theory was that it assured the parent that his child would develop well, thereby freeing him of guilt if he could not assist in that development.

14. Lears makes this point in discussing popular literature: "Sentimental literature, by contributing to the evasive banality of the official culture, actually helped to legitimize modern industrial capitalism. The common pattern of culture involved a denial of the conflicts in modern capitalistic society, an affirmation of continuing harmony and progress" (17). He does not discuss the boy book but does reiterate his point—with an important addition—in terms of childhood in general: "On the one

hand, an exaltation of childishness pointed to a critique of adult conventions; on the other, it accommodated adults to those conventions by providing a brief, imaginary escape from them. Both tendencies emerged fullblown during the late nineteenth century" (144).

15. Like the work of the early humorists, Peck's Bad Boy stories, which began appearing in 1882, were originally published as newspaper columns. The first of several collections of these columns was published in 1883 as *Peck's Bad Boy and His Pa*. The sobriquet "bad boy" obviously recalls Aldrich; the timing of the book's publication meant that Peck's work took its place alongside the boy book in the marketplace. Shillaber also figured in the same marketplace. His early work introduced Mrs. Partington and her mischievous nephew Ike in a series of newspaper sketches collected under the title *Life and Sayings of Mrs. Partington* (1854). Now he too took advantage of the interest in boy books. *Ike Partington; or, The Adventures of a Human Boy and His Friends* (1879) was the first of a series of books that focused on Ike.

16. One author wrote a prequel: Grant Showerman's *A Country Chronicle* (1916) was followed by *A Country Child* (1917), an account of the same characters, a year younger.

17. Louisa May Alcott's *Little Men* (1871), Martha Finley's *An Old Fashioned Boy* (1871), and Frances Hodgson Burnett's *Little Lord Fauntleroy* (1886) present rather feminized images of boyhood, as their titles suggest. Frances Boyd Calhoun's *Miss Minerva and William Green Hill* (1909) is an amusing exception to this pattern.

## 2. Thomas Bailey Aldrich and Charles Dudley Warner

1. There are no contemporary biographies of either writer. See Ferris Greenslet on Aldrich, Mrs. James T. Fields and Thomas R. Lounsbury on Warner. The work on Warner is particularly sketchy. Charles E. Samuels's study of Aldrich includes some biographical information but does not go beyond Greenslet.

2. Fields quotes a letter from Warner to Howells in response to his review of *Being a Boy:* "I feel greatly encouraged by your opinion of 'My Only Boy.' Isn't he a little like your 'John' [Howells's son]? . . . I cannot hope that anyone will enter into the spirit of the 'Boy' as you did. I suspect that you saw him a good deal through the form of your dear 'John,' and it is too much to expect that you will lend 'John' to all the people who ought to read and buy the book. . . . The notice is thoroughly charming, the most sympathetic in the world. It quite takes away my power to give you ordinary thanks. I wish the book were half as good as the notice" (90–91).

3. In the rather imprecise fashion of biographers of his period, Greenslet observes of *Story of a Bad Boy,* "So great was its success in the

periodical [*Our Young Folks*] that several thousand subscribers were promptly added to the circulation, and after its publication in book form . . . it speedily ran through some eleven editions, a notable record for a book of its kind in those days" (92). Mott lists the book as a "better seller," a book that does well but unlike a best-seller does not sell a number of copies equal to 1 percent of the population of the United States (303, 322). *Tom Sawyer*, however, was a best-seller (Mott 310). Warner's book did not do nearly as well as these two. In his 1897 Preface, he acknowledged "The volume originally made no sensation. . . . It started a brook, and a brook it has continued" (x).

4. Habegger observes: "The many boy books that were written by Americans in the Gilded Age suggest that the father had very little influence on his son's developing masculinity. . . . It was not the father that enabled the boy to escape women's sphere and define his own masculinity. The most important institution that enabled boys to do so was composed of other boys, not adults. This institution was the outlaw gang—the comitatus that commanded the ultimate loyalty of boys" (205). This observation is abundantly borne out in the boy books. What interests me, however, is how often the emotional center of these books is not the boy's relationship to the gang but his relationship to his absent or inadequate male parent.

## 3. Mark Twain

1. Charles A. Norton suggests that the first eight chapters of *Tom Sawyer* are what remain of this initial phase of composition. In his reconstruction of the composition of the book, he claims that Twain wrote nearly four times this amount of material in 1872–73 and discarded three-fourths of it (6–7). No one else has come to this conclusion; no one else commits himself to exactly what was written in this phase of composition either. The question of discarded material is irrelevant to my consideration of the book; the similarity in form and the dependence on autobiographical material do suggest that these eight chapters were written together.

2. Howells was much taken by this description of Twain's childhood; it evidently ignited a shock of recognition. He repeated it first in a letter to Aldrich in 1900 as he brooded about his own attraction to autobiography "in spite of the small pleasure and pride the past gives me" (*Life in Letters* 2: 129) and remembered it ten years later when he came to write "My Mark Twain."

3. Twain speaks warmly of his mother in his autobiography, calling her his "first and closest friend" (27) and praising her plucky spirit, her lively interest in others, and her compassion. But he also notes that his was an undemonstrative family, and he recalls asking his mother, then an

elderly woman, about his sickly childhood: "'I suppose that during all that time you were uneasy about me?' 'Yes, the whole time.' 'Afraid I wouldn't live?' After a reflective pause—ostensibly to think out the facts—'No—afraid you would'" (12). Tom Sawyer's never-ending campaign to elicit proof of Aunt Polly's love probably reflects Twain's relationship to his mother. My reading of *Tom Sawyer* and *Huck Finn* together, however, suggests that for Twain it was the failure of his father, of the same-sex parent, that was felt most keenly and was most damaging. This being the case, it is not surprising that he would speak so warmly of his mother.

4. Forrest G. Robinson discusses the darker aspects of *Tom Sawyer* more extensively than any other critic (68–76, 79–89). He observes that "Tom's interior life is conducted at a very high emotional pitch, and it is virtually always focused, either directly or obliquely, on guilt or fear" (104–05). With a different focus than mine, he locates the sources of trouble in Tom's relationship with his culture. Also see Cynthia Griffin Wolfe's discussion of *Tom Sawyer,* which attributes Tom's difficulties to the absence of suitable father figures and notes the different forms his resentment of his situation takes.

5. See Christopher Lasch (*Narcissism* 74–75) and Alice Miller (30–48) for psychoanalytically informed accounts of the narcissistic personality. Both allege that pathological narcissism is not simple egotism but instead is a range of responses to an inner emptiness. Miller locates the source of trouble in the mother's attempt to use her child to satisfy her own unmet needs rather than to respect the child for what he is. This assumption is based on the fact that the mother is the first and often primary caretaker. It is likely that the same-sex parent on whom the child must model himself is equally or more important in forming the child's self-image.

6. In his study of Twain, Masters expressed admiration for both *Tom Sawyer* and *Huck Finn;* nevertheless, he was critical of Twain's faulty use of dialect and extravagant incident (122–36). His own *Mitch Miller* consciously corrects these "faults." The result is a dull boy book that nevertheless merits some attention because Masters's innovative strategy is to tell his boyhood story by telling the story of his best friend, and because Skeeters Kirby, the autobiographical character, and Mitch believe Tom Sawyer to be a real person. They try to model their lives on his and to visit him—an interesting tribute to the influence of the boy book.

7. Right before Pap "reforms," Huck reports that Pap and the Widow had taken the issue of Huck's custody to the law, and the new judge had refused to separate Huck from his father. Huck does not say he was present at the hearing, but he may well have been. It is clear that he is not present when the judge takes Pap into his home.

8. Timothy M. Rivinus and Brian W. Ford discuss Huck's passivity as his response to victimization by an alcoholic father. Twain's anger at the alcoholic father has no real-life parallel, but it does serve to rationalize his antagonism toward Pap, an antagonism extreme enough to permit him to violate Huck's point of view in order to include Pap's backsliding.

9. Janet Holmgen McKay examines the same material Smith does and comes to a similar conclusion from a narratological perspective: "Once Twain got going in Huck's speech, the drama of the event rather than the need for narrative consistency won out" (161). From here on, McKay argues that Huck as a narrator is overshadowed by Twain himself: "Having eliminated the external authority and perspective and having created a supremely subjective narrative, he was forced to reimpose order on his story in order to bring it to a close" (188).

## 4. William Dean Howells

1. John W. Crowley summarizes: "One important cause of Winifred's breakdown in 1880 [the beginning of her decline] was her mental stress about authorship: conflicts between her hope for poetic greatness and her fear of failure (and, to some extent, of success); between her desire to please her parents (especially her father) and her dread of disappointing them; between her wish to stand apart from her father's fame and her need to be sheltered by it" (*Mask of Fiction* 102).

2. Howells does not seem to have been a very astute judge of what would appeal to the child reader. In his 1911 introduction to Thomas Hughes's *Tom Brown's School-Days,* an English boy book/school book, Howells justifies the moralizing narrator. Although he recognizes that Hughes's style is that of an earlier time, he seems to forget that he had earlier praised *Story of a Bad Boy* and *Tom Sawyer* for not preaching, thereby holding the boy book author to the same standard that he holds any author to. Now he claims that the unsophisticated readership of Hughes's book justifies the offense:

The author openly preaches and praises himself for preaching; he does not hesitate to slip into the drama and deliver a sermon; he talks the story out with many self-interruptions and excursions; he knows nothing of the modern method of letting it walk along on its own legs, but is always putting his hands under its arms and helping it, or his arm across its shoulder and caressing it. In all this, which I think wrong, he is probably doing quite right for boys who formed and will always form the greatest number of readers; boys like to have things fully explained and commentated, whether they are grown up or not. (ix)

The popularity of Hughes's book long after writers for children stopped overt moralizing suggests that children liked *Tom Brown's School Days* despite, not because of, its moralizing.

3. I am indebted to John Crowley for this information.

4. Tom H. Towers argues that "my boy"'s brother and father help "bring forth that natural goodness that at last brings 'my boy' out of savagery into civilization" (508). In fact, we never see this process in the book. Thomas Cooley notes Howells's "anthropological" (87) approach to the boy life he describes and argues that "by treating his boy as an artifact, Howells complicates those elements of his narrative that contribute to making it a story of initiation and education. But the education theme is there just the same" (90–91). To arrive at this conclusion, he compares the opening and closing sections of the book. While these two sections differ, Howells does not tell us how or when change occurred.

5. Cooley notes some of the formal means by which Howells obscures "my boy"'s singularity and suggests reasons why he needed to do so (85–86, 87–88). I deal somewhat differently with the same subjects in "William Dean Howells's (Auto)biography: A Reading of *A Boy's Town*."

6. Howells's biographers dispute his claim that Mary Howells was an impartial mother. Lynn, for example, cites the frequent expressions of closeness in Will's autobiographies and letters (noted above), as well as the great reluctance with which Mary Howells saw her son leave home and establish a life of his own. Cady also finds Mary Howells a partial mother; however, he suggests that it was her first-born son Joe whom she favored (*Road to Realism* 58)—a situation that increased, rather than decreased, Will's attachment.

7. Rodney D. Olsen provides a useful discussion of Howells's parents' philosophies of child rearing. William Cooper Howells sought to encourage his children by "affectionate means" (19), a gentle, loving sort of moral suasion that proved very restrictive; Mary Howells was more temperamental than her husband and less consistently nurturing to her children (24–25).

# 5. Hamlin Garland

1. Jean Holloway, Joseph B. McCullough, B. R. McElderry, Jr., and Donald Pizer concur in tracing the genesis of *Boy Life on the Prairie*. Pizer provides the most detailed discussion of the early sketches (*Early Work* 54–56).

2. Readers familiar with the partial serialization of an early version of *A Son of the Middle Border,* however, would have been confused: the serialization was narrated by Lincoln Stewart, while Garland's Intro-

duction both claimed and denied that the work was autobiographical (Holloway 221–24).

3. Garland directs the reader to the emotional content of his poetry in his Foreword to *Prairie Songs:* "The prairies are gone. I held one of the ripping, snarling, breaking plows that rolled the hazel bushes and the wild sunflower under. I saw the wild steers come into pasture and the wild colts come under harness. I saw the wild fowl scatter and turn aside; I saw the black sod burst into gold and lavender harvests of wheat and corn—and so there comes into my reminiscences an unmistakable note of sadness. I do not excuse it or conceal it. I set it down as it comes to me" (3). The guilt that Garland hints at here is missing from *Boy Life on the Prairie*, perhaps because in that book Garland recalls the personal cost of taming the prairie.

4. This poem was revised for inclusion in *Boy Life on the Prairie*. The revisions are small but intensify the sense of loss. The most significant are the "myriad varied years" (*Prairie Songs* 94) in the middle of the original, changed to "a million vanished years" (179), and the original ending—"the grinding roar/ Of ceaseless tumult in the street below/ Comes back and welters me again" (*Prairie Songs* 94)—changed and expanded as my text indicates.

5. Discussion of the structure of *Boy Life on the Prairie* has been brief at best. McElderry suggests that "unity is achieved by emphasis on the change in the prairie, which parallels and intensifies the boy's growing up" (vi), but he also speaks of the "apparent discursiveness of the book" (vi). Pizer describes the book as "a cyclical narrative of farm activities" (*Son* 80) that spans seven years; more specifically, he notes the pattern of a year's cycle in Part 1, but finds Part 2 "a non-chronological account of various prairie experiences" (*Son* 81). Leland Krauth points to the yearly cycle in both parts and suggests that "a boy's gradual growth to manhood" is "at the heart of both sections" (25). He describes this as a simple structure complicated only by the fondly recollective point of view of the poems. My own essay, "The Flood of Remembrance and the Stream of Time: Hamlin Garland's *Boy Life on the Prairie*," is an earlier version of this chapter; it does not treat the book as autobiography, but it does describe the form of the book as I do here.

6. The chapter on the circus is the only one in which there is no indication of the time of year. *A Son of the Middle Border* identifies the circus as a spring event; readers of *Boy Life on the Prairie* could deduce that it takes place in spring because the chapter precedes one on a June camping trip.

7. Garland's similarity to his father is particularly evident in *A Son of the Middle Border*, which focuses on the father-son rivalry. Pizer notes that a central pattern in that book is the son's taking on his father's role as head of the family. He summarizes: "Garland's changing relationship

with his parents, from rebellion and desertion to guilt and rescue [of his mother from the hardship of prairie life and from his father's domination] is the emotional center of the book" (*Son* 87).

# 6. Stephen Crane

1. Thomas Beer, John Berryman, R. W. Stallman, and James B. Colvert concur on the biographical matters I discuss in this chapter. See Joseph Katz (227–31) for a discussion of the problems raised by the work of the first three. Colvert's work appeared after Katz's review and is valuable as a factual, rather than an interpretive, account. Louis Zara's research-based novel about Crane is interesting and suggestive.

2. Lee Clark Mitchell notes our tendencies to reject the premises of naturalistic texts by fleshing out characters as if they were realistic characters (15) and by discounting the repetition that denies the possibility of change as stylistic awkwardness (22). Solomon's and Holton's readings of *Whilomville Stories* demonstrate these tendencies.

3. J. C. Levenson follows Crane's biographers in identifying Port Jervis with Whilomville (xi–xiv); he also cites Crane's brothers Edmund and William as models for Dr. Trescott (xii, lix). This does not mean that we need rule out Jonathan Townley Crane, Stephen's father, as a model as well. A child with adult brothers must feel he has many fathers; in fact, this blurring of paternal identity might be one of the sources of the ineffectual fathers in *Whilomville Stories*.

4. "The Angel-Child" ("The Stove" had not yet appeared) interested a New York editor who asked Crane if he could write more of the same for her. "I would approach the little-girl-life with no assurance," he wrote. He then added, "However if you think the 'little Cora' of the Magazine stories could be transported to her own New York and there suffer a few experiences—I think I might manage" (*Correspondence* 2: 593). Crane's willingness to try his hand at girl life, but to try it only in New York, suggests that for him Whilomville life was necessarily boy life, a response we would expect, given the autobiographical origin of the Whilomville stories. His response also reveals his reluctance to give up any opportunity to make some money. He did not live to try his hand at more "little Cora" stories.

5. Cora Crane gave Margery Pease, a friend of the Cranes, the manuscripts of "The Angel-Child" and "The Lover and the Tell-Tale." She wrote, "You can see that Michael [the Peases' son] for the moment is 'Jimmie'" (*Correspondence* 2: 431), a remark that may or may not mean Michael was the model for Jimmie. But even if Michael's experience inspired Jimmie's letter writing, Jimmie's confrontation with his classmates and teacher are of a piece with his experience throughout the Jimmie Trescott stories.

6. Dr. Trescott in "The Monster" is a man of greater moral integrity and force than Dr. Trescott in *Whilomville Stories*. Nevertheless, Crane also shies away from showing him confronting his son. In Chapter 1 of "The Monster," a guilt-stricken Jimmie, behaving very unlike the Jimmie of *Whilomville Stories*, calls his father's attention to a flower that he broke in careless play. After the child has initiated the dialogue, his father suggests that the boy restrict his play. In Chapter 21, Dr. Trescott seeks to explain to Jimmie why he and his friends must not annoy the deformed Henry Johnson. We see Dr. Trescott holding his confused son and saying " 'I want to explain to you—' " (57), and then the scene shifts.

# 7. Booth Tarkington

1. Biographical information is taken from Tarkington's own autobiographies, "As I Seem to Me" and *The World Does Move* and from James Woodress's study. Keith J. Fennimore adds a few interpretive words.

2. In the "Dedicatory Word" that introduces *Penrod: His Complete Story*, a book in which the three Penrod books are reprinted (with some changes), Tarkington notes, "This book owes its existence to a lady connected by marriage with the writer, for at the time of her consent to become thus related she made virtually the condition that he should write something about a boy" (v) and continues on in this vein. Tarkington's recollection is interesting, not only because it verifies Susanah's role in the creation of the Penrod books, but also because Tarkington casts himself in the role of put-upon male, a role he shares with Penrod.

3. In his letter to Woollcott, in addition to recalling the appearance of *Whilomville Stories*, Tarkington recalls having read *Helen's Babies* (1876, by John Habberton; a novel based on his experiences with his two small children) fifty years earlier. He read Owen Johnson's *Lawrenceville Stories* (*The Prodigious Hickey*, 1909; *The Varmint*, 1910; and *The Tennessee Shad*, 1911, all school stories) when they first appeared and claimed that they "had given me more pleasure than anything I had ever read" (quoted by Schwed vii). As I note, he recalls parts of *Tom Sawyer* in *Penrod*. He does not allude to *Huck Finn* (unless Penrod's name is from Brer Penrod, one of the gossips at the Phelps's farm in Chapter 41; Tarkington's niece, Susanah Mayberry, however, says phone books were the source of many of Tarkington's names [66]), but it is unlikely that he would have known *Tom Sawyer* and not its well-known sequel.

4. Susanah Mayberry offers an assessment of the women in Tarkington's life in *My Amiable Uncle*. When she sought information on Tarkington's first wife, some family members told her that "she was a lovely artistic, sensitive woman, who was no match for her mother-in-law and sister-in-law. . . . To say that Uncle Booth's feminine relatives

were possessive is to understate. . . . My grandmother [Tarkington's sister] was so powerful and had such a hold on the men in her family that they rarely fought for their beleaguered wives. . . . One woman, though, stood her ground and won hands down, and that was Uncle Booth's second wife, Susanah" (31). Tarkington's comment on his unmarried maternal uncle is also revealing for what it says about his father: "Uncle Newton's lightest word was law to my mother, and my father never argued" ("As I Seem to Me" 23 August 1941, 80).

5. Woodress speaks of Tarkington's love for the family house on Pennsylvania Street, in which he lived for forty-six years, until urban blight drove him uptown in 1923. He lists the many emotional ties Tarkington had to the house and tells us what happened: "The house finally was torn down in 1940 to make way for a parking lot. Even before its ignominious end, however, the front lawn had been invaded by a hamburger stand, and in his last years Tarkington could not bear going to town by way of Pennsylvania Street" (26–27). Tarkington's elegiac commemoration of Hoosier life in "As I Seem to Me," written a year after demolition of the house, owes some of its intensity to his knowledge of what happened to the family home.

6. The detailed record of Tarkington's publishing history in Dorothy Ritter Russo's and Thelma L. Sullivan's bibliography allows us to trace the process of revision.

# WORKS CITED

Adams, Henry. *The Education of Henry Adams.* 1907. New York: Modern Library-Random, 1931.

Adams, Timothy Dow. *Telling Lies in Modern American Autobiography.* Chapel Hill: University of North Carolina Press, 1990.

Alcott, Louisa M. *Little Men: Life at Plumfield with Jo's Boys.* Boston: Roberts, 1871.

———. *Little Women: or, Meg, Jo, Beth and Amy.* Parts 1 and 2. Boston: Roberts, 1868.

Aldrich, Thomas Bailey. *An Old Town by the Sea.* 1893. Boston: Riverside-Houghton, 1917.

———. Preface to *The Story of a Bad Boy,* iii–viii. Boston: Riverside-Houghton, 1894.

———. *The Story of a Bad Boy.* 1869. Boston: Riverside-Houghton, 1914.

Anderson, Sherwood. *Winesburg, Ohio: A Group of Tales of Ohio Small-Town Life.* New York: Modern Library-Random, 1919.

———. *Tar: A Midwest Childhood.* New York: Boni and Liveright, 1926.

Andrews, Kenneth R. *Nook Farm: Mark Twain's Hartford Circle.* 1950. Hamden: Archon, 1967.

Bakan, David. "Adolescence in America: From Idea to Social Fact." *Daedalus* 100 (1971): 979–95.

Beard, D. C. *The American Boy's Handy Book.* 1882. Boston: Godine, 1983.

Beattie, Ann. Preface to *The Story of a Bad Boy,* by Thomas Bailey Aldrich, v–viii. New York: Garland, 1976.

Beaver, Harold. *Huckleberry Finn.* London: Allen, 1987.

Beer, Thomas. *Stephen Crane.* New York: Knopf, 1923.

Berryman, John. *Stephen Crane.* New York: Sloan, 1950.

Bettelheim, Bruno. *The Uses of Enchantment: The Meaning and Importance of Fairy Tales.* New York: Knopf, 1976.

Blair, Walter. *Mark Twain & Huck Finn.* Berkeley: University of California Press, 1960.

————. "When Was *Huckleberry Finn* Written?" *American Literature* 30 (1958): 1–25.

Bourne, Randolph S. "The Two Generations." *Atlantic Monthly,* May 1911: 591–98.

Bridgman, Richard. "Mark Twain and Dan Beard's Clarence: An Anatomy." *Centennial Review* 31 (1987): 212–27.

Burnett, Frances Hodgson. *Little Lord Fauntleroy.* New York: Scribners, 1886.

Butler, Ellis Parker. *Swatty: A Story of Real Boys.* 1915. Boston: Riverside-Houghton, 1920.

Byers, John R., Jr. "A Hannibal Summer: The Framework of *The Adventures of Tom Sawyer.*" *Studies in American Fiction* 8 (1980): 81–88.

Cady, Edwin H. *The Light of Common Day: Realism in American Fiction.* Bloomington: Indiana University Press, 1971.

————. *The Realist at War: The Mature Years 1885–1920 of William Dean Howells.* Syracuse: Syracuse University Press, 1958.

————. *The Road to Realism: The Early Years 1837–1885 of William Dean Howells.* Syracuse: Syracuse University Press, 1956.

————. *Stephen Crane.* Rev. ed. Boston: Twayne, 1980.

Calhoun, Frances Boyd. *Miss Minerva and William Green Hill.* Chicago: Reilly, 1909.

Chubb, Percival. *Boy Life.* New York: Harpers, 1909.

Coe, Richard N. *When the Grass Was Taller: Autobiography and the Experience of Childhood.* New Haven: Yale University Press, 1984.

Colvert, James B. *Stephen Crane.* New York: Harcourt, 1984.

Comer, Cornelia A. P. "A Letter to the Rising Generation." *Atlantic Monthly,* February 1911: 145–54.

Commager, Henry Steele. *The American Mind: An Interpretation of American Thought and Character Since the 1880's.* 1950. Toronto: Bantam, 1970.

Cooley, Thomas. *Educated Lives: The Rise of Modern Autobiography in America.* Columbus: Ohio State University Press, 1976.

Coolidge, Susan. *What Katy Did.* Boston: Roberts, 1873.

Crane, Stephen. *The Correspondence of Stephen Crane.* Edited by Stanley Wertheim and Paul Sorrentino. 2 vols. New York: Columbia University Press, 1988.

————. *Stephen Crane: Letters.* Edited by R. W. Stallman and Lillian Gilkes. New York: New York University Press, 1960.

————. *Tales of Whilomville: "The Monster," "His New Mittens," Whilomville Stories.* 1899, 1900. Edited by Fredson Bowers. Introduction by J. C. Levenson. Vol. 7 of *The Works of Stephen Crane.* Charlottesville: University Press of Virginia, 1969.

Crowley, John W. *The Black Heart's Truth: The Early Career of W. D. Howells.* Chapel Hill: University of North Carolina Press, 1985.

———. *The Mask of Fiction: Essays on W. D. Howells.* Amherst: University of Massachusetts Press, 1989.

Cummings, Sherwood. *Mark Twain and Science: Adventures of a Mind.* Baton Rouge: Louisiana State University Press, 1988.

Degler, Carl. *The Age of Economic Revolution 1876–1900.* Glenville: Scott, 1967.

Demos, John. *Past, Present, and Personal: The Family and the Life Course in American History.* New York: Oxford University Press, 1986.

Demos, John, and Virginia Demos. "Adolescence in Historical Perspective." *Journal of Marriage and the Family* 31 (1969): 632–38. Reprinted in *The American Family in Social-Historical Perspective,* edited by Michael Gordon, 209–21. New York: St. Martin's, 1973.

DeVoto, Bernard. *Mark Twain at Work.* 1942. Boston: Riverside-Houghton, 1967.

Dubbert, Joe L. *A Man's Place: Masculinity in Transition.* Englewood Cliffs: Prentice, 1979.

Eakin, Paul John. *Fictions in Autobiography: Studies in the Art of Self-Invention.* Princeton: Princeton University Press, 1985.

Eastman, Charles. *Indian Boyhood.* New York: McClure, 1902.

Egan, Susanna. "'Self'-Conscious History: American Autobiography after the Civil War." In *American Autobiography: Retrospect and Prospect,* edited by Paul John Eakin, 70–94. Madison: University of Wisconsin Press, 1991.

Eggleston, Edward. *The Hoosier School-Boy.* New York: Scribners, 1883.

Ehrenreich, Barbara, and Deirdre English. *For Her Own Good: 150 Years of the Experts' Advice to Women.* Garden City: Anchor-Doubleday, 1978.

Fasteau, Marc Feigen. *The Male Machine.* 1975. New York: Delta-Dell, 1976.

Fennimore, Keith J. *Booth Tarkington.* New York: Twayne, 1974.

Fetterly, Judith. "The Sanctioned Rebel." *Studies in the Novel* 3 (1971): 293–304.

Fields, Mrs. James T. *Charles Dudley Warner.* New York: McClure, 1904.

Filene, Peter G. *Him/Her/Self: Sex Roles in Modern America.* 2nd ed. Baltimore: Johns Hopkins University Press, 1986.

Finley, Martha. *Elsie Dinsmore.* New York: Dodd, 1867.

———. *An Old Fashioned Boy.* Philadelphia: Evans, 1871.

Frederic, Harold. *The Damnation of Theron Ware or Illumination.* 1896. Text established by Charlyne Dodge. History of the text by Stanton Garner. Vol. 3 of *The Harold Frederic Edition.* Lincoln: University of Nebraska Press, 1985.

Garland, Hamlin. *Boy Life on the Prairie.* 1899, 1926. Lincoln: University of Nebraska Press, 1961.

———. *My Friendly Contemporaries: A Literary Log.* New York: Macmillan, 1932.

———. *Prairie Songs: Being Chants Rhymed and Unrhymed of the Level Lands of the Great West.* Cambridge: Stone, 1893.

———. *A Son of the Middle Border.* New York: Macmillan, 1917.

Gerber, John C. Introduction to *The Adventures of Tom Sawyer, Tom Sawyer Abroad, Tom Sawyer Detective,* by Mark Twain, 3–30. Vol. 4 of *The Works of Mark Twain.* Berkeley: University of California Press, 1980.

———. Explanatory Notes to *The Adventures of Tom Sawyer, Tom Sawyer Abroad, Tom Sawyer Detective,* by Mark Twain, 467–97. Vol. 4 of *The Works of Mark Twain.* Berkeley: University of California Press, 1980.

Gould, Stephen Jay. *Ontogeny and Phylogeny.* Cambridge: Belknap-Harvard University Press, 1977.

Greenslet, Ferris. *The Life of Thomas Bailey Aldrich.* Boston: Riverside-Houghton, 1908.

Gribben, Alan. "'I Did Wish Tom Sawyer Was There': Boy-Book Elements in *Tom Sawyer* and *Huckleberry Finn.*" In *One Hundred Years of* Huckleberry Finn: *The Boy, His Book, and American Culture,* edited by Robert Sattelmeyer and J. Donald Crowley, 149–70. Columbia: University of Missouri Press, 1985.

———. "Manipulating a Genre: *Huckleberry Finn* as Boy Book." *South Central Review* 5 (1988): 15–21.

Habberton, John. *Helen's Babies.* Boston: Loring, 1876.

Habegger, Alfred. *Gender, Fantasy, and Realism in American Literature.* New York: Columbia University Press, 1982.

Hale, Edward Everett. *A New England Boyhood.* Boston: Cassell, 1893.

Hall, G. Stanley. *Adolescence: Its Psychology and its Relations to Physiology, Anthropology, Sociology, Sex, Crime, Religion and Education.* 2 vols. 1904. Vol. 1. New York: Appleton, 1911.

Handlin, Oscar, and Mary F Handlin. *Facing Life: Youth and the Family in American History.* Boston: Little, 1971.

Hantover, Jeffrey P. "The Boy Scouts and the Validation of Masculinity." *Journal of Social Issues* 34 (1978): 184–95. Reprinted in *The American Man,* edited by Elizabeth H. Pleck and Joseph H. Pleck, 285–301. Englewood Cliffs: Prentice, 1980.

Harris, Joel Chandler. *On the Plantation: A Story of a Georgia Boy's Adventures during the War.* 1892. Athens: University of Georgia Press, 1980.

Hart, James D. *The Popular Book: A History of America's Literary Taste.* 1950. Berkeley: University of California Press, 1963.

Hays, Samuel P. *The Response to Industrialism 1885–1914.* Chicago: University of Chicago Press, 1957.

Higham, John. "The Reorientation of American Culture in the 1890's." In *The Origins of Modern Consciousness*, edited by John Weiss, 25–48. Detroit: Wayne State University Press, 1965.

Hill, Hamlin L. "The Composition and the Structure of *Tom Sawyer.*" *American Literature* 32 (1961): 379–92.

Hinz, Joseph. "Huck and Pluck: 'Bad' Boys in American Fiction." *South Atlantic Quarterly* 51 (1952): 120–29.

Hoffman, Frederick J. *Freudianism and the Literary Mind.* 2nd ed. Baton Rouge: Louisiana University Press, 1957.

Holloway, Jean. *Hamlin Garland: A Biography.* Austin: University of Texas Press, 1960.

Holton, Milne. *Cylinder of Vision: The Fiction and Journalistic Writing of Stephen Crane.* Baton Rouge: Louisiana State University Press, 1972.

Howells, W. D. *A Boy's Town.* New York: Harper, 1890.

———. *The Flight of Pony Baker: A Boy's Town Story.* New York: Harper, 1902.

———. Introduction to *Tom Brown's School-Days*, by Thomas Hughes, ix–xii. New York: Harper, 1911.

———. *Life in Letters of William Dean Howells.* Edited by Mildred Howells. 2 vols. Garden City: Doubleday, 1928.

———. *Literary Friends and Acquaintance: A Personal Retrospect of American Authorship.* Edited by David F Hiatt and Edwin H. Cady. Vol. 32 of *A Selected Edition of W. D. Howells.* Bloomington: Indiana University Press, 1968.

———. "Novel-Writing and Novel-Reading: An Impersonal Explanation." 1899. Vol. 2 of *The Norton Anthology of American Literature.* 3rd ed. Edited by Nina Baym, et al., 266–82. New York: Norton, 1989.

———. "A Pocketful of Money." *Youth's Companion* 16, 23 November 1899: 602–03, 617–18.

———. Review of *The Adventures of Tom Sawyer* by Mark Twain. *Atlantic Monthly*, May 1876: 621–22.

———. Review of *Being a Boy* by Charles Dudley Warner. *Atlantic Monthly*, December 1877: 763–64.

———. Review of *A Son of the Middle Border* by Hamlin Garland. *New York Times Review of Books*, 26 August 1917: 309, 315.

———. Review of *The Story of a Bad Boy* by Thomas Bailey Aldrich. *Atlantic Monthly*, January 1870: 124–25.

———. *Selected Letters of W. D. Howells.* Edited by George Arms, Christoph K. Lohmann, et al. 6 vols. Boston: Twayne, 1979–1983.

———. *A Traveler from Altruria.* 1894. *The Altrurian Romances,* 5–179. Introduction and Notes by Clara and Rudolf Kirk. Text established by Scott Bennett. Vol. 20 of *A Selected Edition of W. D. Howells.* Bloomington: Indiana University Press, 1968.

———. *Years of My Youth and Three Essays.* 1916, 1918, 1919. Edited by

David J. Nordloh. Vol. 29 of *A Selected Edition of W. D. Howells.* Bloomington: Indiana University Press, 1975.

Hunter, J. "Mark Twain and the Boy-Book in 19th Century America." *College English* 24 (1963): 430–38.

Jacobson, Marcia. "The Flood of Remembrance and the Stream of Time: Hamlin Garland's *Boy Life on the Prairie.*" *Western American Literature* 17 (1982): 227–41.

———. *Henry James and the Mass Market.* University: University of Alabama Press, 1983.

———. "The Mask of Fiction: William Dean Howells's Experiments in Autobiography." *biography* 10 (1987): 55–67.

———. "William Dean Howells's (Auto)biography: A Reading of *A Boy's Town.*" *American Literary Realism* 16 (1983): 92–101.

James, Henry. Preface to *What Maisie Knew/ In The Cage/ The Pupil,* v–xxii. Vol. 11 of *The Novels and Tales of Henry James.* New York: Scribners, 1908.

Johnson, Owen. *The Eternal Boy; Being the Story of the Prodigious Hickey.* New York: Dodd, 1909.

———. *The Tennessee Shad.* New York: Baker, 1911.

———. *The Varmint.* New York: Baker, 1910.

Johnson, Rossiter. *Phaeton Rogers: A Novel of Boy Life.* 1881. New York: Scribners, 1893.

Katz, Joseph. "Afterword: Resources for the Study of Stephen Crane." In *Stephen Crane in Transition: Centenary Essays,* edited by Joseph Katz, 205–31. De Kalb: Northern Illinois University Press, 1972.

Keniston, Kenneth. *The Uncommitted: Alienated Youth in American Society.* New York: Delta-Dell, 1965.

Kett, Joseph F. *Rites of Passage: Adolescence in America 1790 to the Present.* New York: Harper Colophon-Basic, 1977.

Kipling, Rudyard. *Kim.* London: Macmillan, 1901.

Krauth, Leland. "*Boy Life on the Prairie:* Portrait of the Artist as a Young Man." *Markham Review* 11 (1982): 25–29.

Larcom, Lucy. *A New England Girlhood Outlined from Memory.* Boston: Riverside-Houghton, 1889.

Lasch, Christopher. *The Culture of Narcissism: American Life in an Age of Diminishing Expectations.* New York: Warner, 1979.

———. *Haven in a Heartless World: The Family Besieged.* New York: Harper Colophon-Basic, 1977.

Lears, T. J. Jackson. *No Place of Grace: Antimodernism and the Transformation of American Culture 1880–1920.* New York: Pantheon, 1981.

Lejeune, Philippe. "The Autobiographical Pact." 1975. In *On Autobiography,* 3–30. Edited by Paul John Eakin. Translated by Katherine Leary. Minneapolis: University of Minnesota Press, 1989.

————. "Autobiography in the Third Person." Translated by Annette and Edward Tomarken. *New Literary History* 9 (1977–78): 27–50.

————. "The Ironic Narrative of Childhood: Vallès." 1980. In *On Autobiography*, 53–69. Edited by Paul John Eakin. Translated by Katherine Leary. Minneapolis: University of Minnesota Press, 1989.

Leuchtenburg, William E. *The Perils of Prosperity 1914–32.* Chicago: University of Chicago Press, 1958.

Levenson, J. C. Introduction to *Tales of Whilomville,* by Stephen Crane, xi–lx. Vol. 7 of *The Works of Stephen Crane.* Charlottesville: University Press of Virginia, 1969.

Liebling, A. J. "The Dollars Damned Him." *The New Yorker,* 5 August 1961: 48–72. Reprinted and abridged in *Stephen Crane: A Collection of Critical Essays,* edited by Maurice Bassan, 18–26. Englewood Cliffs: Prentice, 1967.

Lounsbury, Thomas R. Biographical Sketch, i–xxxviii. Vol. 15 of *Complete Writings of Charles Dudley Warner.* Hartford: American, 1904.

————. Editor's Note to *Being a Boy,* by Charles Dudley Warner, [i]. Vol. 7 of *Complete Writings of Charles Dudley Warner.* Hartford: American, 1904.

Lynn, Kenneth S. *Mark Twain and Southwestern Humor.* Boston: Little, 1959.

————. *William Dean Howells: An American Life.* New York: Harcourt, 1971.

McCullough, Joseph B. *Hamlin Garland.* Boston: Twayne, 1978.

McElderry, B. R., Jr. Introduction to *Boy Life on the Prairie,* by Hamlin Garland, v–xviii. Lincoln: University of Nebraska Press, 1961.

McKay, Janet Holmgen. *Narration and Discourse in American Realistic Fiction.* Philadelphia: University of Pennsylvania Press, 1982.

Macleod, David I. *Building Character in the American Boy: The Boy Scouts, YMCA, and Their Forerunners, 1870–1920.* Madison: University of Wisconsin Press, 1983.

Mailloux, Steven. *Rhetorical Power.* Ithaca: Cornell University Press, 1989.

Martin, Jay. "The Genie in the Bottle: Huckleberry Finn in Mark Twain's Life." In *One Hundred Years of* Huckleberry Finn: *The Boy, His Book, and American Culture,* edited by Robert Sattelmeyer and J. Donald Crowley, 56–81. Columbia: University of Missouri Press, 1985.

————. *Harvests of Change: American Literature, 1865–1914.* Englewood Cliffs: Prentice, 1967.

Masters, Edgar Lee. *Mark Twain: A Portrait.* New York: Scribners, 1938.

————. *Mitch Miller.* New York: Macmillan, 1920.

May, Henry F. *The End of American Innocence: The First Years of Our Own Time 1912–1917.* New York: Knopf, 1959.

Mayberry, Susanah. *My Amiable Uncle: Recollections about Booth Tar-kington.* West Lafayette: Purdue University Press, 1983.

Miller, Alice. *Prisoners of Childhood.* Translated by Ruth Ward. New York: Basic, 1981.

Mitchell, Lee Clark. *Determined Fictions: American Literary Naturalism.* New York: Columbia University Press, 1989.

Mott, Frank Luther. *Golden Multitudes: The Story of Best Sellers in the United States.* New York: Macmillan, 1947.

Norris, Frank. "Child Stories for Adults." 1902. In *The Responsibilities of the Novelist and The Joyous Miracle,* 83–88. Garden City: Doubleday, 1928.

Norton, Charles A. *Writing Tom Sawyer: The Adventures of a Classic.* Jefferson, N.C.: MacFarland, 1983.

Olsen, Rodney D. *Dancing in Chains: The Youth of William Dean Howells.* New York: New York University Press, 1991.

Osherson, Samuel. *Finding Our Fathers: The Unfinished Business of Manhood.* New York: Free Press-Macmillan, 1986.

Otis, James. *Toby Tyler or Ten Weeks with a Circus.* New York: Harper, 1880.

Paine, Albert Bigelow. *Mark Twain: A Biography.* 4 vols. New York: Harper, 1912.

Pascal, Roy. *Design and Truth in Autobiography.* Cambridge: Harvard University Press, 1960.

Peck, George W. *Peck's Bad Boy and His Pa.* 1883. New York: Dover, 1958.

Peterson, Svend. "Splendid Days and Fearsome Nights." *Mark Twain Quarterly* 8 (1949): 3–8, 15.

Pizer, Donald. *Hamlin Garland's Early Work and Career.* Berkeley: University of California Press, 1960.

———. "Hamlin Garland's *A Son of the Middle Border:* Autobiography as Art." In *Essays in American and English Literature Presented to Bruce Robert McElderry, Jr.,* edited by Max F. Shultz with William D. Templeman and Charles R. Metzger, 76–107. Athens: Ohio University Press, 1967.

"The Point of View: Second Childhood in Literature." *Scribners Magazine,* January 1898: 123–24.

Porter, Eleanor. *Pollyanna.* Boston: Page, 1913.

Prioleau, Elizabeth Stevens. *The Circle of Eros: Sexuality in the Work of William Dean Howells.* Durham: Duke University Press, 1983.

Raphael, Ray. *The Men from the Boys: Rites of Passage in Male America.* Lincoln: University of Nebraska Press, 1988.

Rideing, W. H. *The Boyhood of Living Authors.* New York: Crowell, 1887.

Rivinus, Timothy M., and Brian W. Ford. "Children of Alcoholics in Literature: Portraits of the Struggle." Part 1. *Dionysos* 1 (1990): 13–23.

Robinson, Forrest G. *In Bad Faith: The Dynamics of Deception in Mark Twain's America*. Cambridge: Harvard University Press, 1986.

Ross, Dorothy. *G. Stanley Hall: The Psychologist as Prophet*. Chicago: University of Chicago Press, 1972.

Roth, Henry. *Call It Sleep*. New York: Ballou, 1934.

Rotundo, E. Anthony. "Boy Culture: Middle-Class Boyhood in Nineteenth Century America." In *Meanings for Manhood: Constructions of Masculinity in Victorian America,* edited by Mark C. Carnes and Clyde Griffin, 15–36. Chicago: University of Chicago Press, 1990.

Russo, Dorothy Ritter, and Thelma L. Sullivan. *A Bibliography of Booth Tarkington: 1869–1946*. Indianapolis: Indiana Historical Society, 1949.

Samuels, Charles E. *Thomas Bailey Aldrich*. New York: Twayne, 1965.

Schwed, Peter. Foreword to *The Lawrenceville Stories,* by Owen Johnson, vii–viii. New York: Touchstone-Simon, 1987.

Seelye, John D. "The Marvelous Boy—Penrod Once Again." *Virginia Quarterly Review* 37 (1961): 591–604.

Seton, Ernest Thompson. *Boy Scouts of America: A Handbook of Woodcraft, Scouting and Life Craft*. New York: Doubleday, 1910.

———. *Two Little Savages: Being the Adventures of Two Boys Who Lived as Indians and What They Learned*. 1903. Garden City: Doubleday, 1912.

Shillaber, B. P. *Ike Partington; or, The Adventures of a Human Boy and His Friends*. Boston: Lee, 1879.

———. *Life and Sayings of Mrs. Partington*. 1854. Upper Saddle River, N.J.: Gregg, 1969.

Showerman, Grant. *A Country Child*. New York: Century, 1917.

———. *A Country Chronicle*. New York: Century, 1916.

Shute, Henry A. *The Real Diary of a Real Boy*. Boston: Everett, 1902.

Slater, Philip. *Footholds: Understanding the Shifting Sexual and Family Tensions in Our Culture*. New York: Dutton, 1977.

Smith, Henry Nash. *Democracy and the Novel: Popular Resistance to Classic American Writers*. New York: Oxford, 1978.

———. *Mark Twain: The Development of a Writer*. Cambridge: Belknap-Harvard University Press, 1962.

Solomon, Eric. *Stephen Crane: From Parody to Realism*. Cambridge: Harvard University Press, 1966.

Sparapani, Henry R. "The American Boy-Book: 1865–1915." Ph.D. dissertation, Indiana University, 1971.

Stallman, R. W. *Stephen Crane: A Biography*. New York: Braziller, 1968.

Starobinski, Jean. "The Style of Autobiography." In *Literary Style: A Symposium,* edited by Seymour Chatman, 285–96. London: Oxford,

1971. Reprinted in *Autobiography: Essays Theoretical and Critical,* edited by James Olney, 73–83. Princeton: Princeton University Press, 1980.

Stearns, Peter N. *Be a Man! Males in Modern Society.* 2nd ed. New York: Holmes, 1990.

Stevenson, Robert Louis. *Treasure Island.* London: Cassell, 1883.

Stone, Albert E. *The Innocent Eye: Childhood in Mark Twain's Imagination.* 1961. Hamden: Archon, 1970.

Tannen, Deborah. *You Just Don't Understand: Women and Men in Conversation.* 1990. New York: Ballantine, 1991.

Tanner, Tony. *The Reign of Wonder: Naivety and Reality in American Literature.* 1965. New York: Perennial-Harper, 1967.

Tarkington, Booth. *Alice Adams.* Garden City: Doubleday, 1921.

——. "An Appreciation." *The Adventures of Tom Sawyer,* by Mark Twain, xi–xiv. New York: Gabriel Wells, 1923.

——. "As I Seem to Me." *Saturday Evening Post,* 5 July–23 August 1941. 7 parts.

——. Introduction to *The Adventures of Huckleberry Finn,* by Mark Twain, 5–11. New York: Limited Editions Club, 1933.

——. *Penrod.* 1914. Bloomington: Indiana University Press, 1985.

——. *Penrod: His Complete Story.* Garden City: Doubleday, 1946.

——. *Penrod and Sam.* 1916. New York: Grosset, n.d.

——. *Penrod Jashber.* 1929. New York: Grosset, n.d.

——. *Seventeen: A Tale of Youth and Summer and the Baxter Family Especially William.* New York: Harper, 1916.

——. "What I Have Learned from Boys." *The American Magazine,* January 1925: 5–7, 146, 148.

——. *The World Does Move.* New York: Doubleday, 1928.

——. *Your Amiable Uncle: Letters to His Nephews.* Edited by David Lawrence Chambers and John T. Jameson. Indianapolis: Bobbs, 1949.

Thoreau, Henry David. From Journals and Letters. Vol. 1 of *The Norton Anthology of American Literature.* 3rd ed. Edited by Nina Baym et al., 1848–73. New York: Norton, 1989.

Tomsich, John. *A Genteel Endeavor: American Culture and Politics in the Gilded Age.* Stanford: Stanford University Press, 1971.

Towers, Tom H. "Savagery and Civilization: The Moral Dimensions of Howells's *A Boy's Town.* *American Literature* 40 (1969): 499–509.

Trachtenberg, Alan. *The Incorporation of America: Culture and Society in the Gilded Age.* New York: Hill and Wang-Farrar, 1982.

Trensky, Anne. "The Bad Boy in Nineteenth Century American Fiction." *Georgia Review* 27 (1973): 503–17.

Trowbridge, J. T. "The American Boy." *North American Review,* February 1889: 217–25.

——. *Jack Hazard and His Fortunes.* Philadelphia: Porter, 1871.

Twain, Mark. *Adventures of Huckleberry Finn.* 1884. Edited by Walter

Blair and Victor Fischer. *The Mark Twain Library*. Berkeley: University of California Press, 1986.

——. *The Adventures of Tom Sawyer*. 1876. Foreword and Notes by John C. Gerber. Text established by Paul Baender. *The Mark Twain Library*. Berkeley: University of California Press, 1982.

——. *The Autobiography of Mark Twain*. Edited by Charles Neider. New York: Perennial-Harper, 1959.

——. *A Connecticut Yankee in King Arthur's Court*. 1889. Edited by Bernard L. Stein. *The Mark Twain Library*. Berkeley: University of California Press, 1984.

——. *Huck Finn and Tom Sawyer Among the Indians and Other Unfinished Stories*. Foreword and Notes by Dahlia Armon and Walter Blair. Text established by Dahlia Armon et al. *The Mark Twain Library*. Berkeley: University of California Press, 1989.

——. *Mark Twain-Howells Letters: The Correspondence of Samuel L. Clemens and William D. Howells*. Edited by Henry Nash Smith and William Gibson. 2 vols. Cambridge: Belknap-Harvard University Press, 1960.

——. *Mark Twain's Letters*. Edited by Albert Bigelow Paine. 2 vols. New York: Harper, 1917.

——. *Mark Twain's Letters to Will Bowen*. Edited by Theodore Hornberger. Austin: University of Texas Press, 1941.

——. *Tom Sawyer Abroad and Tom Sawyer Detective*. 1894, 1896. Foreword and Notes by John C. Gerber. Text established by Terry Firkins. *The Mark Twain Library*. Berkeley: University of California Press, 1982.

Warner, Charles Dudley. *Being a Boy*. 1877. Boston: Riverside-Houghton, 1880.

——. Preface to *Being A Boy*, vii–x. Boston: Riverside-Houghton, 1897.

Wecter, Dixon. *Sam Clemens of Hannibal*. Boston: Riverside-Houghton, 1952.

Wells, Robert V. "Demographic Change and the Life Cycle of American Families." In *The Family in History: Interdisciplinary Essays*, edited by Theodore K. Rabb and Robert I. Rotberg, 85–94. New York: Harper Torchbooks-Harper, 1971.

Wertheim, Stanley. "Stephen Crane and the Wrath of Jehovah." *Literary Review* 7 (1964): 499–508. Reprinted in *Stephen Crane: Modern Critical Views*, edited by Harold Bloom, 41–48. New York: Chelsea, 1987.

Westbrook, Max. "Whilomville: The Coherence of Radical Language." In *Stephen Crane in Transition: Centenary Essays*, edited by Joseph Katz, 86–105. De Kalb: Northern Illinois University Press, 1972.

White, William Allen. *The Court of Boyville*. 1899. New York: Macmillan, 1910.

Wiggin, Kate Douglas. *Rebecca of Sunnybrook Farm*. Boston: Houghton, 1903.

Wishy, Bernard. *The Child and the Republic: The Dawn of Modern American Child Nurture*. Philadelphia: University of Pennsylvania Press, 1968.

Wolfe, Cynthia Griffin. "*The Adventures of Tom Sawyer:* A Nightmare Vision of American Boyhood." *Massachusetts Review* 21 (1980): 637–52.

Woodress, James. *Booth Tarkington: Gentleman from Indiana*. Philadelphia: Lippincott, 1955.

Woollcott, Alexander. *Woollcott's Second Reader*. New York: Viking, 1937.

Wright, Richard. *Black Boy: A Record of Childhood and Youth*. New York: Harper, 1945.

Zara, Louis. *Dark Rider: A Novel Based on the Life of Stephen Crane*. Cleveland: World, 1961.

Ziff, Larzer. "Authorship and Craft: The Example of Mark Twain." *The Southern Review* ns 12 (1976): 246–60.

# ABOUT THE AUTHOR

Marcia Jacobson is Hargis Professor of American Literature, Auburn University. She received her B.A., M.A., and Ph.D. degrees from the University of California, Berkeley. She is author of *Henry James and the Mass Market* (1983).

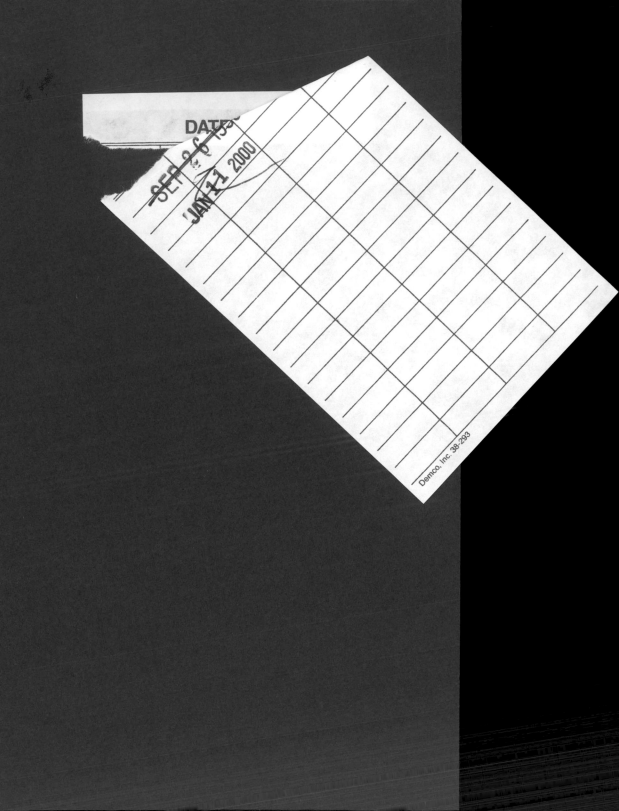